INDIVIDUAL EVALUATION PROCEDURES IN READING (IEP/r)

Thomas A. Rakes
Memphis State University

Joyce S. Choate
Northeast Louisiana University

Gayle Lane Waller
Richland Parish Schools

PRENTICE-HALL, INC. ENGLEWOOD CLIFFS, NEW JERSEY 07632

Library of Congress Cataloging in Publication Data

Rakes, Thomas A.
Individual evaluation procedures in reading (IEP/r)

Bibliography.
Includes index.
1. Reading—Ability testing. 2. Individualized reading instruction. 3. Reading comprehension.
I. Choate, Joyce S. II. Waller, Gayle Lane. III. Title.
LB1050.46.R34 1983 428.4'3 82-23132
ISBN 0-13-457226-2
ISBN 0-13-457218-1 (pbk.)

Editorial/production supervision and
interior design: Jeanne Hoeting
Cover design: Miriam Recio
Manufacturing buyer: Ron Chapman

Printed in the United States of America

10 9 8 7 6 5 4 3 2 1

ISBN 0-13-457226-2
ISBN 0-13-457218-1 {pbk.}

Prentice-Hall International, Inc., *London*
Prentice-Hall of Australia Pty. Limited, *Sydney*
Editora Prentice-Hall do Brasil, Ltda., *Rio de Janeiro*
Prentice-Hall Canada Inc., *Toronto*
Prentice-Hall of India Private Limited, *New Delhi*
Prentice-Hall of Japan, Inc., *Tokyo*
Prentice-Hall of Southeast Asia Pte. Ltd., *Singapore*
Whitehall Books Limited, *Wellington, New Zealand*

Susan B Katz
Pam Westbrook
Lamoine J Miller
Ouachita Parish Schools
Bernard Shadoin
Ozite A Shinault
Jo C Adams
Don W Locke
M J Batey
Henry Hazlitt
Marjorie S Snyder
Melba Shoemaker
W J Lyles
John Taylor
Will Waller
Memphis State University
W P Moore
Jannie Nelson
Claud Ezell
Jerry J Choate
Kathy McDonald
Tillie Adams
Sharon B Rakes
Lana Smith
Dixie Brand
Jane Puderer
Glynn Putnam
Spain J Shinault, jr
William R Powell
Northeast Louisiana University
Sharon Swearingen
Orville Elkin
Brian Enright

A VERY SPECIAL THANK YOU
TO ALL THESE
WHO FIELD TESTED, CRITIQUED,
SUPPORTED, AND DEMONSTRATED THE NEED
FOR IEP/r

tar jsc glw

Franklin Parish Schools
Charlotte Wilton Breard
Barbara Cottingham
Catherine Beach
Alice Henry
Harry B Miller
Sondra K Kutzman
Field Test Participants
Pat Dosher
Louisiana Educational Assessment Program
Jodie Lane
Sharon Roth
JoAnn Bassett
Ocie P Rakes
Jion Yen
J E Choate
Charles Pryor
Trish Leeney
Wayne Greenleaf
Henry L Smith
Teresa Choate
Gertrude Lane
Robert A Kaiser
Toni Bennett
Charles Tillman
Jackie Shipp
Laney Hatch
Carolyn Holtzclaw
William Waller
Haven Lowry
Betty Stapp
Henrietta Bradley
Barney Cottingham
Alison Choate
Angel Choate
Richland Parish Schools
Jeanne Hoeting
Emily Vowell

Contents

Preface

Individual Evaluation Procedures for Reading (IEP/r) was developed for use by teachers, prospective teachers, and clinical personnel concerned with diagnosis and prescription in reading. Particular attention has been given to both the tryout and construction of IEP/r to address the special differences in exceptional youngsters as well as the needs of students in regular classes. Because of this, IEP/r is unique in its treatment of several important areas of diagnostic procedure.

The range of criterion-referenced tests includes a carefully controlled section of sixty-six graded passages which are representative of three different subject area sources. Difficulty levels range from primer through grade ten. Following these tests are auditory, visual, and vocabulary screening instruments plus a word analysis survey, an ecological assessment and a recommended procedure for determining a student's projected achievement level. The book also contains two other major sections: ready-to-use Individual Educational Prescriptions (IEPs) in behavioral objective format, cross-indexed with the reading skills analyses; and a skills reference guide to many major textbooks in special education and reading. We consider the need for integrating the process of diagnosis and prescription to be of great importance. IEP/r reflects this concern. Thus, using this single volume, IEP/r, one may determine a child's relative reading strengths and weaknesses and formulate a plan tailored to the individual student's observed reading skills. The authors suggest that student pages be laminated for repeated use. Permission is granted for the reproduction of teacher copy and record-keeping pages for classroom use.

For the user, IEP/r represents a teacher-tested grouping of tests and strategies designed for use with exceptional and regular students. The directions should be read carefully prior to administering any test in the book. It is further recommended that a teacher use four or five practice sessions to become familiar with administration, scoring, and interpretation procedures. Finally, the user may notice that, while a traditional informal reading inventory format is apparent in IEP/r, more than a few "different" aspects are involved in using the tests. These changes were developed with a special learner population in mind and were fostered by the authors' compulsion to be specific in identifying target reading skills for each student and in appropriately relating the observed reading patterns to a practical individualized plan for improving reading performance.

T.A.R J.S.C G.L.W.

Using IEP/r: A Rationale

The tests in IEP/r were developed and refined over a period of three years beginning in 1979. These criterion-referenced tests underwent three major revisions prior to becoming the final instruments in this volume. Numerous changes in procedure and content have evolved as a result of actually using the tests with more than 1,150 youngsters in five states. The following discussion is not essential for the successful use of the tests, but it may be of interest to those who are curious about the development of the major components and the authors' reasons for administration, interpretation, and related suggestions within this book.

There are two word recognition lists, Form A and Form B. The lists were developed entirely from high frequency word counts of seven popular basal reading series. They are intended to help locate a probable starting level for using the graded passages. The lists offer a reliable and quick means of identifying a starting point for using the graded passages. They also provide some indication of a reader's general skills in word recognition in isolation.

The graded passages were developed on difficulty levels ranging from primer through grade ten. Readability was controlled through the use of readability formulas, uniform sentence lengths, and a carefully controlled volume of words per level according to a core of basal reader vocabulary. Tables I and II represent the story strands with accompanying counts for total words and sentences for each of the 66 stories. Vocabulary used in the graded passages, primer through grade six, was taken from high frequency counts from the following basal reader series:

Basics in Reading, Scott, Foresman & Company, 1978

Bookmark Reading Program, Harcourt Brace Javonivich, Inc., 1979

Houghton Mifflin Reading Program, 1980

Keytext Program, The Economy Company, 1978

Reading 720, Ginn & Company, 1976

Reading Basics Plus, Harper & Row, 1976

Series r, Macmillan Publishing Company, 1975

Passages seven through ten were written using vocabulary from the mentioned basal series containing texts at appropriate levels plus words by frequency level as found in the *Word Frequency Book* (Carroll, Davies, and Richman, 1971). Both A and B forms contain three complete sets of graded passages in literature, history, and science. The passages and questions were field tested on an intact basis. Equivalence of forms is in part accomplished through control of readability, vocabulary load, and source, as well as through results from field testing.

Table I Number of Words, Sentences, and Average Sentence Lengths for Graded Passages, Form A

	FORM A								
GRADE LEVEL	TOTAL WORDS			TOTAL SENTENCES			AVERAGE SENTENCE LENGTH		
	[a]*L*	[b]*S*	[c]*H*	*L*	*S*	*H*	*L*	*S*	*H*
Primer	68	68	67	13	13	13	5.2	5.2	5.2
One	80	80	81	12	12	12	6.7	6.7	6.75
Two	102	103	102	13	13	13	7.8	7.9	7.8
Three	121	125	121	14	14	14	8.6	8.9	8.6
Four	137	137	142	15	15	15	9.1	9.1	9.5
Five	151	152	150	14	14	14	10.7	10.9	10.8
Six	159	159	163	13	14	13	11.4	11.4	11.6
Seven	172	172	176	12	12	12	14.3	14.3	14.7
Eight	178	179	179	12	12	12	14.8	14.9	14.9
Nine	191	192	191	11	11	11	17.4	17.4	17.4
Ten	203	201	202	10	10	10	20.3	20.1	20.2

[a] Literature

[b] Science

[c] History

Table II Number of Words, Sentences, and Average Sentence Lengths for Graded Passages, Form B

GRADE LEVEL	TOTAL WORDS			FORM B TOTAL SENTENCES			AVERAGE SENTENCE LENGTH		
	L[a]	*S*[b]	*H*[c]	*L*	*S*	*H*	*L*	*S*	*H*
Primer	68	62	68	13	12	13	5.2	5.2	5.2
One	78	83	81	12	12	12	6.5	6.9	6.75
Two	102	103	101	13	13	13	7.8	7.9	7.8
Three	128	122	121	14	14	14	9.1	8.7	8.6
Four	138	136	142	15	15	15	9.2	9.1	9.5
Five	150	150	142	14	14	13	10.7	10.7	10.9
Six	162	160	157	14	14	14	11.6	11.4	11.2
Seven	172	174	173	12	12	12	14.3	14.5	14.4
Eight	179	180	177	12	12	12	14.9	15.0	14.8
Nine	190	193	191	11	11	11	17.3	17.5	17.4
Ten	201	201	201	10	10	10	20.1	20.1	20.1

[a] Literature
[b] Science
[c] History

Field try-outs of all instruments were conducted under the supervision of the authors. Eighty-one examiners and 1171 children participated in using various components of IEP/r; concomitantly, examiners were involved in refining the word recognition lists and graded passages. Examiners were representative of five types: (1) special education assessment teachers; (2) reading specialists; (3) regular classroom teachers; and (4) graduate reading and (5) special education majors. An additional 47 undergraduate students majoring in special education and elementary education participated as examiners during the final stages of development. The major modification resulting from field-testing was in adjusting passage readability and the progression of difficulty. Much revision was required of many of the comprehension questions in an attempt to control for passage dependency for literal questions and also to try out the criterion levels on a cross-section of readers, including those with special learning handicaps. The student population for the field-testing included students enrolled in special education programs and students attending special reading classes, as well as youngsters enrolled in regular school programs.

During the development of IEP/r the authors recognized a wide variability among examiner preference for scoring, interpretation, and procedural styles. The directions that follow are specific to the point that a new teacher can, with practice, successfully use any of the tests in IEP/r. However, numerous options or alternatives are also noted throughout the book for those examiners who have already developed a personal style which can, of course, be used while administering IEP/r instruments. The recommended format of IEP/r is intended to bring structure to making clinical observations of reading and related behaviors. Based upon the field-testing of IEP/r, procedures were developed to accommodate the special differences of special education children. Such adjustments, we believe, bring clarity and specificity to the diagnostic process for both classroom and clinical situations. It is also apparent to us that students in regular education classes may receive a more complete evaluation using these techniques than they could receive using more traditional procedures and scoring criteria. Guidelines are given for determining when and how to use the specialized tests, vocabulary lists, ecological survey, projected achievement level formula, Individual Educational Prescriptions, and Prescriptive Resource Guide. It is ultimately the examiner's decision as to which items are needed. We do, however, recommend that when doubt exists as to whether an additional test or procedure is needed, the examiner should usually administer the test(s) in question. It is generally easier and more accurate to develop an instructional program based upon ample diagnostic input than on too little information.

The tests in IEP/r are intended to be used as

they appear, and therefore the record sheets may be reproduced for classroom use. The book may also serve as a model upon which clinicians and teachers may base their own tests. The original concept of informal testing was to keep a diagnostic link between the student and instructional content. By using actual basal vocabulary, IEP/r does in part maintain this link and provide several aides to developing instructional plans for all types of learners.

GETTING READY TO USE IEP/r

To use Individual Evaluation Procedures in Reading it will be necessary to locate specific types of tests and record-keeping pages before actually beginning to test. For most tests there are student response copies and an examiner's record form. To administer a test, the Word Recognition List A for example, it will be necessary to tear out or copy those pages identified as record forms for this test. While administering the test a child will pronounce words from one copy while the examiner records responses on a record form. To maintain a more permanent record of performance these pages should be duplicated. If a record is needed on a short term basis, the record sheets may be laminated and marked with an erasable marker. Examiners frequently wish to laminate student copy pages also. When this is done the test pages last longer and are generally easier to manage. Permission is granted to reproduce, for single classroom use, student response pages in IEP/r.

Before administering any test, all directions in the front section of this manual and any examiner directions that appear on the examiner's record forms and student test pages should be read. The directions appearing on the record forms and tests are minimal but will help to insure consistency of test administration.

To use a test, the administration guide for the test should first be read. Then the actual test page(s) and accompanying record form should be surveyed. At this point, a practice session or two using the test is necessary. Practice sessions will help an examiner become familiar with each test and will allow later administration and interpretation of the test to be conducted with confidence and accuracy.

Tests should always be administered in a quiet area, as free from noise and distraction as possible. The testing period should be a private time without interruptions. In some cases it is helpful to use a tape recorder to maintain a record of performance during auditory and oral testing procedures.

It is generally best to seat the child either directly across the table from the examiner or at one end of the table. This allows direct viewing of the reader and provides some degree of freedom for arranging tests and making notes. The child should be informed that careful notes will be taken during the testing session.

How to Know Which Test to Use. Looking over the tests will reveal that the auditory, visual, and word analysis tests are more basic tests, some of which can be used to screen non-readers and lower elementary-age children. The word recognition lists and graded passages should be used for most students who can read on first grade through grade ten levels. It is usually appropriate to use a word recognition list to determine where to begin reading in context and to screen for children who cannot read and therefore need to be administered a number of the special tests included in IEP/r. It is also likely that some children who can read will exhibit reading problems during oral reading that indicate the need for follow-up testing using one or more of the special tests.

Directions for using each test are discussed under a three part description that includes (1) a description of the test and its potential uses; (2) directions for administering the test; and (3) suggestions for interpreting test results. By using these short explanations an examiner will be able to complete a skill-specific analysis of a child's reading performance.

After testing has been completed several helpful aids are available in IEP/r for use in preparing an educational program. The Ecological Survey, Projected Achievement Level Formula, Individual Educational Prescriptions, and the Prescriptive Resource Guide provide procedures and information for integrating diagnostic data with treatment strategies.

Basic Reading Levels. For the purpose of clarifying terminology three basic reading levels are referred to throughout the inventory. These levels are:

1. The *independent level* refers to the reading level at which a reader can read easily. No assistance is needed and comprehension is nearly perfect.
2. The *instructional level* represents the optimal level upon which instruction should occur. A reader can read and understand material but some assistance is needed.
3. The *frustration level* is the level at which the

reader is unable to comfortably read the material. Word recognition and/or comprehension performance falls below minimum acceptable levels.

Throughout this section of IEP/r, reference will be made to the basic reading levels and most often to the instructional level. Little mention will be made of the frustration level as this is the level to be avoided. Remember that these grade level designations are approximations of reader performance for the graded passages, word lists, and other tests and should not be used as the only criterion or test score for grouping and other educational planning. The levels may be helpful in guiding the development of instructional programs or for initial placement purposes.

STEPS IN ADMINISTERING IEP/r

Listed below is a cursory explanation of the steps involved in administering the IEP/r. The examiner is referred to the sections which follow this one for a detailed discussion of the use and interpretation of tests and/or procedures.

1. STUDENT INTEREST SURVEY
   First, establish student's story strand by asking questions from the assessment form, Student Interest Survey.
2. WORD RECOGNITION LISTS
   A. *Determining Level to Begin Student.* Begin the word recognition list one level below the student's probable reading level, based on the report of the teacher or on the examiner's subjective evaluation.
   B. *Procedure and Scoring.* Have the student read the words aloud. As the student attempts to read each word, mark on the Word Recognition Record Form those words correctly pronounced by placing a check in the column to the left of the word. If no attempt is made to pronounce the word, urge the reader to try. If it becomes apparent that the student has little ability to pronounce the word, suggest that the next word be attempted. When the reader completes an entire list without five errors, the next higher list is administered. Testing continues in this fashion until the student mispronounces at least six words in a list.
3. GRADED PASSAGES
   A. *Determining Level to Begin Student.* Present the correct interest strand of the graded passages, starting one level below the one on which the student successfully recognized at least 75 percent, or 15, of the words on the Word Recognition Lists. Have the student read orally from Form A.
   B. *Procedure and Scoring.* The student should be asked to begin oral reading of passages, and then answer comprehension questions. If the student scores less than instructional level on word recognition in context according to the record sheet, or less than instructional level on comprehension, go back one paragraph at a time until the instructional level is reached. If the student scores above instructional level in word recognition/context or in comprehension, continue on to the higher paragraphs until *both oral comprehension and word recognition/context fall below the instructional levels.*
   C. *Determining Oral and Silent Levels.* Once the oral instructional level is determined, have the student silently read the same level paragraph in Form B. Determine silent comprehension instructional level according to record sheet.
   D. *Determining Listening Level.* Listening comprehension should be determined by reading aloud to the student the story one level above oral or silent instructional level; examiner reads aloud comprehension questions, continuing testing at higher levels until student misses more comprehension questions than are allowed for instructional level.
   E. *Using Specialized Tests.* The specialized tests should be used when a deficit is suspected in those areas of reading and/or related subskill areas measured by IEP/r, or when estimating pre-reading skills.
   F. *Diagnostic Information.* Reading levels should be recorded, along with diagnostic information, on the IEP/r Student Summary Sheet and the Student Planning Sheet for Reading Prescription.
   G. *Individual Educational Prescriptions in Reading.* Sample IEP goal statements and objectives are provided as beginning points for planning the student's prescriptive reading program.
   H. *Prescriptive Resource Guide.* The Prescriptive Resource Guide provides substantive infor-

mation from some of the most outstanding authorities in the fields of reading and special education. The references are useful for locating specific sources from which instructional procedures may be located.

Student Interest Survey

This procedure and the accompanying interest survey are optional items. For some readers, personal interest in a particular topic will often affect the level of performance on a given passage. Diagnosticians are presented two (2) choices in accounting for the student interest factor: the interest factor may be capitalized upon by allowing the student to select the topic of greatest interest; or an attempt may be made to partially neutralize the interest factor by presenting the student with neither his/her first nor last topic choice. Using the form entitled "Student Interest Survey," the examiner may elect either procedure. The purpose of these procedures is to (1) locate either a high interest area or a probable neutral interest area from among the three subject areas of the graded passages; and (2) provide a quick projective type interest survey.

USING STUDENT INTEREST SURVEY

The procedure for the first portion of this form should take no longer than sixty seconds. Ask the child to select a first and second choice from three interest areas:

Literature—real people
Science—animals and insects
History—true stories of long ago

The first choice topic is the story strand of highest interest to the student. When capitalizing on interest factor, this is the story strand in which oral reading begins *after* completion of the Form A Word Recognition Lists. When attempting to select a more neutral interest topic, student's second choice represents the story strand in which to begin oral reading *after* Form A Word Recognition Lists are completed.

The second portion of the interest form is optional and can be completed using one of two administration procedures. Procedure one requires reading items to the child and should be used with youngsters who cannot read the statements or would be unable to write their responses. An examiner may also wish to administer the survey orally to those who could complete the form independently if he/she wishes to use the time to interact with the client. As a warm-up, the use of an oral completion-type inventory can help an examiner establish rapport.

For older clients or children the examiner already knows, the form may be completed independently. When administered as an independent survey, a child should be told to attempt to spell words correctly. If help is needed to spell a word or for any other reason, assistance should be provided.

INTERPRETATION OF RESULTS

It is anticipated that the reading of passages from the reader's first choice of topics may show performance at a level higher than would be expected on topics of lesser interest. Thus, if this procedure is utilized the diagnostician *must* note in interpretation of results that the reading scores so derived represent the particular student's performance when reading high interest materials.

It is expected that the reading of passages from the reader's second choice or neutral subject area strand will be representative of an appropriate sample of reading behaviors. The performance levels and diagnostic information should be of a practical nature rather than information based upon an artificially high or low achievement level due to reader interest. Interpretation of this information will be conducted in a manner consistent with recommendations provided under the section for the graded reading passages.

How useful the responses on the interest survey are will be based upon how honestly each item will be completed. If the examiner can elicit such responses, the information may be used for background purposes in preparing diagnostic summaries and instructional programs. The process of completing the interest survey during the early stages of a diagnostic session should help relax the client and thereby create a more desirable testing climate.

Word Recognition Lists (Forms A and B)

Two forms of graded word lists are available in IEP/r. Forms A and B include nine lists of 20 words each beginning on a primer level and ending on an eighth grade level. The lists are to be administered prior to using any of the graded passages. The lists are intended to provide a quick estimate of a reader's word recognition level in isolation. The resulting level represents the reading level on which the use of graded passages should "most likely" begin.

USING THE WORD RECOGNITION LISTS

To begin, both the student copy of the word list and the examiner's record sheet should be located. Testing should *begin* one or two levels below the reader's anticipated level of performance. Regardless of a child's current grade placement, it is appropriate to begin on a level below where performance is expected. The reader should be told, "I am going to show you several lists of words. You may know some of the words; others may be new to you. I want you to read down each list and pronounce each word. If you do not know a word, try to say the word or word parts anyway. I cannot help you say the words."

As the child is reading, notes should be made on the record form to indicate correct and incorrect attempts as well as any mispronunciations or other errors in parts of the words. If a child refuses to attempt a word, the refusal should be noted with an "R" in the blank for that word and the student told to move on to the next word. If on any one list, the student misses six words, that list should be discontinued and the next lower level list should be presented.

INTERPRETATION OF RESULTS

A reader should continue pronouncing words until the total number of incorrect responses is more than five words. The minimum acceptable level for a word list is 75% correct. If a reader attained 90% on primer level, 80% on grade one, 75% on grade two, and 70% on grade three, the "instructional" level would be grade two. Grade two represents the highest level at which 75% or higher was attained. The user should refer to the performance of the following five readers to practice determining instructional levels. See Table III. Appropriate instructional levels would be: Sandy 4, Betty 2, Ricky 1, Lou 5, and Neil 6.

If testing begins on list three, and a child's performance falls below 75% for this list, the next *lower* level (list two) is presented. Less difficult lists are presented until a minimum level of 75% correct is reached. If at least a 75% score is not reached on the primer level list, several conclusions would be appropriate. These are:

1. Reading should begin on a primer level passage.
2. Supplemental word lists should be used to screen vocabulary (e.g., Sixteen Essential Sight Words, Survival Vocabulary I & II).
3. Several of the special tests in IEP/r will be needed to adequately screen the child's performance (Auditory, Visual and Word Analysis Surveys).

Once an instructional level is determined using the word recognition list, oral reading should begin one level *below* this level. For the five children in this sample oral reading would begin

Table III Word Recognition List, Form A

	PRIMER	FIRST	SECOND	THIRD	FOURTH	FIFTH	SIXTH
Sandy	—	—	19/20	17/20	14/20	18/20	—
Betty	—	20/20	16/20	12/20	—	—	—
Ricky	20/20	20/20	14/20	—	—	—	—
Lou	—	—	18/20	17/20	16/20	18/20	13/20
Neil	—	—	19/20	17/20	17/20	18/20	15/20

_____ Reflects the reader's instructional level on the Word Recognition List

☐ Reflects the suggested starting point for beginning the oral reading passages on these levels: Sandy 3, Betty 1, Ricky primer, Lou 4 and Neil 5. The user will notice that Neil was able to attain a level of six on this test. When a reader scores on a sixth grade level, it is appropriate to begin oral reading on a fifth or sixth grade level.

The purpose of the vocabulary lists is to suggest a level at which to begin oral reading. While specific types of errors and words missed should be noted on the record sheet, errors made in isolation are not considered to be representative of actual reading. Therefore the type and frequency of pronunciation miscues provide only minimal input toward the preparation of remediation plans. More meaningful information will be gained from the graded passages which are representative of a child's actual reading behavior.

Graded Passages (Forms A and B)

The graded passages are the core component of IEP/r. There are 66 passages representing a total of six graded passages for each of eleven grade levels of difficulty. While there are only two forms there are actually *three* complete strands of stories (primer—grade ten) within each form. The grouping of passages is as follows:

Form A

Literature	Primer—grade ten
Science	Primer—grade ten
History	Primer—grade ten

Form B

Literature	Primer—grade ten
Science	Primer—grade ten
History	Primer—grade ten

Each passage level is marked according to grade levels of difficulty. These notations appear in the upper right corner of each student's page and the upper right corner on the examiner's record form. Table IV contains a list of these levels and their corresponding code designations.

For each graded passage there is a student copy, containing only the story, and an examiner's record form, containing the passage, comprehension questions, and several scoring aids. The passages are used to evaluate reading performance by observing word recognition in context, measuring reading comprehension through the use of four types of questions, and identifying levels of reading ability. The broad levels of reading ability are called independent, instructional, and frustration levels of reading performance. A listening level should also be determined as an additional indication of a child's listening comprehension.

Table IV Levels of Difficulty for Graded Passages

FORM A		FORM B	
Ai	—primer	Bi	—primer
AI	—grade one	BI	—grade one
AII	—grade two	BII	—grade two
AIII	—grade three	BIII	—grade three
AIV	—grade four	BIV	—grade four
AV	—grade five	BV	—grade five
AVI	—grade six	BVI	—grade six
AVII	—grade seven	BVII	—grade seven
AVIII	—grade eight	BVIII	—grade eight
AIX	—grade nine	BIX	—grade nine
AX	—grade ten	BX	—grade ten

USING THE GRADED PASSAGES

After first administering the Word Recognition List, Form A, and determining a probable starting level for the graded passages, a three-part testing procedure is suggested. The procedure includes sampling a child's oral reading performance and oral comprehension, screening silent reading comprehension, and determining listening comprehension. If the high or neutral interest strand is being used (as discussed under "Student Interest Survey"), the oral reading begins using Form A, Graded Passages (either literature, history or science) on the level indicated from the results of the Word Recognition List, Form A. If the interest survey procedure is not used, the story strand that is believed to be "most appropriate" for the reader should be selected. This decision should be based on consideration of the reader's age, interests, and any other available information that might help in selecting a content strand. After selecting a series of passages from Form A the testing of the student's oral reading should begin.

The major benefit of using graded passages is to obtain diagnostic information relative to a reader's skill-specific strengths and weaknesses while reading. Scoring guides appear on every graded passage record form. These guides allow for a determination of both level and error ratios. These criteria were developed for use specifically in IEP/r. There is a progression of difficulty between some grade levels for the evaluation of the word recognition performance. Between grades two and three and grades six and seven in particular, the criteria for word recognition performance increases in difficulty. Similar comprehension levels are maintained throughout all levels of IEP/r graded passages.

Oral Reading. The reader should be told, "I want you to read several stories aloud. After you finish reading orally to me, I will take each story back and then ask you some questions about what you have just read. If you come to a word you do not know, try to say the word. I cannot help you."

Next, the introductory statement for the passage should be read to the student. This statement appears on the top of each examiner's record page. The statement is used to provide a mind set for each story and, in a small way, to help prepare the reader for what is about to be read. While the child is reading, the examiner's task is to listen carefully and record what the reader says on the record sheet provided for each passage. The procedure for marking oral reading "miscues" may be influenced by personal preferences as to the types of marking and recording of reader comments. The following system is provided as a general guide to marking oral reading miscues and should be adapted to suit each examiner's own recording system. There are eight types of oral reading miscues to be considered in scoring the IEP/r graded passages. The miscues and suggested marking system appear in Table V.

As a child reads orally, it is important that all deviations from text be noted. If necessary, a tape recorder may be used to aid in the later transcribing of oral reading miscues. Immediately after the student has finished reading a passage, it should be removed from view for the comprehension questions to be asked. Each question is to be read orally by the examiner, with ample time allowed for responses. Care should be taken to note correct and incorrect answers, and to record what is said, particularly on incorrect answers. If no response is attempted, "R" for refusal is marked beside the question. Oral reading is continued until *both word recognition and comprehension* fall below instructional levels indicated on the examiner's record form. After completing this portion of the reading, proceed to *silent reading.*

Data obtained from the administration of the oral reading test should be considered in two major skill areas: word recognition in context and comprehension. Unlike other reading inventories, each of these areas will be analyzed as intact skills and their resulting instructional level designations *will not* be combined to yield a composite instructional reading level. A separate score or instructional level will be reported for word recognition in context (oral reading) and for oral comprehension.

Silent Reading. It is usually necessary to evaluate both oral and silent reading performance, as well as listening skills. It is not uncommon for there to be one or more years difference between the three reading types for the same child. The evaluation of a reader's silent reading should begin on a passage equal to the highest successful level of "comprehension" completed on the oral reading test. If grade four was found to be a child's instructional level for oral reading comprehension, silent reading should begin on level four using the Graded Passages, Form B. If a particular interest strand was used for oral reading (Graded Passages, Form A), then the same interest strand should be continued for the analysis of silent reading comprehension.

To begin the silent reading test the reader should be told, "I am going to ask you to read some stories silently to yourself. After you have read each passage I will take the story back and then ask you some questions about what you have read." The brief introductory statement appearing at the top of each examiner's record page is read orally by the examiner, and then the student's copy of the passages is handed to the reader. After silent reading of each story is finished, the passage is taken by the examiner and the comprehension questions are asked orally by the examiner. Reader's responses to each question are recorded, along with any additional comments that seem appropriate. Partial credit may be given if an answer is half correct based upon the story content, and not on reader experience. The reading should continue until the comprehension level falls below an instructional level, that is, below 60% accuracy for the number of questions attempted on any passage. These comprehension instructional levels are computed for the examiner on each record form.

Listening Comprehension. A listening comprehension test should be administered next. There are individuals who consider listening comprehension to be representative of a reader's

Table V Oral Reading Miscues and Marking Guide

TYPE OF TEXTUAL DEVIATION	NOTATION	EXAMPLE
Insertions	Write the inserted word(s) above the line.	very He was a ‸ very nice person.
Mispronunciations[a]	Write the mispronounced word or words below the original word.	Tony talked to his taked teacher.
Omissions	Circle the omitted word or punctuation mark.	Some people want (new) homes.
Refusals[b]	Write 'R' above the unpronounced word.	Cathy said to keep on R trying.
Repetitions	Underline the word or words that are repeated.	This keeps out the dirt.
Reversals	Use a curved line to note reversed letters or words.	She was pleased to be picked.
Substitutions[c]	Write the substitute word or word part above the original word.	They want to go here home.
Phrasing[d]	Use a slash to indicate inappropriate hesitations or choppy reading.	We worked/hard to do better.

[a] Mispronunciations are considered to be a nonword or dialectical pronunciation of a word.
[b] Refusals occur when a reader will not attempt to pronounce a word. When this happens the reader should be directed to continue reading with the next word.
[c] Substitutions occur when a reader pronounces a word that is not one at which he/she is looking.
[d] Phrasing is the one miscue that is marked but *not* counted in the determination of total reading miscues for each passage.

reading capacity. For youngsters who are able to listen on a level higher than their oral or silent reading comprehension instructional level, it may be suggested that the reader is capable of reading on a higher level, or at a level at least equal to listening skills. However, aside from reading capacity level, it is important to determine if listening activities represent a viable teaching technique. That is, determining that a student's listening comprehension is higher than either the silent or oral comprehension instructional level provides documentation for the efficacy of asking a peer, parent, or aide to read difficult material to the student. If listening comprehension is found to be at or below oral and silent reading levels, then such a practice would probably not be a useful activity.

A listening test should be started at the same level or one level higher than a reader's silent reading comprehension instructional level. For this procedure, passages from *another interest strand* in Form B are needed. For a reader with a silent reading instructional level of sixth grade, listening passages should begin on grade six or seven. The student should be told: "I am going to read to you. After each passage I will ask you some questions. Listen carefully so you will be able to answer the questions." This procedure should continue until the performance level of the reader falls below 60% correct responses. The highest level at which 60% is attained is the instructional level for listening comprehension.

Through age 12 or 13, listening comprehension is generally considered an acceptable means of predicting reading capacity. If a student attains a listening instructional level that is higher than the measured oral or silent reading level, many specialists and teachers would conclude that the reader should be able to read at a higher level. If however, a reader demonstrates a listening comprehension performance that is lower than the oral or silent reading performance, perhaps the student is reading near capacity.

The listening test should, however, be considered for more than its possible value as a predictor of reading capacity. This comprehension score is best used as a factor to compare with scores from other tests in IEP/r. When a student's listening level is higher or lower than performance on other tests, instructional implications are apparent. If listening is a strength, instructional procedures should be provided to capitalize on the strength. When listening comprehension appears to be a weakness, the user should be particularly careful to note performance on other related auditory tests. If a pattern of weakness is evident, based on results from these tests, compensatory and/or remediation strategies would probably be appropriate.

INTERPRETATION OF ORAL READING MISCUES

The word recognition/context level can be determined by counting the total number of recorded miscues (excluding phrasing miscues). By comparing the total number of miscues with the word recognition scoring on the examiner's record form, the appropriate level can be determined quickly for each completed passage. A tally should also be made of the types of oral miscues that were noted. The frequency count will reveal the symptomatic problems that appear to cause the most difficulty and thereby indicate areas of possible need for instructional intervention. Miscues should be counted until a frustration level is reached.

A summary sheet is provided on page 129. By using this sheet an examiner can see any range or pattern of performance and also compare the relative strengths and weaknesses of a reader. The information provided on Table VI illustrates a completed examiner's record page with miscues noted and a completed scoring guide.

To obtain an adequate sample of oral reading behavior testing should continue until *both the oral reading miscues and comprehension performance* reach frustration levels. If a child reaches frustration level in word recognition in context before comprehension, administration of the graded passages should continue until the oral comprehension also reaches frustration level. If a child reaches frustration level on comprehension but not word recognition in context, continue the word recognition portion (oral reading without asking questions) until a frustration level is reached. Such a procedure means that for some readers, the word recognition instructional level will be higher or lower than the comprehension instructional level. Any attempt to combine the two will result in camouflaging the actual level of performance for each, thereby distorting the information upon which an instructional or remediation program would be based.

when to stop

For many years the accepted procedure for determining an oral reading instructional level has been to combine the word recognition and comprehension scores to equal one instructional level. Such a procedure is not recommended when using IEP/r. When both levels match, the idea is excellent. However, more often than not, the two levels will not match and instruction should be provided on the specific level indicated for each skill area. A combined score does not accurately reflect either the word recognition in context or the oral comprehension levels.

When counting oral reading miscues it is recommended that all miscues, except phrasing problems, be counted. Synonym substitutions, omissions of function words, dialect-related mispronunciations, and any reader deviation from the text should be scored as a miscue. This score will be reported separately from the comprehension level and should accurately reflect the reader's actual oral reading behavior. If such miscues were not to be scored, then the final instructional level would be unnecessarily inflated. When a reader reaches more difficult material or moves into a higher grade in school, the neglect or lack of accountability for these miscues may become evident. Instructional improvement must be based upon observed weaknesses. For this reason, counting miscues as such is recommended; if several of the recorded miscues do not affect the meaning of the passage, the resulting comprehension score should reflect this performance. By reporting two separate levels, one each for word recognition in context and oral comprehension, instructional decisions can be based upon actual performance in each of the specific areas with the reported levels of performance being representative of what was measured, rather than a partial miscue analysis.

The authors realize some specialists recommend not scoring dialect-related, synonym- and semantically-correct miscues as errors. There is a body of linguistic support to reflect not counting all "oral reading miscues" as errors. It is also acknowledged that a major purpose of counting miscues is to help determine the types of problems a reader is experiencing. While the level of word recognition is important, the analysis of miscues is generally considered to be of more importance in developing an instructional program.

If the user of this inventory is a highly trained specialist, thoroughly familiar with using miscue analysis, perhaps the use of a more linguistically-accepted scoring procedure would be appropriate. However, one of the criticisms of informal testing instruments has been the debate over the ability or inability of examiners to accurately record and in-

introduction

Read this story to find out about a different kind of fish.

WORD RECOGNITION ERRORS
Insertions ______
Mispronunciations ______
Omissions ______
Refusals ______
Repetitions ______
Reversals ______
Substitutions ______
Phrasing ______
Other: ______

WORD REC/CONTEXT ERRORS		
Ind	Inst	Frus
0–3	4–8	9→

We know fish can swim.

Did you know some fish can fly?

But a flying fish does not have wings.

It is not like a bird.

It moves like a paper plane.

Big fish sometimes go after it.

It can fly over the water.

It can only fly for a short time.

Then it comes down.

Sometimes a big fish is still after it.

It can take off again.

This is the way a flying fish takes care of itself.

MI ✓ 1. Give this story a good name. (Flying Fish; A Different Kind of Fish; or any appropriate title)

D ✓ 2. How long can flying fish fly, according to the story? (a short time) a little while

WM X 3. In the story, the "flying fish can TAKE OFF"; What does TAKE OFF mean? (begin to fly, leave the water, fly in the air) jump, hop

D ✓ 4. What sometimes goes after the flying fish in the story? (a big fish)

WM X 5. The story tells that big fish "GO AFTER it." What does GO AFTER mean? (chase; try to catch) catch something

D ✓ 6. Where does the story say that the flying fish fly? (over the water)

I X 7. Why would being able to fly be helpful to a fish? (to escape from danger; for protection; to stay safe) don't know

D X 8. The story stated that flying fish could move like what kind of plane? (paper) air

	TOTAL COMPREHENSION			FACTUAL (Even #'s)			INTERPRETIVE (Odd #'s)		
Levels:	Ind	Instructional	Frus	Ind	Inst	Frus	Ind	Inst	Frus
Question Errors	0–1	2–3	4→	0	1	2→	0	1	2→
Approx Grade Equiv	Late 1 (1.7–1.9)	Mid 1 (1.4–1.6)	Below 1	Item Analysis: MI__/1; D__/4; I__/1; WM__/2					

terpret oral reading miscues. Equal concern has been voiced regarding the ability of examiners to use data to arrive at an instructional reading level due to differences in scoring procedures. By recording and scoring each deviation from text as an error, the scoring procedure is simplified. The need to categorize a reader's errors by type (e.g., omission, substitution . . .) remains a helpful aid in developing remediation procedures. If several of a reader's miscues are dialect-related or are not considered to promote a loss in understanding, the examiner may state this observation and plan instruction accordingly.

INTERPRETATION OF COMPREHENSION RESPONSES

Reading comprehension is measured by assessing the student's ability to answer comprehension questions immediately after reading each graded passage. Four types of questions are used to determine comprehension of the IEP/r Graded Passages: main idea, detail, word meaning, and inference. The minimum acceptable level, the instructional level, is about 60% correct which equals five of eight or six of ten questions correct per passage. In considering a child's responses to questions it is necessary to use careful judgment. The answers provided in parentheses on the examiner's record form are intended as guides. Factual responses are usually taken directly from the passage. Inferential responses are, for the most part, passage dependent, but will sometimes elicit acceptable responses that are not suggested on the record form. Practical user judgment is necessary to be sure a child's answers are acceptable. It is appropriate to give half credit when a child provides a partially correct response. Answers must be based upon the passage content. An accurate response may be given based on prior knowledge and, except for the inference questions, should not be counted as correct unless information from the passage is used or considered as a basis for the response.

The comprehension level should be reported in three parts. One level for total comprehension and one each for literal (even-numbered questions) and interpretive (odd-numbered questions) comprehension. Such a division makes possible the analysis of a reader's actual performance. As in the use of word recognition levels, by determining a skill-specific level for literal and interpretive type questions, one is better able to develop useful intervention strategies. Table VI illustrates the three-part comprehension scoring for one story.

SUMMARIZING RESULTS

After completing the oral, silent, and listening tests, it is necessary to look over the examiner's record forms carefully. Information on these pages should be recorded on the "Student Summary Sheet for Reading." This form provides means of sorting the diagnostic information under specific skill categories. There is also a "Student Planning Sheet for Reading Prescription." This form should be used to reflect acquired and needed skills for preparation of tutorial recommendations or development of Individual Educational Programs.

It is on these two forms that the student's "Comprehension Style" will be recorded. Comprehension Style is determined by comparing oral and silent reading comprehension instructional levels. The higher level is considered to be a student's preferred reading comprehension style or "Comprehension Style," because this is the manner in which the student best understands what is read. Examiner comments are an important part of the analysis. Care should be taken to be as specific as possible when describing reading behaviors. Examples, frequencies of occurrence, and any observed behaviors such as pointing, fidgeting, or unusual nervousness should be noted.

Special Tests and Procedures

IEP/r contains a total of 21 special tests and procedures classified under eight categories:

1. Visual Tests — Pages 247–56
2. Auditory Tests — Pages 257–58
3. Word Analysis Survey — Pages 261–62
4. Specialized Vocabulary Lists — Pages 263–64
5. Ecological Survey — Page 266
6. Projected Achievement Level Formula — Pages 267–68

7. Individual Educational Prescriptions in Reading Pages 269–75
8. Prescriptive Resource Guide Pages 278–90

Categories one through three include individual tests designed to aid the examiner in evaluating specialized skills. For most students, certain tests should be selected after the Word Recognition and Graded Passages have been administered and scored. Depending upon the results of these two tests, additional follow-up tests of an auditory, visual, or word analysis type could be used to provide more depth and specificity in the evaluation process.

Three specialized vocabulary lists are provided for use in screening for mastery of essential vocabulary. The ecological survey will help determine a reader's "preferred" learning style as well as indicate other environmental conditions that may affect learning for a particular child. Use of the Projected Achievement Level Formula (PAL) will help predict or suggest a realistic expectation of learner minimum progress without the use of an intelligence measure. The Individual Educational Prescriptions in Reading (IEPs) may be used in formulating an individualized reading plan based upon diagnosed strengths and weaknesses of the student. By referring to the Prescriptive Resource Guide, the examiner can locate informational sources of instructional strategies for specific skill needs of a student.

All tests and procedures are not likely to be needed for any one student. However, the range of difficulty and importance of each area necessitates choosing carefully from the tests available. The Word Analysis Survey, Ecological Survey and PAL formula are usually administered more frequently than the auditory and visual tests in IEP/r. The remaining tests in this section should be used to evaluate more narrow types of abilities and are discussed according to each test category that follows. Use of the IEP and Prescriptive Resource Guide Sections will be determined by examiner need.

VISUAL TESTS

Both the visual and auditory tests are designed for ease of administration and scoring. To administer one of the tests a stimulus form and a copy of the examiner's record form will be needed. Each stimulus form contains a copy of one test which the student will read. The record forms for all visual tests are located on pages 259 and 260. For convenience these record forms also contain the scoring criteria for immediate use after administering each test.

Using Tests of Visual Discrimination. Tests one through six represent a series of visual discrimination tests beginning on a symbol recognition level and ending with tests five and six, Visual Discrimination of Words I and II. To assist in determining which test is needed, consideration should be given to the following description of each of the six visual discrimination tests. From this information and results from other tests an examiner should be able to determine the most appropriate test to administer first.

Test One

Discrimination of Shapes and Symbols As the easiest of the tests, this instrument should be administered when the use of minimal visual discrimination skills is expected. If a child is unable to discriminate between symbols we recommend using pictures or objects to administer a similar informal test of your own. This test is designed primarily for children in grades kindergarten through grade two but may be used with older youngsters whose performance on more difficult visual discrimination tests is unsatisfactory.

Test Two

Discrimination of Letter Shapes This test is intended for those children performing on a kindergarten to first grade level. Test content includes the individual shapes that are used to form upper and lower case letters.

Test Three

Discrimination of Letters (I) Using both upper and lower case letters, the test may be used for children in kindergarten or higher grades.

Test Four

Discrimination of Letters (II) This test includes pairs of upper and lower case letters.

Test Five

Discrimination of Words (I) For youngsters in kindergarten or higher grades, this test uses one-syllable words to screen visual discrimination. Scoring includes attention to specific beginning, medial, and ending parts of words.

Test Six

Discrimination of Words (II) In this test, words containing four letters are used to screen visual discrimination. As in test five, differentiated scoring is suggested for beginning, medial and ending parts of words.

If the test selected yields a satisfactory level of performance, use of the next level of the visual discrimination tests is suggested. If the student's performance falls below an expected level, an easier level of the tests should be administered. Tests one through six are administered in a similar manner. The directions are read orally by examiners from the stimulus form. Both sample items are presented, making sure the student understands what is to be done. The examiner's role is to point to each stimulus symbol, letter, or word, one at a time, and ask the reader to point to the matching item in a row of four choices. Each response should be indicated on the record sheet.

Interpretation of Results. An analysis of reader performance on visual discrimination tests one through six can be made based upon two factors: an acceptable or unacceptable score on the record forms and a description of the level and type of discrimination tasks that were and/or were not successfully completed. For example, problems may be observed recognizing medial parts of words. If a student can complete tasks appropriate for grade placement or ability level, then recommendations would be based upon higher level visual discrimination tasks, and prioritized according to student need.

When a student is reading orally it is necessary to notice the word recognition miscues for some indication of possible visual problems; mispronunciations of words may indicate such a problem. By following up with visual discrimination tests, one may not only be able to confirm the problem but also to identify specifically where the problem occurs (perhaps on a symbol, letter, or word). Some youngsters are able to visually discriminate symbols and letters, but not words. Others have difficulty with letter shapes but not symbols. For these children, corrective instruction should include experiences involving the use of single letters in a variety of instructional formats. The procedure for using the IEP/r visual discrimination tests is mainly one of locating the optimal level of performance, and then making suggestions for student progress.

Using Tests of Visual Memory. Three tests are included for screening visual memory. These items measure the ability to recall a symbol, letter, or group of letters. Beginning with test seven, the visual memory tests increase in difficulty.

The appropriate stimulus form and a copy of the examiner's record form should be located prior to test administration. The directions should be read to the student before folding each page along the dotted line. Using the folded page, stimulus symbols or letters are exposed one at a time. The stimulus symbol or letter(s) should be exposed one–two seconds for Visual Memory Tests seven and eight and five seconds for test nine. After each exposure the page is turned over for the student to point to the item that is the same as the stimulus item. The same procedures are suggested for all three of the visual memory tests.

Interpretation of Results. The test(s) are scored according to the scoring key provided on the record form. If the student's performance is acceptable on test seven or eight, the next test is administered. If the performance is not acceptable, visual testing is discontinued. This is the point at which intervention strategies will be recommended and prioritized according to other instructional needs.

The ability to remember visual information is important in learning to read. If words can be pronounced and/or understood, but cannot be remembered, reading ability will be limited. Tests such as the IEP/r tests of visual memory are useful, not so much for leveling or categorizing a reader, but for determining if instruction is indicated and, if so, to approximate a beginning point.

Using Test Ten: Visualizing Sounds in Words. This test requires the examiner to say words and have the child locate words with the same beginning, medial, or ending sounds. The test should be located on page 256 and the record form on page 260 prior to administering the test. The record form indicates the words to be read to the student. The directions on the stimulus page are read to the student; each stimulus word is read from the record form to the student. The two sample items are presented each time a new section is started. Before each section of beginning, medial, and ending sounds, two practice items are provided. All stimulus words are provided on the record form for this test.

The test begins at the bottom of the stimulus page with number one and moves up the page toward the examiner. The examiner points to each row after saying the key word.

Interpretation of Results. Results for this test are based upon the number of correct responses for children in grades one through four. The scoring key is located on the response form. The reader's level of performance as well as the analysis of skills in initial medial and ending sounds should be noted. If one or more of these areas is unacceptable, instruction is indicated.

AUDITORY TESTS

Three auditory tests are included in IEP/r. The tests may be used if a student's performance on other tests indicates a possible auditory problem. If results from oral reading, listening comprehension, or the Word Analysis Survey reveal a suspected auditory difficulty, use of one or more of the auditory tests may be indicated. The most frequently used test is test one, Auditory Discrimination of Words. Tests two and three, Auditory Memory of Words and Auditory Memory of Sentences, are used to confirm a suspected deficiency in recalling auditory information. If, for example, a reader's listening comprehension instructional level is lower than the observed oral or silent reading levels, one or both of the auditory memory tests should be administered.

Using the Test of Auditory Discrimination of Words. The test may be found on page 257. It will indicate the extent to which a student is able to recognize sound differences between parts of similar words. Differences are provided in beginning, medial, and ending portions of words. The level of difficulty spans approximately grades one through three, although older students may be tested if they exhibit possible auditory discrimination problems during oral reading.

To administer the Auditory Discrimination of Words test a quiet room will be needed. The student is seated with his/her back to the examiner. The examiner reads aloud the directions on the test sheet. When testing young children, it is often helpful to explain the directions on a more personal basis using their first names. For example, when working with Bryan say, "Are these two words the same: Bryan-Tommy; Bryan-Bryan; and Betty-Bryan?" Then the four sample items on the stimulus page should be presented.

When pronouncing the word pairs the examiner should try to speak in a natural tone of voice. It is also wise to test no more than three or four children within the same hour. Constant pronunciation of the words can cause an examiner to exaggerate or slur sounds. Each yes/no response is recorded as given.

Interpretation of Results. The scoring guide is provided on the response form. If a student's performance is unsatisfactory, it is possible that auditory discrimination may be a problem. Results from this test should be considered in conjunction with information from the oral reading sample and the Word Analysis Survey. By comparing the types of miscues from these tests a pattern may become evident. If beginning, medial, or ending sounds are confused on more than one test, there is an observed confirmation of a specific difficulty. Such patterns or supportive information may then be used as the basis for making suggestions for improvement.

Using Tests of Auditory Memory. This test is used when a student's ability to remember oral information is suspect. When a student exhibits difficulty following oral directions or appears confused by simple oral requests, one or both of the auditory memory tests should be administered. When a student's listening comprehension instructional level is lower than oral and/or silent reading instructional levels, these tests should be given. Testing begins with Auditory Memory of Words Test on page 257. For this test and the following test, the examiner's response form is also needed.

The directions are read to the student using the sample items at the top of the page. Testing continues until the student is unable to recall the information on two successive numbers. When a reader is able on the first try to correctly recall all information, either in sequence or random order for words, or in paraphrased form for sentences, the second item of the same length is omitted and testing continued to the next level of difficulty.

Interpretation of Results. Two types of information are recorded: the greatest number of words (or longest sentence) recalled in order; and the greatest number of total words recalled. For test three, the latter score would be for the longest sentence correctly paraphrased. While there are no age or grade equivalents for scoring these tests, the student's test performance should be carefully compared to the classroom demands placed upon the student to perform in related areas.

The auditory memory tests are appropriate for the purpose of confirming or rejecting suspected difficulties of an auditory nature. A poor performance on the auditory memory test(s) may indicate the need for direct intervention to improve performance in auditory memory tasks. A low score may also indicate the need to rely more heavily on visual tasks as a means of instruction. In the latter situation the auditory mode may not be the student's best means of learning.

WORD ANALYSIS SURVEY

This test is intended to measure phonic and structural analysis performance. The initial section (tests I–X) of the test is designed to measure specific phonic sounds using nonsense letter combinations. Tests XI–XIV measure word structure skills. A summary of the 14 skill areas appears on the bottom of the record form on page 262. The test should be administered to students who:

1. Demonstrate multiple oral reading miscues
2. Exhibit word recognition problems during reading or completion of the word recognition lists
3. Participate in a phonetic reading program
4. Indicate a preference for auditory learning experiences

Using the Word Analysis Survey. For this test, the student stimulus copy on page 261 and a copy of the Word Analysis Record Form are needed. During this test the student will be required to pronounce nonsense words. The student should be told, "I am going to show you lists of words which you probably have not seen before. Look at each word, then pronounce the word. If you are not sure how to say the word, please try anyway. If you do not know all the word, say the parts you do know." As each word is pronounced, each correct response is marked with a check and incorrect responses are circled on the record form. If it becomes apparent that the test items are too difficult for the student, testing is discontinued.

Some youngsters are easily distracted or confused by the lists of nonsense words. These students should be administered this test in a manner requiring each word to be printed on a card. A 3″ × 5″ or 1½″ × 2½″ unlined index card is recommended. Each word card may be shown to the child for pronunciation and then scored using the same procedure suggested for using the word lists. If the task then appears to be too frustrating for the student, the examiner should discontinue use of this test and rely upon item analysis of word recognition tests to determine the student's acquired phonic and structural analysis skills.

Interpretation of Results. After the test is completed the recorded incorrect responses will need to be tallied under each test section at the bottom of the record form. From this summary, it will be possible to determine acquired and needed skills under item 3B on the Student Planning Sheet. Individual Educational Programs (IEP's) may then be developed based upon this summary of information.

SPECIALIZED VOCABULARY LISTS

The three lists may be used as diagnostic tools or as sources of useful vocabulary for instructional purposes. Two survival lists contain important word and word groups that are necessary for everyday reading. Many of the words appear on signs and doors. Still others can be considered to be of a "basic sight word" nature. List III, *Sixteen Essential Sight Words,* was developed from the frequency counts of the seven basal series used in the development of IEP/r. These sixteen words represent the most frequently used sixteen words appearing in all seven series for levels primer through grade six. The list makes an excellent short sight word screening test. Any words a reader does not know should be taught.

THE ECOLOGICAL SURVEY: CHECKLIST OF STUDENT LEARNING PREFERENCE

This survey is an optional assessment, not only of learner characteristics, but also of those features of the youngster's learning environment which contribute to academic success or failure. Ideally, this instrument should be completed by the student's classroom teacher who is most familiar with the conditions under which performance is greatest. A teacher who has not previously analyzed the effects of specific ecological factors upon the student may require two or three days to observe the youngster and note findings on a copy of the Ecological Survey. When a classroom teacher is unavailable to complete this form, the examiner may want to partially complete the survey, based upon diagnostic observations, and in the case of older students, through direct questioning of students. It may be impractical to attempt to determine environmental learning needs of some students; professional judgment must evaluate the applicability of the Ecological Survey.

The summary of ecological needs should be explained to the teacher who is responsible for the major portion of a youngster's reading instruction. The instructional implications of the findings of the Ecological Survey should be translated into instructional prescriptions according to student needs.

THE PROJECTED ACHIEVEMENT LEVEL

The Projected Achievement Level is used to estimate the *minimum* progress a student is expected to make during a specified period of instruction, following the prescribed instructional plan. It is also appropriate for setting realistic reading goals for a student. Among the criteria to be followed in formulating long-term goals are the student's past achievement during the years in school, the present or actual achievement level, and the amount of treatment time. With these criteria in mind, the minimum Projected Achievement Level (PAL) may be determined by referring to the PAL formula, page 267.

The PAL may then be inserted into IEP statements. Following the instructional period, retest scores may be compared to the PAL scores to roughly estimate effectiveness of instruction.

INDIVIDUAL EDUCATIONAL PRESCRIPTIONS/reading (IEPs)

Beginning on page 269 is a collection of Individual Educational Prescriptions (IEP's). The IEP's are written as behavioral objectives and categorized according to skill areas measured by the tests in this book. The objectives can be used to plan educational programs, used in tutorial lessons, included in case reports, or used as a resource for the type of experiences that can be used to correct various skills difficulties. The statements are written in a manner that allows for easy adaptation for classroom use. They are not intended to be inclusive or representative of a sequence of suggested objectives. They are, however, concise and in sufficient quantity to provide a starting point for developing instructional procedures to correct observed difficulties or relative weaknesses located using the various IEP/r tests.

For each skill area tested by the IEP/r, sample annual goals are listed. These present not only suggested instructional goals, but also represent an estimate of the progress a student will make during a specified period of instruction (usually one year) following the prescribed instructional plan. The Projected Achievement Level (PAL) is appropriate for inclusion in the goal statements.

For each goal, cross-indexed with skill areas on the Student Planning Sheet, several objectives are suggested. These objectives are appropriate to increased achievement in each of the major areas of reading. However, because each student presents a unique profile of acquired and needed skills, as well as individual learning preferences, these objectives may have to be adjusted accordingly. The examiner is cautioned to carefully consider all available data and select objectives appropriate to each individual student's diagnosed needs. Upon implementation of selected objectives, observation of student performance may suggest modifications of, or changes in, objectives.

Included in the short-term objectives are indices of mastery. A teacher may, and probably should, consider alternate methods of determining mastery, according to the individual student's profile.

To use the prescriptions, it is necessary to first complete the Student Planning Sheet on page 130, indicating acquired and needed skills. Skills should be prioritized according to the degree of student instructional need, as well as the importance of each skill area to the student's classroom progress. Once needed skills are prioritized, the number of the indicated skill area(s) is also the number of the suggested instructional objectives in the Individual Educational Prescriptions for reading section on page 269. If a youngster is found to need skills in the area of comprehension, main idea, (skill area #5A on Student Planning Sheet), the matching number is then located in the prescriptions. By referring to the sample goal statement listed for number 5, the student's instructional goal may be written. Using the objectives under 5A, the examiner may either select or modify one of those suggested, or formulate an objective more specific to the needs of the student. In most cases, those objectives listed are ordered from least to most difficult. The examiner must exercise professional judgment in determining where, in an instructional sequence, a youngster's program should begin. The reader will note that some objectives contain blanks to be filled in by the examiner; this information should be taken from the Student Summary Sheet.

PRESCRIPTIVE RESOURCE GUIDE

The guide consists of a listing of resources referenced by page for textbooks in reading and special education. The skill areas of the Student Planning Sheet are listed and cross-indexed to the textbooks. The numbers of each referenced skill area correspond with the numbers on the Student Planning Sheet. The information on each of the referenced textbooks is directly related to the specific skill for which it is listed. The references include sample teaching activities, suggested instructional procedures, and discussions about what to do for specific reading problems. The guide can be helpful in locating sources in which one may determine how to remediate the problems of a particular reader. When used in conjunction with IEP's appearing before this section, the educator can refer to appropriate sources to better plan a prescriptive reading program. At the end of the Resource Guide is a blank form to be used to personalize the guide. If the user has additional references the form may be helpful for adding to the present guide.

STUDENT INTEREST SURVEY

NAME ______________________ DATE ______________________

Examiner should read aloud to student only Question 1 if the intent is to measure student reading performance on stories of high interest; to assess student performance when reading stories of a more neutral interest, both questions should be asked.

1. "When YOU choose the stories you read, which kind do you choose FIRST: stories about REAL PEOPLE; ones about ANIMALS AND INSECTS; or TRUE STORIES OF LONG AGO?" ______________
2. "Which stories would you choose NEXT?" ______________

The student will read the story strand chosen as "first" if high interest performance is to be measured; if the more neutral interest performance is examiner's goal, the story strand chosen by student as "next," or second choice, is the theme of the inventory strand which student will read, as indicated below:

Theme	Inventory Strand
Real People—	Literature
Animals and Insects—	Science
True Stories of Long Ago—	History

If rapport with the student has been established previously, proceed directly to the Word Recognition List, and then the selected inventory strand.

When presenting the inventory to a student who is not known well by examiner, it is advisable to administer the following General Reading Interest Survey as an initial step. This procedure may help to establish rapport, in addition to yielding important information about the student. Examiner should ask student to orally complete each sentence read aloud to him/her.

GENERAL READING INTEREST SURVEY

1. Your favorite subject in school is ______________
2. The reason you like this subject is ______________
3. The school subject you like least is ______________
4. The reason you dislike this subject is ______________
5. The books you like best are ______________
6. The magazines you like to read are ______________
7. Your favorite place to read is ______________
8. Your favorite story is ______________
9. You enjoy reading most when ______________
10. When you read you feel ______________
11. Your favorite TV show is ______________
12. Your favorite sports are ______________
13. On weekends you enjoy ______________
14. When you read aloud at school you feel ______________
15. You get the books you read from ______________

IEP/r

FORM A

IEP/r
WORD RECOGNITION IN ISOLATION

List A

(i)	(I)	(II)
1. of	1. way	1. move
2. am	2. care	2. able
3. fish	3. about	3. stood
4. say	4. people	4. love
5. tree	5. every	5. air
6. ask	6. never	6. unhappy
7. very	7. any	7. few
8. have	8. write	8. tall
9. dog	9. I'm	9. begin
10. man	10. page	10. should
11. fox	11. slow	11. children
12. some	12. were	12. try
13. bed	13. eyes	13. middle
14. first	14. many	14. different
15. talk	15. take	15. return
16. water	16. from	16. himself
17. house	17. thing	17. smile
18. cake	18. paper	18. shine
19. they	19. call	19. learn
20. funny	20. room	20. does

IEP/r
WORD RECOGNITION IN ISOLATION

List A

(III)	(IV)	(V)
1. travel	1. hero	1. stern
2. suit	2. theater	2. intense
3. appear	3. balance	3. bureau
4. hour	4. flutter	4. reef
5. sharp	5. ram	5. ceremony
6. month	6. ancient	6. horizon
7. built	7. pollution	7. prosper
8. grown	8. gorge	8. generation
9. understand	9. beckon	9. extent
10. caused	10. survive	10. companion
11. quite	11. communicate	11. orbit
12. escape	12. recognize	12. region
13. single	13. design	13. investigation
14. direction	14. observe	14. facility
15. family	15. direct	15. prairie
16. promise	16. modern	16. miracle
17. enjoy	17. enormous	17. concentrate
18. language	18. planet	18. ravine
19. toward	19. original	19. weary
20. joined	20. develop	20. fascinating

IEP/r
WORD RECOGNITION IN ISOLATION

List A

(VI)	(VII)	(VIII)
1. precision	1. delta	1. appall
2. transfer	2. literal	2. intrigue
3. contracted	3. virtually	3. stifled
4. abruptly	4. alternative	4. condense
5. hoist	5. tundra	5. apprehension
6. symbol	6. poise	6. docile
7. native	7. abstract	7. oppressive
8. glaze	8. tolerate	8. simultaneously
9. outlandish	9. compose	9. anguish
10. amateur	10. refuge	10. formidable
11. depress	11. manuscript	11. nonchalant
12. apparatus	12. heralded	12. circuit
13. flail	13. render	13. scholarship
14. score	14. elusive	14. remote
15. archaeologist	15. nomadic	15. endurance
16. flourished	16. predators	16. ingenious
17. specimen	17. gaunt	17. physiology
18. associated	18. isolated	18. reluctantly
19. menacing	19. retreat	19. indifferent
20. instinct	20. implication	20. habitat

IEP/r
WORD RECOGNITION IN ISOLATION

List A: Record Sheet for: ________________________________ (name)

(i)	(I)	(II)
1.__of ________	1.__way ________	1.__move________
2.__am ________	2.__care ________	2.__able ________
3.__fish________	3.__about________	3.__stood________
4.__say________	4.__people ________	4.__love ________
5.__tree________	5.__every________	5.__air________
6.__ask ________	6.__never________	6.__unhappy ______
7.__very ________	7.__any________	7.__few ________
8.__have ________	8.__write ________	8.__tall________
9.__dog________	9.__I'm________	9.__begin________
10.__man ________	10.__page ________	10.__should ________
11.__fox ________	11.__slow ________	11.__children ______
12.__some ________	12.__were ________	12.__try________
13.__bed________	13.__eyes ________	13.__middle ________
14.__first________	14.__many________	14.__different ______
15.__talk________	15.__take ________	15.__return ________
16.__water ________	16.__from ________	16.__himself________
17.__house________	17.__thing ________	17.__smile________
18.__cake ________	18.__paper________	18.__shine________
19.__they ________	19.__call________	19.__learn________
20.__funny________	20.__room ________	20.__does ________

(III)	(IV)	(V)
1.__travel________	1.__hero ________	1.__stern________
2.__suit________	2.__theater ________	2.__intense ________
3.__appear ______	3.__balance ________	3.__bureau ________
4.__hour ________	4.__flutter________	4.__reef ________
5.__sharp ________	5.__ram ________	5.__ceremony______
6.__month________	6.__ancient ________	6.__horizon________
7.__built ________	7.__pollution ______	7.__prosper________
8.__grown________	8.__gorge________	8.__generation ____
9.__understand____	9.__beckon ________	9.__extent ________
10.__caused ______	10.__survive ________	10.__companion ____
11.__quite ________	11.__communicate____	11.__orbit________
12.__escape______	12.__recognize ______	12.__region ________
13.__single________	13.__design ________	13.__investigation____
14.__direction______	14.__observe ________	14.__facility ________
15.__family________	15.__direct________	15.__prairie ________
16.__promise ______	16.__modern ________	16.__miracle________
17.__enjoy ________	17.__enormous ______	17.__concentrate ____
18.__language ____	18.__planet________	18.__ravine ________
19.__toward ______	19.__original ________	19.__weary ________
20.__joined________	20.__develop ________	20.__fascinating ____

IEP/r

WORD RECOGNITION IN ISOLATION

List A: Record Sheet for: ______________________________(name)

(VI)	(VII)	(VIII)
1.__precision ______	1.__delta ________	1.__appall __________
2.__transfer________	2.__literal________	2.__intrigue ________
3.__contracted______	3.__virtually ____	3.__stifled __________
4.__abruptly ______	4.__alternative____	4.__condense ________
5.__hoist __________	5.__tundra ______	5.__apprehension ____
6.__symbol ________	6.__poise ________	6.__docile ___________
7.__native ________	7.__abstract_______	7.__oppressive ______
8.__glaze __________	8.__tolerate _______	8.__simultaneously____
9.__outlandish______	9.__compose ____	9.__anguish__________
10.__amateur ______	10.__refuge ______	10.__formidable ______
11.__depress ________	11.__manuscript __	11.__nonchalant ______
12.__apparatus______	12.__heralded ____	12.__circuit __________
13.__flail __________	13.__render ______	13.__scholarship ______
14.__score __________	14.__elusive ______	14.__remote __________
15.__archaeologist____	15.__nomadic ____	15.__endurance ______
16.__flourished______	16.__predators ____	16.__ingenious ________
17.__specimen ______	17.__gaunt________	17.__physiology ______
18.__associated______	18.__isolated ______	18.__reluctantly ______
19.__menacing ______	19.__retreat ______	19.__indifferent ______
20.__instinct ________	20.__implication __	20.__habitat __________

CONSISTENT WORD RECOGNITION PATTERNS

Acquired Skill	Needed Skill	Skill	Sample Error(s)
		Beginning Consonants Ending Consonants Short Vowels Long Vowels Silent e Blends Digraphs Special Vowel Sounds Prefixes Suffixes Compound Words Contractions Other. . .	

COMMENTS

Three sisters like to read.
They want to write books.
But girls don't write books.
Boys write books.
The girls use the names of three boys.
They write a book.

People like the first book.
They want more.
The girls write new books.
They do not use boys' names.
They use the girls' names.
More people will read these books.
They will see that girls can write books.

Many years ago a man went to another country.
His name was Teddy.
Teddy saw a small brown bear in a tree.
It had big eyes.
Teddy liked the bear very much.

Teddy went home.
A toy maker made him a toy bear.
It looked like the bear in the tree.
It was called a teddy bear.
Many people saw the toy.
They wanted to own it.
Now teddy bears are made for people all over the world to enjoy.

P. T. Barnum was a great American.

He found many funny people to be in his show.

The show went around the world.

Barnum found a very small man.

He became part of the show.

He stood only as tall as a two-year-old boy.

Barnum also found different animals to be in his show.

Jumbo was the biggest and fattest elephant people had ever seen.

People loved Jumbo very much.

His name became a new word in our language.

Some people came just to see Barnum.

He had found strange animals and people.

Together they made the "Greatest Show on Earth."

When the boy was sixteen, he hurt his knee. The knee appeared to be getting worse. By the time he went to a doctor, the boy had blood poisoning. "I may be able to save the boy's life. I can't save the leg. The poison is quite bad. It may spread to the rest of his body at any hour," explained the doctor to the family.

The boy called his brother. "Please promise to help me," he said. The boy fought for his life for two days and nights. His brother was at his side. On the third day, the boy began to get better.

The boy was a football star that year. Many years later, he became president of his country.

Her father was a teacher but he liked to watch the stars. Maria and her father observed the stars and planets through the telescope every night. Her father taught her how to study the stars. For ten years Maria worked in a library during the day. At night she watched the stars. One night she sighted a moving light. She had discovered an unknown comet. Scientists throughout the world heard of her discovery of the comet. She received many honors and awards.

Maria began teaching at a college for women. For twenty-three years she communicated her knowledge and love of stars. She also campaigned for women to be admitted to all colleges. Maria was recognized as a leader in her field. A crater on the moon was even named after her. Her father had taught her well.

On the south side of the city a young black girl sang. Everyone at the church ceremony was amazed. All who heard her knew that this eight-year-old was a great singer. Marian concentrated on teaching herself to sing. She also taught herself to play the piano. When she was sixteen, Marian was refused admission to a music school in the city. After a few months of intensive training with a black teacher, she sang for a famous voice teacher. He was impressed by her singing. He agreed to teach her.

Later Marian began to give concerts for which she was paid. Winning two singing contests increased her success. She became famous in other countries. As her fame grew in other countries, Americans became impressed with the great singer. In 1955, Marian became the first black singer to be featured with a world famous opera in her own country.

As a boy and as a young man, he spent much of his spare time outdoors. He liked to ride horses, swim, sail, and ice skate. When Franklin was in college, his cousin, Teddy, was President of the United States. Thus Franklin became associated with politics. After he became a New York lawyer, he was elected to the State Senate. During his term as Senator, he contracted polio which left his legs useless.

Franklin had to be hoisted to and from a wheelchair. He could no longer enjoy the outdoor life. From the wheelchair he used a special apparatus to exercise the upper part of his body and make it strong. He wanted to stay active to continue his political career.

Despite his handicap, Franklin Roosevelt was elected President of the United States in 1932. The American people considered him a great leader. They reelected him president three times. No person has been elected president more than four times.

After the American Revolution, the colonists came to realize and value their freedom from foreign reign. For Ben, a young black man, life was exciting and rewarding.

Ben was not only a bright young man, but he was also shrewd and creative. Denied a formal education, he chose the alternative of self-instruction, teaching himself many things in his quest for knowledge. Intrigued by the machines of his time, he once disassembled a watch to examine its tiny parts. He matched each piece of the watch with a larger one which he carved from wood. Thus he assembled and built the first clock made in America. Ben helped survey the land site for the new capital of the United States, Washington, D. C.

One of Ben's most outstanding feats was his publication of an almanac. Many Americans enjoyed reading the almanac. Among them was another American hero, Thomas Jefferson. Jefferson felt that the same freedom which had rendered Ben capable of developing his skills would foster the growth of future Americans.

The only plant breeder ever to achieve world fame was Luther Burbank. Much of his success was achieved because of his patience and willingness to experiment. In 1870, at age twenty-one, he purchased his own farm in Massachusetts. There, he experimented with the small, easily spoiled potatoes that were grown in the area. After three years of patient work, he developed white potatoes with brown skins. Named Burbank potatoes, they were far superior to other kinds. Saving ten of his new potatoes, Burbank reluctantly sold the rights to them to a seed store for $150; with the money, he purchased a train ticket to California.

In Santa Rosa, California, Luther worked with plant breeding for more than fifty years. Throughout the course of his life, he dramatically changed the plant world. He developed improved varieties of plums, cherries, apples, nuts, and berries, as well as new types of vegetables and flowers.

The ingenious work of Burbank with plants stimulated worldwide interest in scientific control of plant development. His successes illustrate the potential rewards of careful and patient study.

Marie Curie is well known for her discovery of radium, but what is not well-known is her life as a child. She was born and raised in Warsaw, Poland. Although she taught herself to read at age four, she was discouraged from reading by her parents, who feared this genius in their little girl and encouraged her in more traditional play activities. Marie's early life was often difficult and painful. Her father, a professor of physics and mathematics, was lowered in his position due to his political views in Russian-controlled Poland. Her mother suffered from tuberculosis for several years. The treatment for this disease, coupled with the reduced income, impoverished the family. During this difficult time in her life, Marie buried herself in her reading, consuming everything from adventure stories to technical journals. While reading, Marie forgot the Russian tsar and his spies, her father's shame, her mother's illness, and all the hardship. Despite all her personal problems, Marie was determined to meet all adversity and to emerge victorious. Indeed, she did just that, providing the world with a new therapeutic treatment and receiving the Nobel Prize in 1903.

Many eventually famous and brilliant persons have had notably unremarkable beginnings in their early schooling, and Albert Einstein was one of these. Although he became an important scientist in his day and a winner of the Nobel Prize, his early years in school were particularly difficult for him; because his grades were frequently lowest in his classes, his teachers branded him as "dull." German schools were extremely strict and harsh in Einstein's youth, and he was frequently punished for asking too many questions or for being inattentive in all classes except mathematics. He had no friends either, for he was inadequate in sports and had goals and aspirations markedly different from the other students. All of this culminated in his being asked to leave the gymnasium, or high school, in Germany just before graduation. Nonetheless, Einstein did eventually receive his diploma in 1897 from a Swiss high school. He completed college in 1900 and began working in the Swiss patent office. Shortly after this, Einstein realized his mother's lifelong dream for him. He became a college professor, first in several European countries, including Switzerland and Austria, and finally in the United States. Einstein was invited to lecture on his theories throughout the world.

Some people don't like apes.
Apes look mean.
They are not.
They are sad in the zoo.
They want to go home.

The home of the apes is in the woods.
They have fun there.
They play with other apes.
They play in trees.
At night mother apes stay in trees.
Baby apes do too.
Father apes don't stay in trees.
They make a bed in the grass.

We know fish can swim.
Did you know some fish can fly?
But a flying fish does not have wings.
It is not like a bird.
It moves like a paper plane.

Big fish sometimes go after it.
It can fly over the water.
It can only fly for a short time.
Then it comes down.
Sometimes a big fish is still after it.
It can take off again.
This is the way a flying fish takes care of itself.

How would you like to begin a long trip in a hot, dry land?

There is little food or water.

A camel does not mind.

It stores enough food and water in its hump.

This will last for many days.

Little food grows in dry places.

The camel does not mind eating bushes and plants.

The wind blows sand and dust.

The camel's long eyelashes keep its eyes safe.

It is able to close its nose.

This keeps out the sand and dust.

It would be dangerous for other animals to travel in hot, dry lands.

But camels are well prepared.

Lions are sometimes called "Kings of the Jungle." Their size and walk appear so grand that they look like kings. Lions may be longer than some cars. The color of these giant cats may be from gray to brown. Most people think that lions are very brave too. But lions may not be quite as brave as everyone thinks.

Lions are afraid of camp fires. People can also scare lions by waving large branches. Many male lions do not even catch their own dinner. At night they just roar loudly. This frightens small animals away from them and toward the female lions. It is the female lions who capture dinner.

Lions may not be the bravest of animals. But they look and act like kings!

Among the most brightly colored birds are hummingbirds. They are also the smallest birds in the world. Some hummingbirds are as tiny as bumblebees with feathers. They may weigh no more than a penny. Their little nests are only about the size of nut shells.

These birds are named for the humming noise of their wings. In flight, their tiny wings flutter thousands of times each minute. The wings move so quickly that it is difficult to see them. Flying at rapid speeds, hummingbirds perform much like helicopters. They can dart in all directions and even balance in mid-air.

Hummingbirds may eat fifty tiny meals a day. They like sweet nectar. Their long, narrow bills reach deep into flowers. People like to observe the tiny birds. If honey is placed in a feeder, sometimes hummingbirds will come.

You may have seen beautiful white birds circling the horizon at beaches and lakes. You may have seen these gulls roaming the reefs or beaches in the early morning. These birds are a special part of beach scenes. Few beach pictures are painted without a gull in the picture. You can hear the sound of the rushing waves and the gulls' shrill cry. They are the sounds of the beach.

Did you know that gulls keep our beaches clean? They are like a small army of trash collectors. They eat the debris thoughtless people have left behind. Shiny trash on the beach is often carried to sea by the birds. After cleaning the beach, gulls fly over the water, snapping up shellfish to eat. The gulls drop the shellfish on a jagged reef. This cracks the shellfish open. The sight and sound of the fascinating gull make the beach a special place.

Bats are often thought of as undesirable and menacing creatures. They are sometimes associated with Halloween and evil spirits. Bats do have some outlandish habits, like sleeping in the daytime in damp, dark caves. But they can be really helpful to people. Powerful wings help the bats fly at rapid speeds. Bats can capture insects which might harm a farmer's crops.

You may have heard it said that someone "is blind as a bat." Bats can see, but they are better known for their ability to use their radar system. In flight, the bat makes a squeaking sound that can be scary. Moving ahead of the bat, the sound bounces off any objects in the bat's path. This enables the bat to travel with precision even in total darkness. By studying the bat's built-in radar apparatus, scientists have been able to refine mechanical radar systems. Studying bats has helped protect people. Still, many people do not like bats.

Prairie dogs have made their homes on the plains of the United States for over one million years. The cute animals resemble squirrels with short tails. So named for their homes and their barks, prairie dogs express their affection for one another by kissing!

Each prairie dog family has an underground house in a permanent town with just a few burrow mounds visible above ground. The interior of the home has many tunnels and entrances, and may have a hidden entrance which is used to take refuge from predators. Each home may have a small nesting room or two. Close to the surface of the ground may be constructed a unique room. The animals can turn around in it. From this room they can also listen to events on the surface. The town is constantly guarded by some town members. Approaching danger is heralded by the urgent barking of the guards from atop their burrow mounds. Given the danger signal, the prairie dogs retreat to the refuge of their underground town.

In the cold barren land of Antarctica is found one of nature's most appealing creatures. The upright stance of penguins, their waddling gait, and short flippers create the appearance of a small man in a black tuxedo. The friendliness of the penguins further adds to their appeal.

The physiology of penguins permits them to withstand the intense cold of the remote Antarctic regions. Their small heads, wings, and feet attached to a robust trunk offer limited surface area to the icy temperatures. Thick layers of fat under the skin help insulate the birds from the harsh weather. The remoteness of their natural habitat aids in protecting the birds from man.

Penguins live in flocks or colonies and share duties; while some parents hunt and fish, others tend the nurseries of penguin chicks. Most penguins are able to fend for themselves and survive the cold and rough habitat. However, some have difficulty in captivity and may become almost helpless. The captured penguins may not learn to feed themselves. These birds must be taught to accept hand fed fish each day.

The whale, an extraordinary animal in numerous respects, has been the subject of fantastic stories starting with Jonah in the Bible. The growth of an animal's body is limited to that size which it is capable of supporting and moving unassisted. Whales have been able to attain their enormous size because water provides the support and vehicle for the whale's movements. Contrary to what many people believe, whales are mammals, not fish. Some scientists believe that whales originally lived on land because they breathe air and are warm-blooded. They have some body hair, and their skeletal structure suggests that they once had legs.

One group of whales, sometimes called "whalebones," has instead of teeth, a fringe of long plates made of a substance somewhat like fingernails. Through these plates, they strain their food. The largest member of this group is the blue whale. It can be as long as ninety feet and weigh as much as one hundred fifty tons, and is the largest creature ever to have existed on earth. It would require approximately thirty enormous elephants or three of the largest dinosaurs ever discovered to equal the weight of this whale.

Goats, animals that have existed since the times of ancient civilizations, are relatives of sheep and, like sheep, they are valuable for their milk and hair. Goats can be either wild or domestic, but we usually consider them to be rugged and, at times, stubborn animals.

Wild goats ordinarily exist in high rocky habitats in Europe and Asia except for Rocky Mountain wild goats. These high spirited animals are vigorous and generally able to withstand extremely harsh winters in the mountainous regions.

Domestic goats can be located in several countries throughout the world; these animals, when fully grown, may weigh more than one hundred twenty pounds. They do not consume aluminum containers as some individuals believe! They prefer grass and foods that are not overly rich, but will, however, chew or lick nearly anything that contains minerals. Goats have a special type of stomach that enables them to swallow their food rapidly, store it, and then later, ruminate or chew the food as a "cud."

In the United States, goats are raised primarily for their milk which is sweet, nutritious, and generally easier to digest than cow's milk. Some people prefer goats as pets on a farm or in a zoo.

Some people want new homes.
They want to go west.
They need to take things with them.
They can take some things on a horse.
They want to take more.
They can take wagons.
Will wagons get there?

They take the wagons.
They ride in wagons.
They put things in them.
They work and work.
The wagons go west.
More people go west to make new homes.

Long ago people in a far away land liked horses.
The horses were pretty.
They could run fast.
They were pets.
People used the horses too.
They helped the people work.
It was fun to watch the horses race.
It was fun to see which horse ran faster.

Some men from a far away place did not want their horses.
They left these horses in a new country.
That is how these horses came there.
People today think these are fine horses.

Many years ago a man began a different kind of school.

It was in his country.

It was a school for little children.

There, they were able to sing, dance, and play.

They could make things.

But the people were unhappy with the school.

They said, "Little children should not go to school."

So they made the man close the school.

Years later, a man in another country began the same kind of school.

Children go to this school at age five.

They like to go.

But they learn more than singing, dancing, and playing.

These children get ready for first grade.

Over two thousand years ago in a far away land, a king ordered a royal road built. The king wanted to improve the country. This road joined the twenty main parts of the country. The king and his helpers traveled the royal road. The road was often used by the royal helpers. They would take news from one part of the country to another.

This special road was convenient. It was the best way to travel. By traveling the royal road, the people could sell their goods. Some people just liked to travel. They would visit with their family and friends.

Now we have roads like the royal road. They join main parts of a country. We call the roads highways.

Near the largest city in China stands an enormous hill. Hundreds of years ago, a very fine white clay was taken from the hill. From the clay, the Chinese people developed a special pottery. It was a hard, shiny white pottery. Some people saw the fine dishes, vases, and bowls. People thought they were beautiful. They were very impressed with the appearance and distinctive design of the pottery. Soon traders from foreign countries began to take the dishes home to sell. They were expensive. People learned to imitate the Chinese dishes. Imitations did not cost as much, but were not as fine. The dishes became known as ''china dishes.''

Today, examples of these ancient dishes may be seen in museums. The custom of calling the dishes ''china'' has survived through the years. Modern pottery dishes which we use at mealtime are still called china.

In the early 1800's, most American cloth was still homemade. Cloth was being made by machines in England. But the cloth was costly and few people could afford it.

A young man from Boston, F. C. Lowell, decided to investigate better ways to make cloth. He toured and studied the cloth factories in England. When he returned home, he and a companion designed their ownpower loom. Lowell built a large factory in Boston. Next to the mill, he built company facilities in which young farm girls could live. It was a chance for the girls to live in a big city. They could also earn their own money. The girls worked in the factory for little pay. But they were given free meals and schooling.

Because the factories and the farm girls prospered, Lowell expanded the factory facilities. Today the region around Boston remains a center of the cloth industry.

On January 24, 1848, James Marshall went to inspect the lumber mill he was building in California. From the nearby water, James picked up a shiny rock which appeared to be gold. Could this possibly be gold? James and his boss, Mr. Sutter, tested the specimen and confirmed that the shiny rock was gold. They wanted to keep the discovery a secret for the six weeks required to complete the mill. But news of the discovery of gold quickly spread across the nation. Their discovery caused a wild race for gold.

Thousands of people abruptly quit their jobs and rushed to California. Storekeepers, farmers, ranchers, and lumbermen abandoned their homes and their work. They traveled to seek their fortune. With so many people mining for gold, food and housing became scarce and expensive. Whenever a person did strike gold, much of the money was spent for necessary living expenses. California flourished. Some men discovered their fortunes in gold during the "Gold Rush."

In the middle 1600's, Alpen dogs were the watchdogs of a group of monks who established a refuge in a mountain pass. Travelers often became lost in sudden snowstorms in the isolated area of the very high pass of the Swiss Alps. The monks took their watchdogs with them on rescue missions. They discovered that Alpen dogs were well equipped for such duties. The huge shaggy dogs, some weighing as much as two hundred pounds, were powerful and strong enough to plow through snowdrifts. They were able to tolerate the harsh climate. The dogs' keen power of scent and hearing aided in detecting people hidden by the snow. Their sense of direction enabled the dogs to lead rescue parties wherever necessary. News of the phenomenal powers of the courageous dogs of the mountain retreat spread.

''Saint Bernard'' was the name of the high mountain pass. The enormous watchdogs were renamed for the pass in the 1800's. Saint Bernards have been credited with rescuing the lives of almost three thousand travelers in the Swiss Alps.

The word "cosmetic" is derived from a Greek word meaning decorating skills; these skills were employed over five thousand years ago in ancient Egypt. There, the physicians used and supplied cosmetics to both men and women. Preparations such as perfumed oils were used to improve their appearance. These oils protected people from the dry heat and harsh climate, and kept their skin soft and unwrinkled. The women darkened their eyebrows, eyelashes and upper eyelids with a fine, black powder made from soot. Dark green cream or powder was applied under the eyes. A plant juice, the color of rust, was used to dye and decorate the feet and fingers.

The last queen of Egypt greatly popularized the art of cosmetic adornment; all who saw the beautiful queen were intrigued by her ingenious use of cosmetics. The queen, world famous for her beauty, was also skilled in making cosmetics.

The use of cosmetics spread from Egypt to other countries. As demand for beauty aids grew, tradesmen began making and selling these products. Today, the cosmetic business is a multibillion dollar industry.

Schools, as we recognize them, were first initiated in the colonies around the 1640's by the people arriving in America from Europe. Massachusetts was the first state to enact legislation requiring that children be taught to read. In most colonies, other laws followed that required schools to be established in one form or another. Both elementary and upper schools, the latter originally being called Latin grammar schools, were common. In 1636, Harvard College was opened, and in the years just before the Revolutionary War, seven or eight more liberal arts colleges opened.

In the Middle and Southern colonies, in addition to public schools, religious and private groups opened schools. It was not until 1821 that the first public high school opened in Boston. By the end of the century, public high schools had almost replaced private academies in many areas of the country.

A new system of schools developed there and abroad through more than three hundred years of lawmaking. Changes have included the addition of science, art, music, language, business, history, homemaking, shop trades, and other areas of study. We are fortunate to live at a time when schools offer so much.

The coming of railroads to America was beset with many problems. The iron horse, as the steam locomotive was nicknamed, was an apt label. Making its steam power from wood and water, the engine erratically snorted, coughed, belched, and jerked in a manner similar to that of a fidgety horse. As early locomotives chugged down the track, they spewed out sparks, cinders, and smoke over unsuspecting passengers in open cars behind. Sometimes the wood supply would run out, and passengers had to forage in nearby forests for more firewood before the train could go on. Perhaps the most distressing characteristic of early locomotives was that they had no brakes. When these trains pulled into the station, townspeople would run out, grab whatever was handy, and pull the train to a stop. All of these difficulties bothered people, and some held protest meetings and wrote newspaper articles against trains. Numerous detractors claimed the cattle would be harmed or that it was unhealthy to travel at the ''dangerous'' speed of fifteen miles an hour, while others feared that they might be blown up if the steam boilers ever exploded. But despite all these problems, the railroads did grow into the world's greatest transportation system.

introduction

This story happened many years ago;
let's pretend that we were there.

WORD RECOGNITION ERRORS
Insertions ______
Mispronunciations ______
Omissions ______
Refusals ______
Repetitions ______
Reversals ______
Substitutions ______
Phrasing ______
Other: ______

Three sisters like to read.

They want to write books.

But girls don't write books.

Boys write books.

The girls use the names of three boys.

They write a book.

People like the first book.

They want more.

The girls write new books.

They do not use boys' names.

They use the girls' names.

More people will read these books.

They will see that girls can write books.

WORD REC/CONTEXT ERRORS		
Ind	Inst	Frus
0–3	4–8	9→

MI ___ 1. Give this story a name. (The Sisters' Books; All About Three Sisters; or appropriate title.)

D ___ 2. What kind of work did the girls do? (writers or wrote books)

WM ___ 3. The story says that people like the FIRST book; what does FIRST mean? (#1; earliest; preceding all others in order)

D ___ 4. What names did the sisters use on their first book? (the names of three boys)

WM ___ 5. The story says that the sisters USED the names of boys; what does USED mean? (called themselves boys' names; put boys' names on their books; signed boys' names)

	TOTAL COMPREHENSION			FACTUAL (Even #'s)			INTERPRETIVE (Odd #'s)		
Levels:	Ind	Instructional	Frus	Ind	Inst	Frus	Ind	Inst	Frus
Question Errors	0–1	2–3	4→	0	1	2→	0	1	2→
Approx Grade Equiv	Early 1st Grade (1.1–1.3)		Below Primer	Item Analysis: MI__/1; D__/4; I__/1; WM__/2					

D ___ 6. How many sisters were in the story? (three)

I ___ 7. After reading this story, why did you think the girls used their own names on their later books? (people liked their first book; people then knew that girls could write good books; they knew that people would not be afraid to read their books just because they were girls.)

D ___ 8. How did the girls in the story feel about reading? (they liked to read)

COMMENTS:

introduction

Read this story to find out about a famous person and a well known bear.

WORD RECOGNITION ERRORS
Insertions ________
Mispronunciations ________
Omissions ________
Refusals ________
Repetitions ________
Reversals ________
Substitutions ________
Phrasing ________
Other: ________

Many years ago a man went to another country.

His name was Teddy.

Teddy saw a small brown bear in a tree.

It had big eyes.

Teddy liked the bear very much.

Teddy went home.

A toy maker made him a toy bear.

It looked like the bear in the tree.

It was called a teddy bear.

Many people saw the toy.

They wanted to own it.

Now teddy bears are made for people all over

the world to enjoy.

WORD REC/CONTEXT ERRORS		
Ind	Inst	Frus
0–3	4–8	9→

MI ___ 1. What would be a good name for this story? (Teddy Finds a Bear; All About Teddy Bears; or appropriate title)

D ___ 2. Where did Teddy visit? (another country)

WM ___ 3. In this story, it says that they wanted to OWN it; what does it mean to OWN something? (wanted it to belong to them; to possess it; to have charge of it)

D ___ 4. When Teddy saw the first bear in the story, where was the bear? (in tree)

WM ___ 5. What is meant by ALL OVER THE WORLD? (in many countries; many places)

D ___ 6. What did the toy maker in the story do? (made a bear like the one Teddy saw; made a toy teddy bear)

I ___ 7. After reading this story, why do you think the toy was called a teddy

	TOTAL COMPREHENSION			FACTUAL (Even #'s)			INTERPRETIVE (Odd #'s)		
Levels:	Ind	Instructional	Frus	Ind	Inst	Frus	Ind	Inst	Frus
Question Errors	0–1	2–3	4→	0	1	2→	0	1	2→
Approx Grade Equiv	Late 1 (1.7–1.9)	Mid 1 (1.4–1.6)	Below 1	Item Analysis: MI__/1; D__/4; I__/1; WM__/2					

bear? (because it was Teddy who first saw it and loved it; because the very first toy bear was made for Teddy)

D ___ 8. According to this story, who enjoys teddy bears? (people all over the world)

COMMENTS:

introduction

Read this story to learn about an interesting person with an unusual job.

WORD RECOGNITION ERRORS
Insertions ______
Mispronunciations ______
Omissions ______
Refusals ______
Repetitions ______
Reversals ______
Substitutions ______
Phrasing ______
Other: ______

P. T. Barnum was a great American.

He found many funny people to be in his show.

The show went around the world.

Barnum found a very small man.

He became part of the show.

He stood only as tall as a two-year-old boy.

Barnum also found different animals to be in his show.

Jumbo was the biggest and fattest elephant people had ever seen.

People loved Jumbo very much.

His name became a new word in our language.

Some people came just to see Barnum.

He had found strange animals and people.

Together they made the "Greatest Show on Earth."

WORD REC/CONTEXT ERRORS		
Ind	Inst	Frus
0–4	**5–10**	**11→**

MI ___ 1. What would be a good title for this story? (The Greatest Show on Earth; P. T. Barnum's Show; appropriate title)

D ___ 2. What great man is this story about? (P. T. Barnum)

WM ___ 3. The story tells about DIFFERENT animals; what does DIFFERENT mean? (unusual; very large or small sized people)

D ___ 4. What was Jumbo? (elephant; famous circus elephant)

WM ___ 5. The people in the story LOVED Jumbo; what does LOVED mean? (liked very much; felt affection for)

D ___ 6. The story tells about a special man that Barnum found; what was so unusual about the man? (small in height; size of a two year old)

	TOTAL COMPREHENSION				FACTUAL (Even #'s)			INTERPRETIVE (Odd #'s)		
Levels:	Ind	Instructional		Frus	Ind	Inst	Frus	Ind	Inst	Frus
Question Errors	**0–1**	**2**	**3**	**4→**	**0**	**1**	**2→**	**0**	**1**	**2→**
Approx Grade Equiv	Late 2 (2.7–2.9)	Mid 2 (2.4–2.6)	Early 2 (2.1–2.3)	Below 2	Item Analysis: MI__/1; D__/4; I__/1; WM__/2					

I ____ 7. After reading this story, what do you think was P. T. Barnum's job with the Greatest Show on Earth? (ringmaster; boss; owner; to find new acts)

D ____ 8. What new word was added to our language because of P. T. Barnum's show? (Jumbo)

COMMENTS:

introduction

This story is about a boy's struggle to stay alive.
Read to find out what happened to him.

WORD RECOGNITION ERRORS
Insertions ______
Mispronunciations ______
Omissions ______
Refusals ______
Repetitions ______
Reversals ______
Substitutions ______
Phrasing ______
Other: ______

WORD REC/CONTEXT ERRORS		
Ind	Inst	Frus
0–5	**6–12**	**13→**

When the boy was sixteen, he hurt his knee. The knee appeared to be getting worse. By the time he went to a doctor, the boy had blood poisoning. "I may be able to save the boy's life. I can't save the leg. The poison is quite bad. It may spread to the rest of his body at any hour," explained the doctor to the family.

The boy called his brother. "Please promise to help me," he said. The boy fought for his life for two days and nights. His brother was at his side. On the third day, the boy began to get better.

The boy was a football star that year. Many years later, he became president of his country.

MI ___ 1. Give this story a good title. (Football Star Becomes President; Struggle for Life; or appropriate title)

D ___ 2. What did the boy in the story become many years later? (president)

WM ___ 3. What did the word SPREAD mean in the phrase "SPREAD to the rest of his body"? (move, infect, reach)

D ___ 4. What did the doctor say about the boy's leg? (could not save the leg)

WM ___ 5. What is meant by AT HIS SIDE? (near; close by; at bedside)

D ___ 6. How many days was the boy very ill? (two–three days)

I ___ 7. How do you know that the boy's leg was saved? (later played football)

D ___ 8. How old was the boy when he became ill? (sixteen)

I ___ 9. After reading this story, why do you think that the boy wanted his brother nearby? (to help him; give him support; because he was scared; he loved him very much and wanted his comfort)

D ___ 10. What kind of poisoning did the boy have? (blood)

	TOTAL COMPREHENSION				FACTUAL (Even #'s)			INTERPRETIVE (Odd #'s)		
Levels:	Ind	Instructional		Frus	Ind	Inst	Frus	Ind	Inst	Frus
Question Errors	**0–1**	**2–3**	**4**	**5→**	**0**	**1–2**	**3→**	**0**	**1–2**	**3→**
Approx Grade Equiv	Late 3 (3.7–3.9)	Mid 3 (3.4–3.6)	Early3 (3.1–3.3)	Below 3	Item Analysis: MI__/1; D__/5; I__/2; WM__/2					

introduction

This story is about a girl named Maria who watched the stars. Read to find out what she did.

WORD RECOGNITION ERRORS
Insertions ______
Mispronunciations ______
Omissions ______
Refusals ______
Repetitions ______
Reversals ______
Substitutions ______
Phrasing ______
Other: ______

WORD REC/CONTEXT ERRORS		
Ind	Inst	Frus
0–5	**6–14**	**15→**

Her father was a teacher but he liked to watch the stars. Maria and her father observed the stars and planets through the telescope every night. Her father taught her how to study the stars. For ten years Maria worked in a library during the day. At night she watched the stars. One night she sighted a moving light. She had discovered an unknown comet. Scientists throughout the world heard of her discovery of the comet. She received many honors and awards.

Maria began teaching at a college for women. For twenty-three years she communicated her knowledge and love of stars. She also campaigned for women to be admitted to all colleges. Maria was recognized as a leader in her field. A crater on the moon was even named after her. Her father had taught her well.

MI ___ 1. Give this story a good title. (The Star Gazer; A Famous Star Watcher; or appropriate title)

D ___ 2. Who was Maria's first and best teacher? (her father)

WM ___ 3. What is a CRATER on the moon? (depression or hole on surface of moon)

D ___ 4. For what did Maria campaign? (for women to be admitted to all colleges)

WM ___ 5. The story stated that Maria CAMPAIGNED; what does CAMPAIGNED mean? (worked or talked in favor of)

D ___ 6. How many years did Maria teach at the college? (twenty-twenty-five years)

	TOTAL COMPREHENSION				FACTUAL (Even #'s)			INTERPRETIVE (Odd #'s)		
Levels:	Ind	Instructional		Frus	Ind	Inst	Frus	Ind	Inst	Frus
Question Errors	**0–1**	**2–3**	**4**	**5→**	**0**	**1–2**	**3→**	**0**	**1–2**	**3→**
Approx Grade Equiv	Late 4 (4.7–4.9)	Mid 4 (4.4–4.6)	Early 4 (4.1–4.3)	Below 4	Item Analysis: MI__/1; D__/5; I__/2; WM__/2					

I ___ 7. After reading this story, why do you think that Maria was a hard worker? (worked both day and night)

D ___ 8. What discovery did Maria make? (unknown comet)

I ___ 9. Why do you think a crater on the moon was named for Maria? (because she was a famous teacher who studied the stars and planets; to honor a famous astronomer)

D ___ 10. Before becoming a teacher, what kind of job did Maria have? (librarian)

COMMENTS:

introduction

This story is about a famous singer named Marian. Read to find out about her.

WORD RECOGNITION ERRORS
Insertions ______
Mispronunciations ______
Omissions ______
Refusals ______
Repetitions ______
Reversals ______
Substitutions ______
Phrasing ______
Other: ______

WORD REC/CONTEXT ERRORS		
Ind	Inst	Frus
0–6	**7–15**	**16→**

On the south side of the city a young black girl sang. Everyone at the church ceremony was amazed. All who heard her knew that this eight-year-old was a great singer. Marian concentrated on teaching herself to sing. She also taught herself to play the piano. When she was sixteen, Marian was refused admission to a music school in the city. After a few months of intensive training with a black teacher, she sang for a famous voice teacher. He was impressed by her singing. He agreed to teach her.

Later Marian began to give concerts for which she was paid. Winning two singing contests increased her success. She became famous in other countries. As her fame grew in other countries, Americans became impressed with the great singer. In 1955, Marian became the first black singer to be featured with a world famous opera in her own country.

MI ___ 1. Give this story a good title. (A Singer Becomes Famous; Marian's Singing Career; or appropriate title)

D ___ 2. How old was Marian when she amazed people at the church ceremony? (eight)

WM ___ 3. The story tells that Marian CONCENTRATED; what does CONCENTRATED mean? (worked hard; studied diligently; focused)

D ___ 4. Who taught Marian to play the piano? (she taught herself)

WM ___ 5. The story speaks of a church CEREMONY; what does CEREMONY mean? (ritual; service)

D ___ 6. Where did the young singer first become famous? (other countries)

I ___ 7. Why do you think everyone was amazed to hear an eight-year-old sing so well? (so young; usually can't sing that well that young; voice usually not that well developed that young)

D ___ 8. In what year did Marian sing with the famous opera in her own country? (1955; 1950's)

	TOTAL COMPREHENSION				FACTUAL (Even #'s)			INTERPRETIVE (Odd #'s)		
Levels:	Ind	Instructional		Frus	Ind	Inst	Frus	Ind	Inst	Frus
Question Errors	**0–1**	**2–3**	**4**	**5→**	**0**	**1–2**	**3→**	**0**	**1–2**	**3→**
Approx Grade Equiv	Late 5 (5.7–5.9)	Mid 5 (5.4–5.6)	Early 5 (5.1–5.3)	Below 5	Item Analysis: MI__/1; D__/5; I__/2; WM__/2					

I ___ 9. After reading this story, how do you know that Marian was not only talented but also a hard worker? (she didn't give up; she taught herself to sing and play piano)

D ___ 10. Why didn't Marian attend music school in the city? (refused admission)

COMMENTS:

introduction

Read this story about a famous American president to see what happened to him.

WORD RECOGNITION ERRORS
Insertions ______
Mispronunciations ______
Omissions ______
Refusals ______
Repetitions ______
Reversals ______
Substitutions ______
Phrasing ______
Other: ______

WORD REC/CONTEXT ERRORS		
Ind	Inst	Frus
0–6	**7–16**	**17→**

As a boy and as a young man, he spent much of his spare time outdoors. He liked to ride horses, swim, sail, and ice skate. When Franklin was in college, his cousin, Teddy, was President of the United States. Thus Franklin became associated with politics. After he became a New York lawyer, he was elected to the State Senate. During his term as Senator, he contracted polio which left his legs useless.

Franklin had to be hoisted to and from a wheelchair. He could no longer enjoy the outdoor life. From the wheelchair he used a special apparatus to exercise the upper part of his body and make it strong. He wanted to stay active to continue his political career.

Despite his handicap, Franklin Roosevelt was elected President of the United States in 1932. The American people considered him a great leader. They reelected him president three times. No person has been elected president more than four times.

MI ___ 1. What would be a good title for this story? (Franklin Overcomes His Handicap; The Most Popular President; or appropriate title)

D ___ 2. Which of Franklin's relatives was president? (his cousin, Teddy)

WM ___ 3. The story tells of Franklin using a special APPARATUS; what does APPARATUS mean? (device; equipment)

D ___ 4. When was Franklin Roosevelt first elected president? (1932; 1930's)

WM ___ 5. The story says he had to be HOISTED; what does HOISTED mean? (lifted; raised)

D ___ 6. What caused Franklin to lose the use of his legs? (polio)

I ___ 7. After reading this story, why do you think that losing the use of his legs was a particular disappoint-

	TOTAL COMPREHENSION				FACTUAL (Even #'s)			INTERPRETIVE (Odd #'s)		
Levels:	Ind	Instructional		Frus	Ind	Inst	Frus	Ind	Inst	Frus
Question Errors	**0–1**	**2–3**	**4**	**5→**	**0**	**1–2**	**3→**	**0**	**1–2**	**3→**
Approx Grade Equiv	Late 6 (6.7–6.9)	Mid 6 (6.4–6.6)	Early 6 (6.1–6.3)	Below 6	Item Analysis: MI__/1; D__/5; I__/2; WM__/2					

ment to Franklin? (he liked to spend his spare time in outdoor sports; he could no longer ride horses, swim, ice skate)

D ___ 8. Name two outdoor sports Franklin enjoyed as a boy. (riding; swimming; sailing; ice skating/any two)

I ___ 9. Based on this story, how do you know that being in a wheelchair did not hurt Franklin's popularity as president? (Elected and then reelected)

D ___ 10. To how many terms was Franklin reelected president? (three)

COMMENTS:

introduction

Read this story about an American hero, Benjamin Bennekar, to find out what he did.

WORD RECOGNITION ERRORS
Insertions ____
Mispronunciations ____
Omissions ____
Refusals ____
Repetitions ____
Reversals ____
Substitutions ____
Phrasing ____
Other: ____

WORD REC/CONTEXT ERRORS		
Ind	Inst	Frus
0–7	**8–17**	**18→**

After the American Revolution, the colonists came to realize and value their freedom from foreign reign. For Ben, a young black man, life was exciting and rewarding.

Ben was not only a bright young man, but he was also shrewd and creative. Denied a formal education, he chose the alternative of self-instruction, teaching himself many things in his quest for knowledge. Intrigued by the machines of his time, he once disassembled a watch to examine its tiny parts. He matched each piece of the watch with a larger one which he carved from wood. Thus he assembled and built the first clock made in America. Ben helped survey the land site for the new capital of the United States, Washington, D. C.

One of Ben's most outstanding feats was his publication of an almanac. Many Americans enjoyed the almanac. Among them was another American hero, Thomas Jefferson. Jefferson felt that the same freedom which had rendered Ben capable of developing his skills would foster the growth of future Americans.

MI ___ 1. What would be a good title for this story? (The Man Who Taught Himself; The Life of a Famous American; or appropriate title)

D ___ 2. Give two words that were used in the story to describe Ben. (shrewd; black; creative; young/any two)

WM ___ 3. The story tells of Ben being INTRIGUED by machines; what does INTRIGUED mean? (fascinated; very interested in)

D ___ 4. What book did Ben publish? (almanac)

	TOTAL COMPREHENSION				FACTUAL (Even #'s)			INTERPRETIVE (Odd #'s)		
Levels:	Ind	Instructional		Frus	Ind	Inst	Frus	Ind	Inst	Frus
Question Errors	**0–1**	**2–3**	**4**	**5→**	**0**	**1–2**	**3→**	**0**	**1–2**	**3→**
Approx Grade Equiv	Late 7 (7.7–7.9)	Mid 7 (7.4–7.6)	Early 7 (7.1–7.3)	Below 7	Item Analysis: MI__/1; D__/5; I__/2; WM__/2					

WM ____ 5. What does it mean to be SHREWD? (cunning; very smart; resourceful)

D ____ 6. How did Ben get his education? (he taught himself)

I ____ 7. Why do you think that life was exciting and rewarding during the time of this story? (Americans first realizing their freedom from foreign reign; America was a young, growing nation; many things happening)

D ____ 8. What did Ben study to learn how to build the clock? (watch)

I ____ 9. After reading this story, why do you think that Ben's publication of the almanac was considered an outstanding feat? (not many publications then; he had no formal education)

D ____ 10. When did this story take place? (after the American Revolution; about two hundred years ago)

COMMENTS:

introduction

This story is about a successful person and his love of plants; read to see what happened.

WORD RECOGNITION ERRORS
Insertions ______
Mispronunciations ______
Omissions ______
Refusals ______
Repetitions ______
Reversals ______
Substitutions ______
Phrasing ______
Other: ______

WORD REC/CONTEXT ERRORS		
Ind	Inst	Frus
0–7	**8–18**	**19→**

The only plant breeder ever to achieve world fame was Luther Burbank. Much of his success was achieved because of his patience and willingness to experiment. In 1870, at age twenty-one, he purchased his own farm in Massachusetts. There, he experimented with the small, easily spoiled potatoes that were grown in the area. After three years of patient work, he developed white potatoes with brown skins. Named Burbank potatoes, they were far superior to other kinds. Saving ten of his new potatoes, Burbank reluctantly sold the rights to them to a seed store for $150; with the money, he purchased a train ticket to California.

In Santa Rosa, California, Luther worked with plant breeding for more than fifty years. Throughout the course of his life, he dramatically changed the plant world. He developed improved varieties of plums, cherries, apples, nuts, and berries, as well as new types of vegetables and flowers.

The ingenious work of Burbank with plants stimulated worldwide interest in scientific control of plant development. His successes illustrate the potential rewards of careful and patient study.

MI ___ 1. What is a good title for this story? (The Plant Breeder; Burbank's Work; or appropriate title)

D ___ 2. With what plant did Burbank experiment first? (potato)

WM ___ 3. The story tells of Burbank RELUCTANTLY selling the rights; what does RELUCTANTLY mean? (hesitantly; unwillingly)

D ___ 4. Where did Burbank move to spend

	TOTAL COMPREHENSION				FACTUAL (Even #'s)			INTERPRETIVE (Odd #'s)		
Levels:	Ind	Instructional		Frus	Ind	Inst	Frus	Ind	Inst	Frus
Question Errors	0–1	2–3	4	5→	0	1–2	3→	0	1–2	3→
Approx Grade Equiv	Late 8 (8.7–8.9)	Mid 8 (8.4–8.6)	Early 8 (8.1–8.3)	Below 8	Item Analysis: MI__/1; D__/5; I__/2; WM__/2					

most of his life? (California; Santa Rosa, California)

WM ___ 5. What does the word INGENIOUS mean in the phrase "INGENIOUS" work with plants? (clever; well conceived; skillful)

D ___ 6. Name two types of fruits he improved. (cherries; plums; apples; berries/any two)

I ___ 7. The story tells of Burbank reluctantly selling the rights to his new potatoes; why did he sell the rights? (to get the money to move to California)

D ___ 8. In what state did Burbank buy his first farm? (Massachusetts)

I ___ 9. After reading the story, why do you think that Burbank wanted to develop the new potato? (the old ones spoiled too easily and were small; people needed improved potato)

D ___ 10. Why, according to this story, was Burbank a successful plant breeder? (because of his careful AND patient study)

COMMENTS:

introduction

Read this story to find out about the childhood of a famous woman.

WORD RECOGNITION ERRORS
Insertions ______
Mispronunciations ______
Omissions ______
Refusals ______
Repetitions ______
Reversals ______
Substitutions ______
Phrasing ______
Other: ______

WORD REC/CONTEXT ERRORS		
Ind	Inst	Frus
0–8	**9–19**	**20→**

Marie Curie is well known for her discovery of radium, but what is not well known is her life as a child. She was born and raised in Warsaw, Poland. Although she taught herself to read at age four, she was discouraged from reading by her parents, who feared this genius in their little girl and encouraged her in more traditional play activities. Marie's early life was often difficult and painful. Her father, a professor of physics and mathematics, was lowered in his position due to his political views in Russian-controlled Poland. Her mother suffered from tuberculosis for several years. The treatment for this disease, coupled with the reduced income, impoverished the family. During this difficult time in her life, Marie buried herself in her reading, consuming everything from adventure stories to technical journals. While reading, Marie forgot the Russian tsar and his spies, her father's shame, her mother's illness, and all the hardship. Despite all her personal problems, Marie was determined to meet all adversity and to emerge victorious. Indeed, she did just that, providing the world with a new therapeutic treatment and receiving the Nobel Prize in 1903.

MI ___ 1. What is the major idea presented in this story about Marie Curie? (how trying her childhood was and how she overcame all)

D ___ 2. What was her home land? (Poland)

WM ___ 3. What does TRADITIONAL mean in "more TRADITIONAL

	TOTAL COMPREHENSION				FACTUAL (Even #'s)			INTERPRETIVE (Odd #'s)		
Levels:	Ind	Instructional		Frus	Ind	Inst	Frus	Ind	Inst	Frus
Question Errors	**0–1**	**2–3**	**4**	**5→**	**0**	**1–2**	**3→**	**0**	**1–2**	**3→**
Approx Grade Equiv	Late 9 (9.7–9.9)	Mid 9 (9.4–9.6)	Early 9 (9.1–9.3)	Below 9	Item Analysis: MI__/1; D__/5; I__/2; WM__/2					

play activities''? (customary or normal)

D ___ 4. How did Marie's family react to her reading at an early age? (they discouraged her; encouraged her to play instead)

WM ___ 5. What does ADVERSITY mean? (trouble; misfortune; calamity)

D ___ 6. What did Marie's father do for a living? (professor of physics, math)

I ___ 7. How do you think her father felt about his change in position? (defiant, but somewhat ashamed)

D ___ 8. What was wrong with Marie's mother? (very sick with tuberculosis; sick with disease)

I ___ 9. What effect did her childhood have on Marie's character? (made her strong, independent, determined to be successful)

D ___ 10. What connection did Marie Curie have with medicine? (provided the world with new therapeutic treatment)

COMMENTS:

introduction

Read this selection to find out about the life of a brilliant scientist.

WORD RECOGNITION ERRORS
Insertions ____
Mispronunciations ____
Omissions ____
Refusals ____
Repetitions ____
Reversals ____
Substitutions ____
Phrasing ____
Other: ____

WORD REC/CONTEXT ERRORS		
Ind	Inst	Frus
0–8	**9–20**	**21→**

Many eventually famous and brilliant persons have had notably unremarkable beginnings in their early schooling, and Albert Einstein was one of these. Although he became an important scientist in his day and a winner of the Nobel Prize, his early years in school were particularly difficult for him; because his grades were frequently lowest in his classes, his teachers branded him as "dull." German schools were extremely strict and harsh in Einstein's youth, and he was frequently punished for asking too many questions or for being inattentive in all classes except mathematics. He had no friends either, for he was inadequate in sports and had goals and aspirations markedly different from the other students. All of this culminated in his being asked to leave the gymnasium, or high school, in Germany just before graduation. Nonetheless, Einstein did eventually receive his diploma in 1897 from a Swiss high school. He completed college in 1900 and began working in the Swiss patent office. Shortly after this, Einstein realized his mother's lifelong dream for him. He became a college professor, first in several European countries, including Switzerland and Austria, and finally in the United States. Einstein was invited to lecture on his theories throughout the world.

	TOTAL COMPREHENSION				FACTUAL (Even #'s)			INTERPRETIVE (Odd #'s)		
Levels:	Ind	Instructional		Frus	Ind	Inst	Frus	Ind	Inst	Frus
Question Errors	**0–1**	**2–3**	**4**	**5→**	**0**	**1–2**	**3→**	**0**	**1–2**	**3→**
Approx Grade Equiv	Late 10 (10.7–.9)	Mid 10 (10.4–10.6)	Early 10 (10.1–10.3)	Below 10	Item Analysis: MI__/1; D__/5; I__/2; WM__/2					

MI ___ 1. Suggest a title for this story. (The Rise of Einstein; or appropriate title)

D ___ 2. What did Einstein's earliest teachers think of him? (dull; slow; stupid)

WM ___ 3. What is a GYMNASIUM in Germany? (high school)

D ___ 4. What happened when Einstein asked too many questions at school? (punished)

WM ___ 5. What does CULMINATED mean? (resulted or climaxed)

D ___ 6. What were the German schools like during Einstein's youth? (strict and harsh)

I ___ 7. Based on this story, how do we know that Einstein probably liked his mathematics class? (didn't pay attention in any class but math)

D ___ 8. Why didn't he graduate from the German high school? (asked to leave just before graduation)

I ___ 9. After reading this story, why do you think Einstein became a college professor? (so intelligent; his mother's dream; to share scientific knowledge)

D ___ 10. Name two countries in which Einstein taught. (any two: Austria, Switzerland, and the United States)

COMMENTS:

introduction

Read this story to find out about giant apes.

WORD RECOGNITION ERRORS	
Insertions	
Mispronunciations	
Omissions	
Refusals	
Repetitions	
Reversals	
Substitutions	
Phrasing	
Other:	

Some people don't like apes.

Apes look mean.

They are not.

They are sad in the zoo.

They want to go home.

The home of the apes is in the woods.

They have fun there.

They play with other apes.

They play in trees.

At night mother apes stay in trees.

Baby apes do too.

Father apes don't stay in trees.

They make a bed in the grass.

WORD REC/CONTEXT ERRORS		
Ind	Inst	Frus
0–3	**4–8**	**9→**

MI ___ 1. What is a good name for this story? (Life of Apes; Where Apes Live; or any appropriate title)

D ___ 2. Where does the father ape sleep at night? (in the grass)

WM ___ 3. The story tells that father apes make a BED in the grass; what does BED mean in this story? (place to sleep)

D ___ 4. Where does a baby ape stay at night? (in a tree)

WM ___ 5. The story says apes look MEAN; what is another word for MEAN? (angry; mad; dangerous)

D ___ 6. How does the story say the apes feel in the zoo? (sad)

I ___ 7. Why do you think the mother and baby apes sleep in trees at night? (to be safe; for protection)

D ___ 8. In this story where do the apes have fun? (at home in the woods)

	TOTAL COMPREHENSION			FACTUAL (Even #'s)			INTERPRETIVE (Odd #'s)		
Levels:	Ind	Instructional	Frus	Ind	Inst	Frus	Ind	Inst	Frus
Question Errors	**0–1**	**2–3**	**4→**	**0**	**1**	**2→**	**0**	**1**	**2→**
Approx Grade Equiv	Early 1st Grade (1.1–1.3)		Below Primer	Item Analysis: MI__/1; D__/4; I__/1; WM__/2					

introduction

Read this story to find out about a different kind of fish.

WORD RECOGNITION ERRORS
Insertions ______
Mispronunciations ______
Omissions ______
Refusals ______
Repetitions ______
Reversals ______
Substitutions ______
Phrasing ______
Other: ______

We know fish can swim.

Did you know some fish can fly?

But a flying fish does not have wings.

It is not like a bird.

It moves like a paper plane.

Big fish sometimes go after it.

It can fly over the water.

It can only fly for a short time.

Then it comes down.

Sometimes a big fish is still after it.

It can take off again.

This is the way a flying fish takes care of itself.

WORD REC/CONTEXT ERRORS		
Ind	Inst	Frus
0–3	4–8	9→

MI ___ 1. Give this story a good name. (Flying Fish; A Different Kind of Fish; or any appropriate title)

D ___ 2. How long can flying fish fly, according to the story? (a short time)

WM ___ 3. In the story, the "flying fish can TAKE OFF." What does TAKE OFF mean? (begin to fly, leave the water, fly in the air)

D ___ 4. What sometimes goes after the flying fish in the story? (a big fish)

WM ___ 5. The story tells that big fish "GO AFTER it." What does GO AFTER mean? (chase; try to catch)

D ___ 6. Where does the story say that the flying fish fly? (over the water)

I ___ 7. Why would being able to fly be helpful to a fish? (to escape from danger; for protection; to stay safe)

D ___ 8. The story stated that flying fish could move like what kind of plane? (paper)

	TOTAL COMPREHENSION			FACTUAL (Even #'s)			INTERPRETIVE (Odd #'s)		
Levels:	Ind	Instructional	Frus	Ind	Inst	Frus	Ind	Inst	Frus
Question Errors	0–1	2–3	4→	0	1	2→	0	1	2→
Approx Grade Equiv	Late 1 (1.7–1.9)	Mid 1 (1.4–1.6)	Below 1	Item Analysis: MI__/1; D__/4; I__/1; WM__/2					

introduction

This story is about an unusual animal, the camel.
Read to learn about camels.

WORD RECOGNITION ERRORS
Insertions ______
Mispronunciations ______
Omissions ______
Refusals ______
Repetitions ______
Reversals ______
Substitutions ______
Phrasing ______
Other: ______

WORD REC/CONTEXT ERRORS		
Ind	Inst	Frus
0–4	**5–10**	**11→**

How would you like to begin a long trip in a hot, dry land?

There is little food or water.

A camel does not mind.

It stores enough food and water in its hump.

This will last for many days.

Little food grows in dry places.

The camel does not mind eating bushes and plants.

The wind blows sand and dust.

The camel's long eyelashes keep its eyes safe.

It is able to close its nose.

This keeps out the sand and dust.

It would be dangerous for other animals to try to travel in hot, dry lands.

But camels are well prepared.

MI ___ 1. What is a good name for this story? (How a Camel Lives in the Desert; All About Camels; or any appropriate title)

D ___ 2. How does a camel's nose protect it? (closes to keep out dust and sand)

WM ___ 3. What is meant by "the camel does not MIND"? (doesn't care; is not bothered)

D ___ 4. What helps a camel protect its eyes? (long eyelashes)

WM ___ 5. What does it mean to be PREPARED? (be ready; have what it needs)

D ___ 6. How long does the story tell that camels can store food and water? (many days)

I ___ 7. After reading this story, why do you think that it would be dangerous for most other animals to travel in hot, dry lands? (they are not prepared; might die; would need more food and water)

D ___ 8. According to the story, what does a camel eat? (bushes and plants)

	TOTAL COMPREHENSION				FACTUAL (Even #'s)			INTERPRETIVE (Odd #'s)		
Levels:	Ind	Instructional		Frus	Ind	Inst	Frus	Ind	Inst	Frus
Question Errors	**0–1**	**2**	**3**	**4→**	**0**	**1**	**2→**	**0**	**1**	**2→**
Approx Grade Equiv	Late 2 (2.7–2.9)	Mid 2 (2.4–2.6)	Early 2 (2.1–2.3)	Below 2	Item Analysis: MI__/1; D__/4; I__/1; WM__/2					

introduction

Read this story to find out more about lions.

WORD RECOGNITION ERRORS
Insertions ______
Mispronunciations ______
Omissions ______
Refusals ______
Repetitions ______
Reversals ______
Substitutions ______
Phrasing ______
Other: ______

WORD REC/CONTEXT ERRORS		
Ind	Inst	Frus
0–5	**6–12**	**13→**

Lions are sometimes called "Kings of the Jungle." Their size and walk appear so grand that they look like kings. Lions may be longer than some cars. The color of these giant cats may be from gray to brown. Most people think that lions are very brave too. But lions may not be quite as brave as everyone thinks.

Lions are afraid of camp fires. People can also scare lions by waving large branches. Many male lions do not even catch their own dinner. At night they just roar loudly. This frightens small animals away from them and toward the female lions. It is the female lions who capture dinner.

Lions may not be the bravest of animals. But they look and act like kings!

MI ___ 1. What would be a good title for this story? (King of Jungle; All About Lions; How Lions Get Food; or appropriate title)

D ___ 2. What does this story say that lions are sometimes called? (Kings of the Jungle)

WM ___ 3. What does it mean to be BRAVE? (not afraid; bold)

D ___ 4. Name 2 ways that this story says people can scare lions. (campfires AND waving branches)

WM ___ 5. The story tells that the lion's walk appears GRAND; what is meant by GRAND? (stately; kingly; strut; great; dignified)

D ___ 6. In this story, how long are some lions? (longer than some cars)

	TOTAL COMPREHENSION				FACTUAL (Even #'s)			INTERPRETIVE (Odd #'s)		
Levels:	Ind	Instructional		Frus	Ind	Inst	Frus	Ind	Inst	Frus
Question Errors	**0–1**	**2–3**	**4**	**5→**	**0**	**1–2**	**3→**	**0**	**1–2**	**3→**
Approx Grade Equiv	Late 3 (3.7–3.9)	Mid 3 (3.4–3.6)	Early 3 (3.1–3.3)	Below 3	Item Analysis: MI__/1; D__/5; I__/2; WM__/2					

I ___ 7. When do the lions in the story usually eat? (at night)

D ___ 8. What color are the lions in this story? (from gray to brown)

I ___ 9. After reading this story, how do you think some kings look and act? (grand; scare people; may be big; walk in a grand manner; in command)

D ___ 10. What do male lions do to capture dinner? (roar; scare small animals toward female lion)

COMMENTS:

introduction

This story is about a tiny bird that enjoys plant nectar. Read to find out about this bird.

WORD RECOGNITION ERRORS
Insertions ______
Mispronunciations ______
Omissions ______
Refusals ______
Repetitions ______
Reversals ______
Substitutions ______
Phrasing ______
Other: ______

WORD REC/CONTEXT ERRORS		
Ind	Inst	Frus
0–5	**6–14**	**15→**

Among the most brightly colored birds are hummingbirds. They are also the smallest birds in the world. Some hummingbirds are as tiny as bumblebees with feathers. They may weigh no more than a penny. Their little nests are only about the size of nut shells.

These birds are named for the humming noise of their wings. In flight, their tiny wings flutter thousands of times each minute. The wings move so quickly that it is difficult to see them. Flying at rapid speeds, hummingbirds perform much like helicopters. They can dart in all directions and even balance in mid-air.

Hummingbirds may eat fifty tiny meals a day. They like sweet nectar. Their long, narrow bills reach deep into flowers. People like to observe the tiny birds. If honey is placed in a feeder, sometimes hummingbirds will come.

MI ___ 1. What would be a good title for this story? (The Smallest Bird; All About Hummingbirds; or any appropriate title)

D ___ 2. Why do we call these birds hummingbirds? (because of humming sound of their wings)

WM ___ 3. What does FLUTTER mean in "their tiny wings FLUTTER"? (move quickly)

D ___ 4. According to this story, how much do some hummingbirds weigh? (no more than a penny)

WM ___ 5. What does OBSERVE the tiny birds mean? (watch them; look at them)

	TOTAL COMPREHENSION				FACTUAL (Even #'s)			INTERPRETIVE (Odd #'s)		
Levels:	Ind	Instructional		Frus	Ind	Inst	Frus	Ind	Inst	Frus
Question Errors	**0–1**	**2–3**	**4**	**5→**	**0**	**1–2**	**3→**	**0**	**1–2**	**3→**
Approx Grade Equiv	Late 4 (4.7–4.9)	Mid 4 (4.4–4.6)	Early 4 (4.1–4.3)	Below 4	Item Analysis: MI__/1; D__/5; I__/2; WM__/2					

D ___ 6. How many times a day does the story state that some hummingbirds eat? (fifty)

I ___ 7. Give two reasons why you think that people enjoy watching hummingbirds. (flutter; so tiny; so fast; dart about; bright colors)

D ___ 8. Describe a hummingbird's bill. (long AND narrow)

I ___ 9. What about the story makes you think that hummingbirds might like honey? (they come to feeder for it; it's like nectar; sweet to eat)

D ___ 10. What size nest do hummingbirds build according to the story? (size of a nut shell)

COMMENTS:

introduction

Read this story to learn about something that happens at the beach.

WORD RECOGNITION ERRORS
Insertions ______
Mispronunciations ______
Omissions ______
Refusals ______
Repetitions ______
Reversals ______
Substitutions ______
Phrasing ______
Other: ______

WORD REC/CONTEXT ERRORS		
Ind	Inst	Frus
0–6	**7–15**	**16→**

You may have seen beautiful white birds circling the horizon at beaches and lakes. You may have seen these gulls roaming the reefs or beaches in the early morning. These birds are a special part of beach scenes. Few beach pictures are painted without a gull in the picture. You can hear the sound of the rushing waves and the gulls' shrill cry. They are sounds of the beach.

Did you know that gulls keep our beaches clean? They are like a small army of trash collectors. They eat the debris thoughtless people have left behind. Shiny trash on the beach is often carried to sea by the birds. After cleaning the beach, gulls fly over the water, snapping up shellfish to eat. The gulls drop the shellfish on a jagged reef. This cracks the shellfish open. The sight and sound of the fascinating gull make the beach a special place.

MI ___ 1. What would be a good title for this story? (Gulls at the Beach; The Sight and Sound of the Beach; All About Gulls; or appropriate title)

D ___ 2. What kind of birds are in the story? (gulls)

WM ___ 3. The story tells of gulls roaming the REEFS; what are REEFS? (jagged rocks, rocks at or near the surface of the ocean water)

D ___ 4. When do the gulls roam the beaches? (early in the morning)

WM ___ 5. The story describes FASCINATING gulls; what is another word for FASCINATING? (intriguing; interesting; unusual)

D ___ 6. According to this story, what are the "sounds of the beach"? (sound of the rushing waves AND gulls' shrill cries)

I ___ 7. After reading this story, why do you think that gulls might like to live near beaches? (plenty to eat; to eat shellfish and beach debris)

	TOTAL COMPREHENSION				FACTUAL (Even #'s)			INTERPRETIVE (Odd #'s)		
Levels:	Ind	Instructional		Frus	Ind	Inst	Frus	Ind	Inst	Frus
Question Errors	0–1	2–3	4	5→	0	1–2	3→	0	1–2	3→
Approx Grade Equiv	Late 5 (5.7–5.9)	Mid 5 (5.4–5.6)	Early 5 (5.1–5.3)	Below 5	Item Analysis: MI__/1; D__/5; I__/2; WM__/2					

D ___ 8. Why do the gulls in the story drop shellfish on reefs? (to crack open the shellfish)

I ___ 9. How, according to the story, do gulls make the beach more enjoyable for people? (their sight and sound are interesting; they clean the beaches)

D ___ 10. What does the story say that gulls often carry to sea? (shiny trash)

COMMENTS:

introduction

Read this story to find out about a strange animal.

WORD RECOGNITION ERRORS
Insertions ______
Mispronunciations ______
Omissions ______
Refusals ______
Repetitions ______
Reversals ______
Substitutions ______
Phrasing ______
Other: ______

Bats are often thought of as undesirable and menacing creatures. They are sometimes associated with Halloween and evil spirits. Bats do have some outlandish habits, like sleeping in the daytime in damp, dark caves. But they can be really helpful to people. Powerful wings help the bats fly at rapid speeds. Bats can capture insects which might harm a farmer's crops.

You may have heard it said that someone is "blind as a bat." Bats can see, but they are better known for their ability to use their radar system. In flight, the bat makes a squeaking sound that can be scary. Moving ahead of the bat, the sound bounces off any objects in the bat's path. This enables the bat to travel with precision even in total darkness. By studying the bat's built-in radar apparatus, scientists have been able to refine mechanical radar systems. Studying bats has helped protect people. Still, many people do not like bats.

WORD REC/CONTEXT ERRORS		
Ind	Inst	Frus
0–6	**7–16**	**17→**

MI ___ 1. Give this story a good title. (Bats Are Not ALL Bad; The Interesting Life of a Bat; The Good Features of Bats; or appropriate title)

D ___ 2. How are bats able to safely fly in darkness? (use their radar to know where to fly)

WM ___ 3. What does it mean to have OUTLANDISH habits? (weird; strange; ridiculous; unusual)

D ___ 4. How do bats help farmers, according to this story? (by capturing harmful insects)

WM ___ 5. What does PRECISION mean in the phrase, "travel with PRECISION"? (exactness; accuracy)

D ___ 6. Where do bats sleep, according to

	TOTAL COMPREHENSION				FACTUAL (Even #'s)			INTERPRETIVE (Odd #'s)		
Levels:	Ind	Instructional		Frus	Ind	Inst	Frus	Ind	Inst	Frus
Question Errors	**0–1**	**2–3**	**4**	**5→**	**0**	**1–2**	**3→**	**0**	**1–2**	**3→**
Approx Grade Equiv	Late 6 (6.7–6.9)	Mid 6 (6.4–6.6)	Early 6 (6.1–6.3)	Below 6	Item Analysis: MI__/1; D__/5; I__/2; WM__/2					

this story? (damp, dark places; caves)

I ___ 7. After reading this story, how do you know that a bat's radar system really works? (they are able to fly with precision in dark; scientists have studied their radar system)

D ___ 8. Why do bats squeak when they fly? (it's part of their radar system; so the sound will bounce off whatever is in their path)

I ___ 9. The story states that "studying bats has helped protect people." How do you think this has helped protect people? (scientists have refined mechanical radar systems which warn them of objects in their path; used on boats, planes, warning devices, etc.)

D ___ 10. According to the story, why do some people not like bats? (think they are undesirable, menacing; associated with Halloween and evil spirits; because of their outlandish habits)

COMMENTS:

introduction

Read this story to find out about some interesting animals.

WORD RECOGNITION ERRORS
Insertions ______
Mispronunciations ______
Omissions ______
Refusals ______
Repetitions ______
Reversals ______
Substitutions ______
Phrasing ______
Other: ______

WORD REC/CONTEXT ERRORS		
Ind	Inst	Frus
0–7	**8–17**	**18→**

Prairie dogs have made their homes on the plains of the United States for over one million years. The cute animals resemble squirrels with short tails. So named for their homes and their barks, prairie dogs express their affection for one another by kissing!

Each prairie dog family has an underground house in a permanent town with just a few burrow mounds visible above ground. The interior of the home has many tunnels and entrances, and may have a hidden entrance which is used to take refuge from predators. Each home may have a small nesting room or two. Close to the surface of the ground may be constructed a unique room. The animals can turn around in it. From this room they can also listen to events on the surface. The town is constantly guarded by some town members. Approaching danger is heralded by the urgent barking of the guards from atop their burrow mounds. Given the danger signal, the prairie dogs retreat to the refuge of their underground town.

MI ___ 1. What is a good title for this story? (Prairie Dog Homes; How Prairie Dogs Live; or appropriate title)

D ___ 2. According to the story, what animals do prairie dogs resemble? (squirrels)

WM ___ 3. The story tells of prairie dogs taking REFUGE; what does it mean to TAKE REFUGE? (take or seek shelter; seek cover; hide; seek safety)

D ___ 4. In what part of the United States do prairie dogs live, according to this story? (the plains of the US)

WM ___ 5. The story tells of prairie dogs escaping from PREDATORS;

	TOTAL COMPREHENSION				FACTUAL (Even #'s)			INTERPRETIVE (Odd #'s)		
Levels:	Ind	Instructional		Frus	Ind	Inst	Frus	Ind	Inst	Frus
Question Errors	**0–1**	**2–3**	**4**	**5→**	**0**	**1–2**	**3→**	**0**	**1–2**	**3→**
Approx Grade Equiv	Late 7 (7.7–7.9)	Mid 7 (7.4–7.6)	Early 7 (7.1–7.3)	Below 7	Item Analysis: MI__/1; D__/5; I__/2; WM__/2					

what is a PREDATOR? (one who preys on, chases, or attempts to capture others)

D ___ 6. Name two rooms that might be found in a prairie dog's home. (Nesting room; listening room; turn-around room; the unique room/any two)

I ___ 7. After reading this story, why do you think that prairie dogs might want to listen to what is happening above ground? (to see if it's safe to go out; to listen for enemies or predators; to check weather)

D ___ 8. How does the story tell that prairie dogs signal danger? (urgent barking)

I ___ 9. Why do you think that prairie dog homes have several entrances? (choice of escape; so they can go out the safe one)

D ___ 10. According to this story, how do prairie dogs express affection? (by kissing)

COMMENTS:

introduction

Read this story about cold weather animals.

WORD RECOGNITION ERRORS
Insertions ________
Mispronunciations ________
Omissions ________
Refusals ________
Repetitions ________
Reversals ________
Substitutions ________
Phrasing ________
Other: ________

WORD REC/CONTEXT ERRORS		
Ind	Inst	Frus
0–7	8–18	19→

In the cold barren land of Antarctica is found one of nature's most appealing creatures. The upright stance of penguins, their waddling gait, and short flippers create the appearance of a small man in a black tuxedo. The friendliness of the penguins further adds to their appeal.

The physiology of penguins permits them to withstand the intense cold of the remote Antarctic regions. Their small heads, wings, and feet attached to a robust trunk offer limited surface area to the icy temperatures. Thick layers of fat under the skin help insulate the birds from the harsh weather. The remoteness of their natural habitat aids in protecting the birds from man.

Penguins live in flocks or colonies and share duties; while some parents hunt and fish, others tend the nurseries of penguin chicks. Most penguins are able to fend for themselves and survive the cold and rough habitat. However, some have difficulty in captivity and may become almost helpless. The captured penguins may not learn to feed themselves. These birds must be taught to accept hand fed fish each day.

MI ___ 1. Give this story a good title. (Penguins of Antarctica; All About Penguins; or appropriate title)

D ___ 2. According to this story, where are penguins found? (Antarctica)

WM ___ 3. The story speaks of the penguin's natural HABITAT; what is a

	TOTAL COMPREHENSION				FACTUAL (Even #'s)			INTERPRETIVE (Odd #'s)		
Levels:	Ind	Instructional		Frus	Ind	Inst	Frus	Ind	Inst	Frus
Question Errors	0–1	2–3	4	5→	0	1–2	3→	0	1–2	3→
Approx Grade Equiv	Late 8 (8.7–8.9)	Mid 8 (8.4–8.6)	Early 8 (8.1–8.3)	Below 8	Item Analysis: MI__/1; D__/5; I__/2; WM__/2					

HABITAT? (home; dwelling; where they live)

D ___ 4. Name two features of penguins which, according to this story, enable them to withstand the intense cold. (Small heads; wings; feet; robust trunk; thick fat/any two)

WM ___ 5. The story tells about REMOTE regions; what does REMOTE mean? (distant; far off; isolated)

D ___ 6. What are the duties of the adult penguins in this story? (share duties for hunting; fishing; tending young/any two)

I ___ 7. Although the story does not state a reason, why do you think that penguins might need protection from people? (might hunt them; attempt to capture them)

D ___ 8. According to this story, what protects penguins from man? (the remoteness of their natural habitat or home)

I ___ 9. After reading this story, why do you think that capturing penguins might be considered cruel? (they may become almost helpless in captivity; can't even feed selves; after capture, have difficulty)

D ___ 10. Name two features of penguins which, according to the story, help to create the appearance of a small man. (upright stance; waddling gait; short flippers; color of "tuxedo"/any two)

COMMENTS:

introduction

Read this story to find out why whales are such interesting creatures.

WORD RECOGNITION ERRORS
Insertions ______
Mispronunciations ______
Omissions ______
Refusals ______
Repetitions ______
Reversals ______
Substitutions ______
Phrasing ______
Other: ______

WORD REC/CONTEXT ERRORS		
Ind	Inst	Frus
0–8	**9–19**	**20→**

The whale, an extraordinary animal in numerous respects, has been the subject of fantastic stories starting with Jonah in the Bible. The growth of an animal's body is limited to that size which it is capable of supporting and moving unassisted. Whales have been able to attain their enormous size because water provides the support and vehicle for the whale's movements. Contrary to what many people believe, whales are mammals, not fish. Some scientists believe that whales originally lived on land because they breathe air and are warm-blooded. They have some body hair, and their skeletal structure suggests that they once had legs.

One group of whales, sometimes called "whalebones," has instead of teeth, a fringe of long plates made of a substance somewhat like fingernails. Through these plates, they strain their food. The largest member of this group is the blue whale. It can be as long as ninety feet and weigh as much as one hundred fifty tons, and is the largest creature ever to have existed on earth. It would require approximately thirty enormous elephants or three of the largest dinosaurs ever discovered to equal the weight of this whale.

	TOTAL COMPREHENSION				FACTUAL (Even #'s)			INTERPRETIVE (Odd #'s)		
Levels:	Ind	Instructional		Frus	Ind	Inst	Frus	Ind	Inst	Frus
Question Errors	**0–1**	**2–3**	**4**	**5→**	**0**	**1–2**	**3→**	**0**	**1–2**	**3→**
Approx Grade Equiv	Late 9 (9.7–9.9)	Mid 9 (9.4–9.6)	Early 9 (9.1–9.3)	Below 9	Item Analysis: MI__/1; D__/5; I__/2; WM__/2					

MI ___ 1. Suggest a title for this story. (The Fantastic Whales; or appropriate title)

D ___ 2. Give two reasons why scientists believe whales once lived on land. (any two: body hair; warm-blooded; breathe air; skeletal structure suggests they once had legs; mammals)

WM ___ 3. What does EXTRAORDINARY mean? (unbelievable; very unusual)

D ___ 4. Name the largest whale. (Blue Whale)

WM ___ 5. What does CONTRARY mean in the phrase "CONTRARY to what many people believe"? (different from; opposite of)

D ___ 6. What does the whalebone group of whales have instead of teeth? (fringe of long plates made of a substance much like fingernails)

I ___ 7. Why do you think the whale is the subject of many fantastic stories? (people are fascinated with large size; mammals that live in water; not many people see whales)

D ___ 8. According to this story, why have whales been able to reach their enormous size? (water supports body and provides vehicle for whales' movements)

I ___ 9. The story tells that whales breathe air, have body hair and may once have had legs; why do you think these facts have led scientists to believe that whales once lived on land? (don't need air, hair, or legs to live in water; these are all characteristics of land animals)

D ___ 10. How many elephants would it take to equal the weight of the blue whale? (about thirty)

COMMENTS:

introduction

This story is about a useful animal.
Read to find out about goats.

WORD RECOGNITION ERRORS
Insertions ______
Mispronunciations ______
Omissions ______
Refusals ______
Repetitions ______
Reversals ______
Substitutions ______
Phrasing ______
Other: ______

WORD REC/CONTEXT ERRORS		
Ind	Inst	Frus
0–8	**9–20**	**21→**

Goats, animals that have existed since the times of ancient civilizations, are relatives of sheep and, like sheep, they are valuable for their milk and hair. Goats can be either wild or domestic, but we usually consider them to be rugged and, at times, stubborn animals.

Wild goats ordinarily exist in high rocky habitats in Europe and Asia except for Rocky Mountain wild goats. These high spirited animals are vigorous and generally able to withstand extremely harsh winters in the mountainous regions.

Domestic goats can be located in several countries throughout the world; these animals, when fully grown, may weigh more than one hundred twenty pounds. They do not consume aluminum containers as some individuals believe! They prefer grass and foods that are not overly rich, but will, however, chew or lick nearly anything that contains minerals. Goats have a special type of stomach that enables them to swallow their food rapidly, store it, and then later, ruminate and chew the food as a "cud."

In the United States, goats are raised primarily for their milk which is sweet, nutritious, and generally easier to digest than cow's milk. Some people prefer goats as pets on a farm or in a zoo.

	TOTAL COMPREHENSION				FACTUAL (Even #'s)			INTERPRETIVE (Odd #'s)		
Levels:	Ind	Instructional		Frus	Ind	Inst	Frus	Ind	Inst	Frus
Question Errors	**0–1**	**2–3**	**4**	**5→**	**0**	**1–2**	**3→**	**0**	**1–2**	**3→**
Approx Grade Equiv	Late 10 (10.7–.9)	Mid 10 (10.4–10.6)	Early 10 (10.1–10.3)	Below 10	Item Analysis: MI__/1; D__/5; I__/2; WM__/2					

MI ___ 1. What would be a good title for this story? (All About Goats; Different Types of Goats: or appropriate title)

D ___ 2. Name two types of goats. (wild AND domestic)

WM ___ 3. What is a CUD? (a lump of grass that goats chew; the food which is ruminated and chewed at leisure)

D ___ 4. What do goats eat? (any one: grass; simple foods; lick items for minerals)

WM ___ 5. The word CONSUME is used in this story; what does it mean? (to eat)

D ___ 6. Name two areas where wild goats are found (any two: Asia; Europe; U.S.; or Rocky Mountains)

I ___ 7. Why do you think wild goats would have to be rugged animals? (any two: to survive; find food; live in the winter; protect themselves)

D ___ 8. Give two reasons why some people prefer goat's milk to cow's milk. (any two: sweet; nutritious; easier to digest than cow's milk)

I ___ 9. After reading this story, why do you think some people believe that goats eat aluminum containers? (because they will chew or lick nearly anything that contains minerals)

D ___ 10. How much did the story say a goat could weigh? (one hundred twenty pounds or more)

COMMENTS:

introduction

This story tells about travel long ago. *Let's pretend that we were there.*

WORD RECOGNITION ERRORS
Insertions ______
Mispronunciations ______
Omissions ______
Refusals ______
Repetitions ______
Reversals ______
Substitutions ______
Phrasing ______
Other: ______

WORD REC/CONTEXT ERRORS		
Ind	Inst	Frus
0–3	4–8	9→

Some people want new homes.

They want to go west.

They need to take things with them.

They can take some things on a horse.

They want to take more.

They can take wagons.

Will wagons get there?

They take the wagons.

They ride in wagons.

They put things in them.

They work and work.

The wagons go west.

More people go west to make new homes.

MI ___ 1. What would be a good name for this story? (Going West; Wagons Go West; or appropriate title)

D ___ 2. Where were the people in the story going? (West)

WM ___ 3. What does WORK mean in the story part that says, "they WORK and WORK"? (they tried very hard; they had much to do; they struggle)

D ___ 4. Why did the people in the story want to go west? (wanted new homes)

WM ___ 5. What does "to MAKE a new home" mean? (build new house in new place; move; move to new home or house)

D ___ 6. How did the people in the story travel? (rode in wagons; horses pulled the *wagons*)

	TOTAL COMPREHENSION			FACTUAL (Even #'s)			INTERPRETIVE (Odd #'s)		
Levels:	Ind	Instructional	Frus	Ind	Inst	Frus	Ind	Inst	Frus
Question Errors	0–1	2–3	4→	0	1	2→	0	1	2→
Approx Grade Equiv	Early 1st Grade (1.1–1.3)		Below Primer	Item Analysis: MI__/1; D__/4; I__/1; WM__/2					

I ___ 7. What kind of things do you think the people wanted to take with them on their trip? (furniture, clothes; things to move into new home)

D ___ 8. Why did more people go west, according to this story? (to make new home)

COMMENTS:

introduction

This story of long ago tells about a special animal.
Read to find out what is so special about this animal.

WORD RECOGNITION ERRORS
Insertions ______
Mispronunciations ______
Omissions ______
Refusals ______
Repetitions ______
Reversals ______
Substitutions ______
Phrasing ______
Other: ______

Long ago people in a far away land liked horses.

The horses were pretty.

They could run fast.

They were pets.

People used the horses too.

They helped the people work.

It was fun to watch the horses race.

It was fun to see which horse ran faster.

Some men from a far away place did not want their horses.

They left these horses in a new country.

That is how these horses came there.

People today think these are fine horses.

WORD REC/CONTEXT ERRORS		
Ind	Inst	Frus
0–3	**4–8**	**9→**

MI ___ 1. What is a good name for this story? (Pet Horses; How Horses Got There; All About Special Horses; or appropriate title)

D ___ 2. Name two things these horses could do. (run fast; work; race/any two)

WM ___ 3. What does FAR AWAY land mean? (one many miles away; a long way off)

D ___ 4. Why did people go to the races in this story? (to see which horse ran faster; fun to watch)

WM ___ 5. The story tells that these are FINE horses; what does FINE mean? (excellent; elegant; handsome; beautiful; wonderful)

D ___ 6. How did these horses get to a new country? (men from far away left them)

I ___ 7. After reading this story, why do you think the horses became pets? (people liked them so much; people petted or pampered them)

D ___ 8. Why did the men in the story leave the horses? (they did not want them)

	TOTAL COMPREHENSION			FACTUAL (Even #'s)			INTERPRETIVE (Odd #'s)		
Levels:	Ind	Instructional	Frus	Ind	Inst	Frus	Ind	Inst	Frus
Question Errors	**0–1**	**2–3**	**4→**	**0**	**1**	**2→**	**0**	**1**	**2→**
Approx Grade Equiv	Late 1 (1.7–1.9)	Mid 1 (1.4–1.6)	Below 1	Item Analysis: MI__/1; D__/4; I__/1; WM__/2					

introduction

Read this story to find out about a special school that was started long ago.

WORD RECOGNITION ERRORS	
Insertions	
Mispronunciations	
Omissions	
Refusals	
Repetitions	
Reversals	
Substitutions	
Phrasing	
Other:	

WORD REC/CONTEXT ERRORS		
Ind	Inst	Frus
0–4	5–10	11→

Many years ago a man began a different kind of school.

It was in his country.

It was a school for little children.

There, they were able to sing, dance, and play.

They could make things.

But the people were unhappy with the school.

They said, "Little children should not go to school."

So they made the man close the school.

Years later, a man in another country began the same kind of school.

Children go to this school at age five.

They like to go.

But they learn more than singing, dancing, and playing.

These children get ready for first grade.

MI ___ 1. What would be a good name for this story? (Little Children Go to School; All About Kindergarten; or appropriate title)

D ___ 2. Where did this kind of school first begin? (The man's country)

WM ___ 3. What does ABLE mean in "to be able to sing"? (can; have the ability)

D ___ 4. Why were people unhappy with the first school? (they thought that little children should not have to go to school; thought the children were too young to go to school)

WM ___ 5. What does UNHAPPY mean in the sentence, "People were UNHAPPY"? (sad; not happy, not cheerful)

D ___ 6. According to the story, at what age do children go to the new school? (age five)

I ___ 7. After reading this story, why do you

	TOTAL COMPREHENSION				FACTUAL (Even #'s)			INTERPRETIVE (Odd #'s)		
Levels:	Ind	Instructional		Frus	Ind	Inst	Frus	Ind	Inst	Frus
Question Errors	0–1	2	3	4→	0	1	2→	0	1	2→
Approx Grade Equiv	Late 2 (2.7–2.9)	Mid 2 (2.4–2.6)	Early 2 (2.1–2.3)	Below 2	Item Analysis: MI__/1; D__/4; I__/1; WM__/2					

think that the children might have liked this school? (could have fun; could sing, dance, and play with other children)

D ___ 8. In the new school, the children get ready for what? (for first grade)

COMMENTS:

introduction

Read this story of long ago to learn about the importance of a road.

WORD RECOGNITION ERRORS
Insertions ______
Mispronunciations ______
Omissions ______
Refusals ______
Repetitions ______
Reversals ______
Substitutions ______
Phrasing ______
Other: ______

WORD REC/CONTEXT ERRORS		
Ind	Inst	Frus
0–5	**6–12**	**13→**

Over two thousand years ago in a far away land, a king ordered a royal road built. The king wanted to improve the country. This road joined the twenty main parts of the country. The king and his helpers traveled the royal road. The road was often used by the royal helpers. They would take news from one part of the country to another.

This special road was convenient. It was the best way to travel. By traveling the royal road, the people could sell their goods. Some people just liked to travel. They would visit with their family and friends.

Now we have roads like the royal road. They join main parts of a country. We call the roads highways.

MI ___ 1. Give this story a good title. (The Royal Road; Long Ago Highways; or appropriate title)

D ___ 2. Who ordered the royal road to be built? (king)

WM ___ 3. The story tells that the road was CONVENIENT; what does CONVENIENT mean? (helpful; handy; comfortable; suitable)

D ___ 4. According to the story, who traveled on the old royal road? (royal helpers; king; people selling goods; travelers/any two)

WM ___ 5. What is the meaning of ORDERED in the phrase "ORDERED a road to be built"? (commanded; gave directions to)

D ___ 6. For what purpose did the royal helpers use the road? (to take news from one part of the country to another)

I ___ 7. How do you know that the royal road was a long road? (story said that it joined the main parts of the country; joined twenty parts of the country)

	TOTAL COMPREHENSION				FACTUAL (Even #'s)			INTERPRETIVE (Odd #'s)		
Levels:	Ind	Instructional		Frus	Ind	Inst	Frus	Ind	Inst	Frus
Question Errors	**0–1**	**2–3**	**4**	**5→**	**0**	**1–2**	**3→**	**0**	**1–2**	**3→**
Approx Grade Equiv	Late 3 (3.7–3.9)	Mid 3 (3.4–3.6)	Early 3 (3.1–3.3)	Below 3	Item Analysis: MI__/1; D__/5; I__/2; WM__/2					

D ___ 8. How many parts of the country were joined by the royal road? (twenty)

I ___ 9. After reading this story, how do you think this road made life easier? (more convenient to travel; travel took less time; could go more places)

D ___ 10. According to this story, what do we now call the roads which are like the royal road? (highways)

COMMENTS:

introduction

Read this story to find out about some very special pottery.

WORD RECOGNITION ERRORS
Insertions ______
Mispronunciations ______
Omissions ______
Refusals ______
Repetitions ______
Reversals ______
Substitutions ______
Phrasing ______
Other: ______

Near the largest city in China stands an enormous hill. Hundreds of years ago, a very fine white clay was taken from the hill. From the clay, the Chinese people developed a special pottery. It was a hard, shiny white pottery. Some people saw the fine dishes, vases, and bowls. People thought they were beautiful. They were very impressed with the appearance and distinctive design of the pottery. Soon traders from foreign countries began to take the dishes home to sell. They were expensive. People learned to imitate the Chinese dishes. Imitations did not cost as much, but were not as fine. The dishes became known as "china dishes."

Today, examples of these ancient dishes may be seen in museums. The custom of calling the dishes "china" has survived through the years. Modern pottery dishes which we use at mealtime are still called china.

WORD REC/CONTEXT ERRORS		
Ind	Inst	Frus
0–5	6–14	15→

MI ___ 1. Give this story a good title. (History of China Dishes; Why We Call Dishes China; or appropriate title)

D ___ 2. What were china dishes made from? (white clay)

WM ___ 3. The story tells of an ENORMOUS hill; what does ENORMOUS mean? (huge; very high)

D ___ 4. Name two things mentioned in the story which are made of china. (dishes; vases; bowls)

	TOTAL COMPREHENSION				FACTUAL (Even #'s)			INTERPRETIVE (Odd #'s)		
Levels:	Ind	Instructional		Frus	Ind	Inst	Frus	Ind	Inst	Frus
Question Errors	0–1	2–3	4	5→	0	1–2	3→	0	1–2	3→
Approx Grade Equiv	Late 4 (4.7–4.9)	Mid 4 (4.4–4.6)	Early 4 (4.1–4.3)	Below 4	Item Analysis: MI__/1; D__/5; I__/2; WM__/2					

WM ___ 5. The story tells of a custom which SURVIVED; what does SURVIVE mean? (lasted; held up)

D ___ 6. Why did the traders in the story take the Chinese dishes home? (to sell them)

I ___ 7. Why do we call all pottery or dishes china? (look something like the original dishes from China)

D ___ 8. If you wanted to see old china dishes, where would you go? (museums)

I ___ 9. After reading the story, how do you know that people really liked the original china dishes? (word still used today; were imitated; still keep in museums)

D ___ 10. According to this story, when did the Chinese people begin making their fine dishes? (hundreds of years ago)

COMMENTS:

introduction

This story is about a man from Boston.
Read about Mr. Lowell's work in the cloth industry.

WORD RECOGNITION ERRORS
Insertions ______
Mispronunciations ______
Omissions ______
Refusals ______
Repetitions ______
Reversals ______
Substitutions ______
Phrasing ______
Other: ______

WORD REC/CONTEXT ERRORS		
Ind	Inst	Frus
0–6	**7–15**	**16→**

In the early 1800's, most American cloth was still homemade. Cloth was being made by machines in England. But the cloth was costly and few people could afford it.

A young man from Boston, F. C. Lowell, decided to investigate better ways to make cloth. He toured and studied the cloth factories in England. When he returned home, he and a companion designed their own power loom. Lowell built a large factory in Boston. Next to the mill, he built company facilities in which young farm girls could live. It was a chance for the girls to live in a big city. They could also earn their own money. The girls worked in the factory for little pay. But they were given free meals and schooling.

Because the factories and the farm girls prospered, Lowell expanded the factory facilities. Today the region around Boston remains a center of the cloth industry.

MI ___ 1. Give this story a good title. (A Cloth Factory in Boston; History of the Power Loom; or appropriate title)

D ___ 2. Who worked in the cloth factory, according to the story? (young farm girls)

WM ___ 3. What does PROSPERED mean in "the girls PROSPERED"? (did well; flourished)

D ___ 4. How was cloth made in England, according to the story? (by machine)

WM ___ 5. What does INVESTIGATE mean in the phrase, "he decided to "INVESTIGATE"? (study; research; look closely)

D ___ 6. According to the story, why didn't Americans want to buy cloth from England? (too expensive)

	TOTAL COMPREHENSION				FACTUAL (Even #'s)			INTERPRETIVE (Odd #'s)		
Levels:	Ind	Instructional		Frus	Ind	Inst	Frus	Ind	Inst	Frus
Question Errors	**0–1**	**2–3**	**4**	**5→**	**0**	**1–2**	**3→**	**0**	**1–2**	**3→**
Approx Grade Equiv	Late 5 (5.7–5.9)	Mid 5 (5.4–5.6)	Early 5 (5.1–5.3)	Below 5	Item Analysis: MI__/1; D__/5; I__/2; WM__/2					

I ___ 7. After reading this story, why do you think Lowell wanted to find better ways to make cloth? (so he could have cheaper cloth; so everyone could afford cloth; he was an ambitious man)

D ___ 8. When did this story take place? (Early 1800's)

I ___ 9. How do you think machine-made cloth has changed our way of life? (more variety of cloth at cheaper prices; more people have cloth)

D ___ 10. What did Lowell and a companion design? (power loom)

COMMENTS:

introduction

Read this story about one of the most exciting times in our history.

WORD RECOGNITION ERRORS	
Insertions	________
Mispronunciations	________
Omissions	________
Refusals	________
Repetitions	________
Reversals	________
Substitutions	________
Phrasing	________
Other:	________

WORD REC/CONTEXT ERRORS		
Ind	Inst	Frus
0–6	**7–16**	**17→**

On January 24, 1848, James Marshall went to inspect the lumber mill he was building in California. From the nearby water, James picked up a shiny rock which appeared to be gold. Could this possibly be gold? James and his boss, Mr. Sutter, tested the specimen and confirmed that the shiny rock was gold. They wanted to keep the discovery a secret for the six weeks required to complete the mill. But news of the discovery of gold quickly spread across the nation. Their discovery caused a wild race for gold.

Thousands of people abruptly quit their jobs and rushed to California. Storekeepers, farmers, ranchers, and lumbermen abandoned their homes and their work. They traveled to seek their fortune. With so many people mining for gold, food and housing became scarce and expensive. Whenever a person did strike gold, much of the money was spent for necessary living expenses. California flourished. Some men discovered their fortunes in gold during the "Gold Rush."

MI ___ 1. Give this story a good title. (The California Gold Rush; or appropriate title)

D ___ 2. Who found the shiny rock near the mill in this story? (James Marshall; James; Marshall)

WM ___ 3. The story tells of testing the SPECIMEN; what does SPECIMEN mean? (sample; example; a portion)

D ___ 4. In about what year did James find the gold? (1848; 1840–1850)

	TOTAL COMPREHENSION				FACTUAL (Even #'s)			INTERPRETIVE (Odd #'s)		
Levels:	Ind	Instructional		Frus	Ind	Inst	Frus	Ind	Inst	Frus
Question Errors	**0–1**	**2–3**	**4**	**5→**	**0**	**1–2**	**3→**	**0**	**1–2**	**3→**
Approx Grade Equiv	Late 6 (6.7–6.9)	Mid 6 (6.4–6.6)	Early 6 (6.1–6.3)	Below 6	Item Analysis: MI__/1; D__/5; I__/2; WM__/2					

WM ___ 5. The story tells of California FLOURISHING; what does FLOURISH mean? (prosper; towns grew and people prospered)

D ___ 6. Name two kinds of workers who left their homes to hunt for gold. (farmers; ranchers; lumbermen; store keepers/any two)

I ___ 7. How do you know from reading this story that everyone did not find a fortune in gold in California? (story says SOME, not all found their fortunes)

D ___ 8. Why did Mr. Sutter and Mr. Marshall want to keep their discovery a secret? (so they could finish building the lumber mill)

I ___ 9. The story tells about the men who found their fortunes in gold; based on what you read, what do you think happened to those who did not discover gold and why? (Returned to old job before money ran out; lost all money because story tells that food and housing became scarce and expensive)

D ___ 10. Why were food and housing so expensive? (too many people and too little food and space)

COMMENTS:

introduction

This story is about Alpen dogs.
Read to find out what they did in the story.

WORD RECOGNITION ERRORS
Insertions ______
Mispronunciations ______
Omissions ______
Refusals ______
Repetitions ______
Reversals ______
Substitutions ______
Phrasing ______
Other: ______

WORD REC/CONTEXT ERRORS		
Ind	Inst	Frus
0–7	**8–17**	**18→**

In the middle 1600s, Alpen dogs were the watchdogs of a group of monks who established a refuge in a mountain pass. Travelers often became lost in sudden snowstorms in the isolated area of the very high pass of the Swiss Alps. The monks took their watchdogs with them on rescue missions. They discovered that Alpen dogs were well equipped for such duties. The huge shaggy dogs, some weighing as much as two hundred pounds, were powerful and strong enough to plow through snowdrifts. They were able to tolerate the harsh climate. The dogs' keen power of scent and hearing aided in detecting people hidden by the snow. Their sense of direction enabled the dogs to lead rescue parties wherever necessary. News of the phenomenal powers of the courageous dogs of the mountain retreat spread.

"Saint Bernard" was the name of the high mountain pass. The enormous watchdogs were renamed for the pass in the 1800s. Saint Bernards have been credited with rescuing the lives of almost three thousand travelers in the Swiss Alps.

MI ___ 1. What is a good title for this story? (The Heroic St. Bernards; All About Alpen Dogs; any appropriate title)

D ___ 2. Where did the dogs in the story live? (Swiss Alps or mountain pass)

WM ___ 3. Explain what it means to TOLERATE the climate. (endure; exist; live in)

D ___ 4. Describe how the dogs in the story looked. (shaggy; big; strong; two hundred lbs./any two)

	TOTAL COMPREHENSION				FACTUAL (Even #'s)			INTERPRETIVE (Odd #'s)		
Levels:	Ind	Instructional		Frus	Ind	Inst	Frus	Ind	Inst	Frus
Question Errors	**0–1**	**2–3**	**4**	**5→**	**0**	**1–2**	**3→**	**0**	**1–2**	**3→**
Approx Grade Equiv	Late 7 (7.7–7.9)	Mid 7 (7.4–7.6)	Early 7 (7.1–7.3)	Below 7	Item Analysis: MI__/1; D__/5; I__/2; WM__/2					

WM ___ 5. What is a mountain RETREAT? (isolated cabin; cabin; lodge; home)

D ___ 6. What breed of dog is discussed in this story? (Alpen or St. Bernard)

I ___ 7. Why do you think, after reading this story, that the dogs were renamed? (in honor of the great deeds performed in the mountain pass; after the region in which they worked)

D ___ 8. About how many people have the dogs been credited with saving in the Swiss Alps? (three thousand; between twenty-five hundred and thirty-five hundred)

I ___ 9. How do you think news of the brave dogs spread? (people talking to other people; through folk tales; people telling travelers and travelers telling their friends at home)

D ___ 10. According to the story, why did travelers become lost in the Alps? (sudden snowstorms)

COMMENTS:

introduction

Read this story to find out about the ancient art of cosmetics.

WORD RECOGNITION ERRORS
Insertions ____
Mispronunciations ____
Omissions ____
Refusals ____
Repetitions ____
Reversals ____
Substitutions ____
Phrasing ____
Other: ____

WORD REC/CONTEXT ERRORS		
Ind	Inst	Frus
0–7	**8–18**	**19→**

The word "cosmetic" is derived from a Greek word meaning decorating skills; these skills were employed over five thousand years ago in ancient Egypt. There, the physicians used and supplied cosmetics to both men and women. Preparations such as perfumed oils were used to improve their appearance. These oils protected people from the dry heat and harsh climate, and kept their skin soft and unwrinkled. The women darkened their eyebrows, eyelashes and upper eyelids with a fine, black powder made from soot. Dark green cream or powder was applied under the eyes. A plant juice, the color of rust, was used to dye and decorate the feet and fingers.

The last queen of Egypt greatly popularized the art of cosmetic adornment; all who saw the beautiful queen were intrigued by her ingenious use of cosmetics. The queen, world famous for her beauty, was also skilled in making cosmetics.

The use of cosmetics spread from Egypt to other countries. As demand for beauty aids grew, tradesmen began making and selling these products. Today, the cosmetic business is a multi-billion dollar industry.

	TOTAL COMPREHENSION				FACTUAL (Even #'s)			INTERPRETIVE (Odd #'s)		
Levels:	Ind	Instructional		Frus	Ind	Inst	Frus	Ind	Inst	Frus
Question Errors	**0–1**	**2–3**	**4**	**5→**	**0**	**1–2**	**3→**	**0**	**1–2**	**3→**
Approx Grade Equiv	Late 8 (8.7–8.9)	Mid 8 (8.4–8.6)	Early 8 (8.1–8.3)	Below 8	Item Analysis: MI__/1; D__/5; I__/2; WM__/2					

MI ___ 1. Give this story a good title. (History of Cosmetics; any appropriate title)

D ___ 2. Where did the use of cosmetics begin? (Ancient Egypt)

WM ___ 3. The story tells of cosmetic ADORNMENT; what is ADORNMENT? (decoration)

D ___ 4. Why were special oils used in ancient Egypt, according to this story? (improve appearance; protect skin from dry heat and climate; and keep skin soft and unwrinkled/any two)

WM ___ 5. What does INGENIOUS mean in the phrase, "INGENIOUS use of cosmetics"? (wise; clever; creative)

D ___ 6. Which queen helped to popularize the use of cosmetics? (*Last* queen of Egypt; Cleopatra)

I ___ 7. Why do you think the use of cosmetics spread from Egypt to other countries? (other people imitated or admired the queen; traders brought cosmetics home; people had some needs)

D ___ 8. Name three parts of the body on which ancient Egyptians used cosmetics. (eyes; feet; fingers; skin/any three)

I ___ 9. How do cosmetics used today on fingers and feet differ from those used by the ancient Egyptians on their fingers and feet? (we use nail polish on our finger and toe nails, but not whole feet or whole finger; use cream on them, but don't dye whole feet and fingers)

D ___ 10. Who supplied cosmetics to the ancient Egyptians? (physicians; doctors)

COMMENTS:

introduction

Read this story to find out about one of our most important activities.

WORD RECOGNITION ERRORS
Insertions ______
Mispronunciations ______
Omissions ______
Refusals ______
Repetitions ______
Reversals ______
Substitutions ______
Phrasing ______
Other: ______

WORD REC/CONTEXT ERRORS		
Ind	Inst	Frus
0–8	**9–19**	**20→**

Schools, as we recognize them, were first initiated in the colonies around the 1640s by the people arriving in America from Europe. Massachusetts was the first state to enact legislation requiring that children be taught to read. In most colonies, other laws followed that required schools to be established in one form or another. Both elementary and upper schools, the latter originally being called Latin grammar schools, were common. In 1636, Harvard College was opened, and in the years just before the Revolutionary War, seven or eight more liberal arts colleges opened.

In the Middle and Southern colonies, in addition to public schools, religious and private groups opened schools. It was not until 1821 that the first public high school opened in Boston. By the end of the century, public high schools had almost replaced private academies in many areas of the country.

A new system of schools developed there and abroad through more than three hundred years of lawmaking. Changes have included the addition of science, art, music, language, business, history, homemaking, shop trade, and other areas of study. We are fortunate to live at a time when schools offer so much.

	TOTAL COMPREHENSION				FACTUAL (Even #'s)			INTERPRETIVE (Odd #'s)		
Levels:	Ind	Instructional		Frus	Ind	Inst	Frus	Ind	Inst	Frus
Question Errors	**0–1**	**2–3**	**4**	**5→**	**0**	**1–2**	**3→**	**0**	**1–2**	**3→**
Approx Grade Equiv	Late 9 (9.7–9.9)	Mid 9 (9.4–9.6)	Early 9 (9.1–9.3)	Below 9	Item Analysis: MI__/1; D__/5; I__/2; WM__/2					

MI ___ 1. What is a good title for this story? (American Education; History of American Education)

D ___ 2. When did schools begin in America? (around 1640)

WM ___ 3. As it was used in the story, what is an academy? (a high school)

D ___ 4. What state passed the first law requiring children to be taught to read? (Massachusetts)

WM ___ 5. What does the word "ESTABLISHED" mean? (to begin; to open; to start)

D ___ 6. In about what year did the first American public high school open? (1821; around 1820; 1820–1830)

I ___ 7. Why do you think laws were passed to require children to be taught to read? (people thought reading was important)

D ___ 8. What college began in 1636? (Harvard College)

I ___ 9. How have schools changed since they began? (appropriate response)

D ___ 10. Name three areas or subjects the story mentions as being added to school offerings. (any three: music; business; art; languages; history; homemaking and shop trades)

COMMENTS:

introduction

Read this selection to learn more interesting facts about the early trains.

WORD RECOGNITION ERRORS
Insertions ______
Mispronunciations ______
Omissions ______
Refusals ______
Repetitions ______
Reversals ______
Substitutions ______
Phrasing ______
Other: ______

WORD REC/CONTEXT ERRORS		
Ind	Inst	Frus
0–8	9–20	21→

The coming of railroads to America was beset with many problems. The iron horse, as the steam locomotive was nicknamed, was an apt label. Making its steam power from wood and water, the engine erratically snorted, coughed, belched, and jerked in a manner similar to that of a fidgety horse. As early locomotives chugged down the track, they spewed out sparks, cinders, and smoke over unsuspecting passengers in open cars behind. Sometimes the wood supply would run out, and passengers had to forage in nearby forests for more firewood before the train could go on. Perhaps the most distressing characteristic of early locomotives was that they had no brakes. When these trains pulled into the station, townspeople would run out, grab whatever was handy, and pull the train to a stop. All of these difficulties bothered people, and some held protest meetings and wrote newspaper articles against trains. Numerous detractors claimed the cattle would be harmed or that it was unhealthy to travel at the ''dangerous'' speed of fifteen miles an hour, while others feared that they might be blown up if the steam boilers ever exploded. But despite all these problems, the railroads did grow into the world's greatest transportation system.

	TOTAL COMPREHENSION				FACTUAL (Even #'s)			INTERPRETIVE (Odd #'s)		
Levels:	Ind	Instructional		Frus	Ind	Inst	Frus	Ind	Inst	Frus
Question Errors	0–1	2–3	4	5→	0	1–2	3→	0	1–2	3→
Approx Grade Equiv	Late 10 (10.7–.9)	Mid 10 (10.4–10.6)	Early 10 (10.1–10.3)	Below 10	Item Analysis: MI__/1; D__/5; I__/2; WM__/2					

MI ___ 1. Give a title to this story. (The Problems of the Early Railroads; or appropriate title)

D ___ 2. What was the nickname for the steam locomotive? (iron horse)

WM ___ 3. What does FIDGETY mean? (nervous; jumpy; uneasy)

D ___ 4. How did the early trains get their power? (steam created by burning wood to heat water)

WM ___ 5. The story speaks of DETRACTORS; what are DETRACTORS? (people who say and/or write unfavorable things about something)

D ___ 6. What happened in the story if a train's wood supply ran out? (passengers had to find more in nearby woods)

I ___ 7. How do you know that some peaceful means were used to halt the spread of railroads? (story told of protest meetings and unfavorable newspaper articles—both peaceful means of complaint)

D ___ 8. What means were used to slow down or stop the early locomotives when they pulled into the station? (townspeople pulled train to a stop)

I ___ 9. How do you know that the detractors were not very successful in stopping railroad expansion? (because railroads grew into the world's greatest transportation system)

D ___ 10. What did some people think about cattle and trains? (cattle would be harmed by trains)

COMMENTS:

IEP/r
GRADED PASSAGE RECORD FORM

____________	____	______	______________	____	____________
Student Name	Age	Grade	Number Yrs/School	Date	Diagnostician

DIRECTIONS: Enter Form and Level of each passage and circle how each story is read (O = Orally; S = Silently; L = Listening). For each passage on which student is tested, indicate correct responses by placing a check (✓) beside appropriate question numbers and write incorrect responses. The number of oral word recognition errors should be noted with appropriate comments offered. As each set of story questions is answered, indicate which comprehension level and word recognition in context level that story represents for that student according to scoring criteria on Teacher's copy by circling Independent, Instructional, or Frustration.

STORY						
LEVEL:	________	________	________	________	________	
FORM:	____	____	____	____	____	
	Read: O S L	Read: O S L	Read: O S L	Read: O S L	Read: O S L	
MI	1. ______	1. ______	1. ______	1. ______	1. ______	MI
D	2. ______	2. ______	2. ______	2. ______	2. ______	D
WM	3. ______	3. ______	3. ______	3. ______	3. ______	WM
D	4. ______	4. ______	4. ______	4. ______	4. ______	D
WM	5. ______	5. ______	5. ______	5. ______	5. ______	WM
D	6. ______	6. ______	6. ______	6. ______	6. ______	D
I	7. ______	7. ______	7. ______	7. ______	7. ______	I
D	8. ______	8. ______	8. ______	8. ______	8. ______	D
I	9. ______	9. ______	9. ______	9. ______	9. ______	I
D	10. ______	10. ______	10. ______	10. ______	10. ______	D
COMP LEVEL:	Ind Ins Frs	Ind Ins Frs	Ind Ins Frs	Ind Ins Frs	Ind Ins Frs	
WR/CON:	# of errors__	# of errors__	# of errors__	# of errors__	# of errors__	
LEVEL:	Ind Ins Frs	Ind Ins Frs	Ind Ins Frs	Ind Ins Frs	Ind Ins Frs	

STORY						
LEVEL:	________	________	________	________	________	
FORM:	____	____	____	____	____	
	Read: O S L	Read: O S L	Read: O S L	Read: O S L	Read: O S L	
MI	1. ______	1. ______	1. ______	1. ______	1. ______	MI
D	2. ______	2. ______	2. ______	2. ______	2. ______	D
WM	3. ______	3. ______	3. ______	3. ______	3. ______	WM
D	4. ______	4. ______	4. ______	4. ______	4. ______	D
WM	5. ______	5. ______	5. ______	5. ______	5. ______	WM
D	6. ______	6. ______	6. ______	6. ______	6. ______	D
I	7. ______	7. ______	7. ______	7. ______	7. ______	I
D	8. ______	8. ______	8. ______	8. ______	8. ______	D
I	9. ______	9. ______	9. ______	9. ______	9. ______	I
D	10. ______	10. ______	10. ______	10. ______	10. ______	D
COMP LEVEL:	Ind Ins Frs	Ind Ins Frs	Ind Ins Frs	Ind Ins Frs	Ind Ins Frs	
WR/CON:	# of errors__	# of errors__	# of errors__	# of errors__	# of errors__	
LEVEL:	Ind Ins Frs	Ind Ins Frs	Ind Ins Frs	Ind Ins Frs	Ind Ins Frs	

COMMENTS: ____

IEP/r
STUDENT SUMMARY SHEET

NAME:_______________ DATE:______ TEACHER:_________________________ GRADE:____
AGE:____ # YRS IN SCHOOL____ CLASSIFICATION:____ DIAGNOSTICIAN:__________

SKILL AREA

1. Visual Skills
A. Visual Discrimination__________
B. Visual Memory__________
C. Sound Visualization__________

2. Auditory Skills
A. Auditory Discrimination__________
B. Auditory Memory__________

3. WORD RECOGNITION PATTERNS
(Isolation & Context)

A. Sight Vocabulary __________

C. Word Recognition in Context____
____

D. Specialized Vocabulary__________
____

B. Word Analysis:__________
1. Beginning Consonants______
2. Ending Consonants______
3. Short Vowels ______
4. Long Vowels ______
5. Silent e______
6. Blends ______
7. Digraphs ______
8. Special Vowels______
9. Prefixes ______
10. Suffixes ______
11. Compounds______
12. Contractions______
13. Other:______

4. ORAL READING

A. Insertions __________
B. Mispronunciations __________
C. Omissions __________
D. Refusals__________
E. Repetitions__________
F. Reversals __________
G. Substitutions__________
H. Phrasing __________
I. Other: __________

5. COMPREHENSION PATTERNS

Total Comprehension Analysis

Questions Correct 3 Instructional Levels | Question Type | Questions Attempted 3 Instructional Levels | Total % Correct

Oral	Silent	Lstng	Total		Oral	Silent	Lstng	Total	Correct
				Main Idea (#1)					% *
				Detail (#2, 4, 6, 8, 10)					% *
				Word Meaning (#3, 5)					% *
				Inference (#7, 9)					% *

Percentages under 70% indicate areas of instructional need

FACTUAL COMPREHENSION (Even # Questions) INTERPRETIVE COMPREHENSION (Odd # Questions)

Ques Correct	Ques Attempted	% Correct	Ques Correct	Ques Attempted	% Correct
		% *			% *

COMPREHENSION STYLE:	**LEVEL:**

IEP/r
STUDENT PLANNING SHEET FOR READING PRESCRIPTION

Name:________________
Grade:______ Age:______
Years in School________
Examiner: ______________
Date: ________________

READING LEVELS:	Comprehension			Word Recognition	
	ORAL	SILENT	LSTNG	SIGHT	CONTEXT
INSTRUCTIONAL					
INDEPENDENT					
*COMPREHENSION STYLE (circle) ORAL SILENT					

Stories Administered (Circle)
Oral—L/A, S/A, H/A Silent—L/B, S/B, H/B Listening—L/B, S/B, H/B

Analysis of Reading Skills

Acquired Skills	IEP # Skill Area	Prioritized Needs	Comments
	1. VISUAL SKILLS		
	A. Visual Discrimination		
	B. Visual Memory		
	C. Visualization of Sounds		
	2. AUDITORY SKILLS		
	A. Auditory Discrimination		
	B. Auditory Memory		
	3. WORD RECOGNITION PATTERNS		
	A. Sight Vocabulary		
	B. Word Analysis		
	1. Beginning Consonants		
	2. Ending Consonants		
	3. Short Vowels		
	4. Long Vowels		
	5. Silent e		
	6. Blends		
	7. Digraphs		
	8. Special Vowel Sounds		
	9. Prefixes		
	10. Suffixes		
	11. Compound Words		
	12. Contractions		
	13. Other: ________________		
	C. Word Recognition in Context		
	D. Specialized Vocabulary		
	4. ORAL READING		
	A. Insertions		
	B. Mispronunciations		
	C. Omissions		
	D. Refusals		
	E. Repetitions		
	F. Reversals		
	G. Substitutions		
	H. Phrasing		
	I. Other: __________________		
	5. COMPREHENSION PATTERNS		
	A. Main Idea		
	B. Detail		
	C. Word Meaning		
	D. Inference		
	E. Other: __________________		

INDIVIDUAL EVALUATION PROCEDURES FOR READING

Summary of Reading Diagnosis

NAME ______________________ BIRTH DATE ______________________
SCHOOL __________ GRADE __________ # YEARS IN SCHOOL __________
HOMEROOM TEACHER ______________ CLASSIFICATION ______________
EXAMINER ______________________ DATE ______________________

INTEREST INVENTORY
High Interest Strand: ______________
Neutral Interest Strand: ______________

WORD RECOGNITION LISTS
Instructional Level: ______________
Independent Level: ______________

GRADED PASSAGES

READING LEVELS:	COMPREHENSION			WORD REC
	Oral	Silent	Listening	Context
Instructional—				
Independent—				
	*COMPREHENSION STYLE: Oral Silent			

VISUAL TESTS

☐ Vis (1) Dis Shapes
Results: __________
☐ Vis (4) Dis Letters II
Results: __________
☐ Vis (7) Mem Symbols
Results: __________
☐ Vis (2) Dis L Shapes
Results: __________
☐ Vis (5) Dis Words
Results: __________
☐ Vis (8) Mem Letters I
Results: __________
☐ Vis (10) Sounds/Words
Results: __________
☐ Vis (3) Dis Letters I
Results: __________
☐ Vis (6) Dis Words II
Results: __________
☐ Vis (9) Mem Letters II
Results: __________

AUDITORY TESTS

☐ Aud (1) Discrim
Results: ______
☐ Aud (2) Mem Words
Results: __________
☐ Aud (3) Mem Letters II
Results: __________

WORD ANALYSIS SURVEY

☐ Phonic Analysis Survey
Results: __________
☐ Structural Analysis Survey
Results: __________

SPECIALIZED VOCABULARY

☐ Survival Voc I
Results: ________
☐ Survival Voc II
Results: ______
☐ 16 Essential Sight Wds
Results: __________

☐ ECOLOGICAL SURVEY
Results: ______________________________

IEP/r

FORM B

IEP/r
WORD RECOGNITION IN ISOLATION

List B

(i)	(I)	(II)
1. they	1. from	1. light
2. pet	2. zoo	2. while
3. bad	3. into	3. plan
4. word	4. anything	4. busy
5. run	5. hand	5. upon
6. frog	6. paint	6. able
7. came	7. sometimes	7. finish
8. all	8. many	8. near
9. that	9. were	9. act
10. bird	10. people	10. turn
11. new	11. over	11. carry
12. tell	12. after	12. their
13. so	13. long	13. anyone
14. help	14. story	14. surprise
15. boy	15. took	15. kept
16. let	16. there	16. push
17. picture	17. same	17. shout
18. some	18. much	18. leave
19. girl	19. found	19. field
20. puppy	20. work	20. easy

IEP/r
WORD RECOGNITION IN ISOLATION

List B

(III)	(IV)	(V)
1. through	1. prefer	1. drift
2. built	2. design	2. mission
3. silent	3. adjust	3. fascinating
4. lesson	4. miserable	4. ornament
5. edge	5. recognize	5. ancestor
6. broke	6. communicate	6. intense
7. travel	7. systems	7. prey
8. plenty	8. reservation	8. geology
9. neighbor	9. vehicle	9. rhythm
10. bother	10. patient	10. borrow
11. quite	11. acrobatics	11. investigating
12. decide	12. drill	12. survey
13. special	13. solar	13. horizon
14. protect	14. interrupt	14. value
15. business	15. perform	15. responsible
16. change	16. champion	16. burden
17. mirror	17. pollute	17. react
18. ordinary	18. original	18. image
19. mystery	19. bacteria	19. navigator
20. half	20. intelligent	20. extinct

IEP/r
WORD RECOGNITION IN ISOLATION

List B

(VI)	(VII)	(VIII)
1. vast	1. species	1. aerial
2. quarry	2. nomadic	2. potential
3. identify	3. conceived	3. endure
4. aggressive	4. prior	4. reluctant
5. transparent	5. terrain	5. besiege
6. precision	6. literally	6. serenity
7. fossil	7. primitive	7. epidemic
8. associated	8. ignite	8. ingenious
9. depression	9. alien	9. skeptical
10. symbol	10. ritual	10. column
11. phenomenal	11. herald	11. tenement
12. flourish	12. prey	12. geology
13. archaeologist	13. afflict	13. simultaneous
14. contract	14. generated	14. intrigue
15. specimen	15. reserve	15. clarity
16. missionary	16. futile	16. jaunt
17. elegant	17. origin	17. impulse
18. abrupt	18. distinct	18. remote
19. native	19. concept	19. oppressive
20. shrine	20. refuge	20. descendant

IEP/r WORD RECOGNITION IN ISOLATION

List B: Record Sheet for:________________________(name)

(i)	(I)	(II)
1.__they ______	1.__from ______	1.__light ______
2.__pet ______	2.__zoo ______	2.__while ______
3.__bad ______	3.__into ______	3.__plan ______
4.__word ______	4.__anything ______	4.__busy ______
5.__run ______	5.__hand ______	5.__upon ______
6.__frog ______	6.__paint ______	6.__able ______
7.__came ______	7.__sometimes ______	7.__finish ______
8.__all ______	8.__many ______	8.__near ______
9.__that ______	9.__were ______	9.__act ______
10.__bird ______	10.__people ______	10.__turn ______
11.__new ______	11.__over ______	11.__carry ______
12.__tell ______	12.__after ______	12.__their ______
13.__so ______	13.__long ______	13.__anyone ______
14.__help ______	14.__story ______	14.__surprise ______
15.__boy ______	15.__took ______	15.__kept ______
16.__let ______	16.__there ______	16.__push ______
17.__picture ______	17.__same ______	17.__shout ______
18.__some ______	18.__much ______	18.__leave ______
19.__girl ______	19.__found ______	19.__field ______
20.__puppy ______	20.__work ______	20.__easy ______

(III)	(IV)	(V)
1.__through ______	1.__prefer ______	1.__drift ______
2.__built ______	2.__design ______	2.__mission ______
3.__silent ______	3.__adjust ______	3.__fascinating ______
4.__lesson ______	4.__miserable ______	4.__ornament ______
5.__edge ______	5.__recognize ______	5.__ancestor ______
6.__broke ______	6.__communicate ______	6.__intense ______
7.__travel ______	7.__systems ______	7.__prey ______
8.__plenty ______	8.__reservation ______	8.__geology ______
9.__neighbor ______	9.__vehicle ______	9.__rhythm ______
10.__bother ______	10.__patient ______	10.__borrow ______
11.__quite ______	11.__acrobatics ______	11.__investigating ______
12.__decide ______	12.__drill ______	12.__survey ______
13.__special ______	13.__solar ______	13.__horizon ______
14.__protect ______	14.__interrupt ______	14.__value ______
15.__business ______	15.__perform ______	15.__responsible ______
16.__change ______	16.__champion ______	16.__burden ______
17.__mirror ______	17.__pollute ______	17.__react ______
18.__ordinary ______	18.__original ______	18.__image ______
19.__mystery ______	19.__bacteria ______	19.__navigator ______
20.__half ______	20.__intelligent ______	20.__extinct ______

IEP/r WORD RECOGNITION IN ISOLATION

List B: Record Sheet for:______________________________(name)

(VI)	(VII)	(VIII)
1.__vast ________	1.__species________	1.__aerial________
2.__quarry ________	2.__nomadic ________	2.__potential ________
3.__identify________	3.__conceived________	3.__endure ________
4.__aggressive________	4.__prior________	4.__reluctant ________
5.__transparent ________	5.__terrain________	5.__besiege ________
6.__precision ________	6.__literally ________	6.__serenity________
7.__fossil________	7.__primitive________	7.__epidemic ________
8.__associated________	8.__ignite ________	8.__ingenious ________
9.__depression________	9.__alien________	9.__skeptical ________
10.__symbol ________	10.__ritual ________	10.__column ________
11.__phenomenal________	11.__herald ________	11.__tenement ________
12.__flourish________	12.__prey________	12.__geology________
13.__archaeologist________	13.__afflict ________	13.__simultaneous________
14.__contract________	14.__generated________	14.__intrigue________
15.__specimen ________	15.__reserve________	15.__clarity ________
16.__missionary ________	16.__futile ________	16.__jaunt________
17.__elegant ________	17.__origin ________	17.__impulse________
18.__abrupt ________	18.__distinct________	18.__remote ________
19.__native ________	19.__concept ________	19.__oppressive________
20.__shrine ________	20.__refuge ________	20.__descendant ________

CONSISTENT WORD RECOGNITION PATTERNS

Acquired Skill	Needed Skill	Skill	Sample Error(s)
		Beginning Consonants Ending Consonants Short Vowels Long Vowels Silent e Blends Digraphs Special Vowel Sounds Prefixes Suffixes Compound Words Contractions Other. . .	

COMMENTS

The boy likes birds.
Some days he just looks at birds.
He draws them.
He goes to school to draw.

As a man, he works.
His wife works.
Then he looks at birds.
He draws birds.
He paints pretty pictures of them.
He makes a book of his pictures.
It is one of the best books on birds.
People like it.
It helps them to see the birds.

Long ago a boy rode a horse to take the mail.
Sometimes Bill had to ride very fast.

One time Bill helped his country.
He looked for bad people.
His country gave him a prize.

As a man, Bill had a show.
It was a cowboy show.
Many of the cowboys could ride fast.
But Bill could ride faster.
They all could use a rope.
Bill was the star.
People came from far away to see the show.

Over a hundred years ago a young girl wanted to write plays.
She wanted to act.
She and her sisters gave plays in their barn.
The girl wrote the plays and acted in them.

The family did not have much money.
The girl worked to help her family.
She taught school, made dresses, and was a nurse.
She wrote a story about her family life.
The story became famous.
Then she wrote more about her life.

She was one of the first Americans to write stories just for boys and girls.
She was able to earn money writing.
She loved her work.

From the first day, the boy did not like school. He bothered the teachers. They said he couldn't learn because he didn't behave. The boy said that the teachers couldn't teach. In the fourth grade, the boy quit school. No one knew then that one day the boy would be quite famous.

His mother began to teach the boy at home. She helped him meet some people. They taught him the mystery of science and machines.

As a man, he invented wax paper and a kind of printing press. He built improved phone parts. His most famous inventions are the record player and the improved light bulb. He created more than one thousand inventions. He said that a little thought and much hard work helped create the inventions.

Long ago a father taught his son about sounds. The boy wanted to understand how people made sounds. He studied hard for many years.

As a young man, he became a teacher. He taught at a special school for deaf children. It was hard for these children to speak because they had never heard the language. But this man taught them to speak and communicate. He helped the teachers too. One student was so special to the teacher that he married her several years later.

Each day he taught classes, but at night he studied sound. While working on the telegraph, he happened to make a noise. It sounded like a voice. He began to develop a system of producing voice sounds. His teaching was interrupted by his work with sound. He designed and built the first phone.

Among the greatest dancers in this century was Dora Duncan. She changed the world of ballet. Her early life held little promise of later fame.

Even as a small child she enjoyed dance. When dancing she forgot the holes in her shoes and her empty stomach. She could ignore the school where few understood her. Dora's mother allowed her to quit school at age eleven when the teacher said Dora could not learn.

Dora and her sister began a dancing school at home. They taught the children nature's fascinating movements. Theirs was not like most dance then seen on stage. Dora said that dance should be an expression of mind and heart. Among her dance movements borrowed from nature were those of whirling leaves and flowers opening.

Many people were impressed with Dora's dancing and teaching. Over the next thirty years the world would recognize the value of expressive dancing.

Churchill found great pleasure in reading. Yet, throughout his school years, Math and Latin were very difficult for him. He was a very active and restless student whose aggressive acts often caused trouble. A teacher once chased him around the school yard to reduce his restlessness in the classroom. Churchill twice failed the test to enter military school. When his father hired a tutor, Churchill passed the test and was admitted.

It was in military school at age nineteen that Churchill began to achieve his first real success. Here, his activity and restlessness were even encouraged. This school marked the beginning of Churchill's vast achievements. He became known as a popular speaker and writer throughout much of the world. His talents and career continued to flourish. For his writing, he was awarded the Nobel Prize. Churchill rose to the highest office in England's government as its leader. He was awarded the greatest honor in his native land when he became a knight.

When the star of the school play became ill, a small boy volunteered to play the girl's part. The class roared with laughter when Clerow Wilson stood up and began to recite the lines perfectly. The boy entertained the school by playing the girl's part in the school program. This performance heralded the beginning of the career of one of today's most famous entertainers, Flip Wilson.

Flip spent his early childhood in a very poor neighborhood. Despite primitive living conditions, Flip always found something to laugh about. He entertained his friends by telling them outlandish stories.

When Flip joined the U. S. Air Force at age sixteen, he continued to entertain the people around him with his wild stories. Here, he acquired the name Flip when someone said that he had "flipped." Flip decided he wanted to become a professional entertainer. Today Flip Wilson has become one of the most successful comedians on stage and TV. Among his distinctive comical acts is one in which he plays the part of a girl.

Although Sarah was extremely poor in her early life, she took great pride in her appearance. Sarah wanted to soften the texture and loosen the curl of her hair. Hers was the problem experienced by many women who were African descendants. She discovered that, with the application of various mixtures, she could soften her hair texture, but not loosen the curl. Reluctant to abandon the project, Sarah continued to experiment. In 1905, she developed an ingenious device to remove or loosen the tight hair curls. By styling her hair with a heated metal comb and oil mixtures, she could achieve this goal.

Later Sarah opened a school to train hair stylists to use the ''Walker System'' of straightening hair. Through the sales of her beauty products and system, Sarah Walker became very wealthy. Part of this wealth was shared through her gifts of money to organizations and black institutions.

For many women the heated comb was the solution to their greatest cosmetic problem. Although some women use the ''Walker System'' today, the modern version is an electric hot comb.

There have been many important women who, over a period of nearly two hundred years, have been active leaders in the women's suffrage movement. They have led the struggle for women's rights which include the right to vote, equal work, dress reform, and temperance. Beginning by forming the Women's State Temperance Society of New York, Susan B. Anthony became one of the most prominent leaders for women's rights. Susan, who spoke out for issues such as dress reform and even wore bloomers herself, was mainly interested in all women having the right to vote.

In 1851, Ms. Anthony met Elizabeth Stanton and, together, they organized a team for women's suffrage. Susan was famous for her speeches and particularly for her work as editor for a controversial magazine, *The Revolution.*

Susan Anthony was a person who lived what she believed. In 1872, she was determined to vote even though, by law, women were not allowed to vote. Fully aware of possible consequences, she voted and was then arrested. Her trial helped to unite many women across her country. Ms. Anthony served as an example of what one person can accomplish for an entire nation.

Margaret Mead was born in 1901, and became one of the most celebrated anthropologists in the world. She was known for her studies of the children and cultures of the Pacific Islands, Russia, and the United States.

Ms. Mead would actually live with the people she studied and, in many instances, ate and acted exactly as they did. For nine months, while studying Samoan adolescents, she lived and interacted with the adolescent girls almost as a sister. This was made possible, in part, due to her small stature; she stood just over five feet tall. Her efforts were the first of any anthropologist, male or female, on such a personal basis.

Margaret Mead, well known for her writing and also for her lectures, was a major influence in scientifically disproving some ideas concerning human behavior. In addition to her studies, Margaret Mead served in important advisory positions for the United States government following World War II. *Coming of Age in Samoa, Growing Up in New Guinea,* and *Sex and Temperament in Three Primitive Societies* are three of the highly acclaimed books which she authored. Margaret Mead's careful studies of children in primitive societies provided fresh insights toward understanding human personality.

Some children like Ladybugs.
They like to play with them.
They think they are pretty.
Ladybugs are good bugs.
They help people.

Some men did not want bad bugs.
So they set fires.
But they liked Ladybugs.
They wanted to help them.
They said, "Ladybug, Ladybug, fly away home."

Now we need the good bugs.
We use new ways to keep Ladybugs.

Skunks are small and pretty.
They are friendly animals.
They like to be near people.
Skunks live near farms and eat bad bugs.
They help farmers.

Many people do not like to be near skunks.
They give off a bad smell.
Skunks are not strong and they cannot run fast.
People run from skunks because they can make people smell bad.
They keep animals away too.
They can make animals smell the same as the skunk.
This is the way skunks stay safe.

Giraffes are the tallest animals in the world.

These tall giants are tame and quiet.

Giraffes eat leaves from tree tops.

Much of their water comes from leaves.

Their long necks help them reach high.

Using their long lips and tongues they are able to pick the leaves.

Their color and spots hide them near the trees.

They travel in herds.

Their long necks help them watch for danger.

These quick animals can run from most enemies.

But, when needed, they kick their long legs.

They hit with their strong necks to keep them safe.

Men have kept some giraffes safe in parks.

Butterflies are quite beautiful insects. Most butterflies have two pairs of wings. Their bodies are covered with small scales or hairs. These give the silent insects their color. The special mouths of butterflies are made like drinking straws. These straws enable the insects to draw juice from flowers. The straws roll up when not in use.

When the weather turns cool, one kind of butterfly flies south. They may fly as many as eighty miles a day. They travel hundreds of miles. There, on a special mountain, they spend the winter. Their body heat becomes the same as the cool outside air. The quiet, still insects look like thousands of fall leaves. In spring the butterflies return north to enjoy the flowers.

Fleas are not well liked. The small fleas prefer to ride on animals, especially dogs and cats. Fleas have been known to ride on people and even chickens. They make the animals miserable because they tickle. It is hard to get rid of the insects because they multiply quickly.

But some kinds of fleas are intelligent. They can be trained to perform acrobatics. They can jump almost twelve inches. The fleas land on their back legs, facing backward. The patient trainers must first teach the insects to walk instead of jump. Then the fleas can be taught to perform many tricks. They can learn to race, jump sticks and hoops, or even pull wagons. Sometimes the trainers exhibit the performing fleas at a fair. These insects can be a bother. They can also be fun to watch.

Sponges are among the most fascinating of the water creatures. All sponges are made of many single cells. But unlike most animals, their systems have no hearts, brains, or lungs. Sponges have no way of moving around in the water.

There are over five thousand known species of sponges. Some live in salt water, while others live in fresh water. Colors may range from the typical tan to bright reds and blues. They range in size from small to large. They may be as small as peas or larger than a man.

Many small animals live among the pores of sponges, and may even share their meals. Sponges protect small sea creatures by hiding them. A broken sponge can attach itself to a new spot and continue to grow. Sponges have extraordinary powers to resist bacteria. By investigating these powers, scientists have developed new ways to help humans resist diseases.

Many species of owls flourish in both hemispheres. Most owls are night creatures, who sleep during the day. Some owls make the familiar ''hoo-hoo'' sound; others have an eerie cry. The unique design of the owls' eyes and ears gives them phenomenal vision and hearing. The feathers on their wings are shorter and rounder than those of other birds, making their flight almost silent. Owls usually live alone or in pairs.

Among the least social of these birds are Great Horned Owls. These enormous and aggressive owls sometimes have a wing spread of five feet. They do not like people. The eerie cry of these birds scares many people.

Among the more social owls are those named for their sad, wailing call. The colors of the feathers of Screech Owls resemble the bark of the trees in which they perch. These owls do not mind having humans for neighbors. Because Screech Owls help keep crops safe, farmers appreciate these birds.

Oysters are small animals who live mostly in warm ocean waters. Shells provide refuge for their soft fleshy bodies. Each shell has two valves attached by a hinge. A strong muscle attaches the oyster's body to the inside of the shell, allowing the oyster to open and close its shell at will. Once an oyster has attached its left valve to a rock or other object on the sea bottom, it stays there for life.

Oyster shells are lined with a fold of tissue which secretes a lime substance. If an alien object or substance enters the shell, it irritates the oyster's body. In order to protect itself, the oyster secretes a white liquid and surrounds the object. This lime liquid hardens, forming thin sheets over the object. Slowly, more circular layers are added until a pearl is formed.

Some species of oysters create pearls which are highly valued by people. The oyster's method of protection not only provides a more comfortable life for the animal, but also produces something of beauty for people.

Termites are considered to be destructive insects; their damage to wooden structures has earned them quite a bad reputation. But certain species of termites are helpful to the ecology of the tropics. There, they loosen and enrich the soil, foster plant growth, and recycle wood matter.

Termites of the tropics have quite an ingenious social structure. The huge columns of the insect mounds may tower six feet above the ground and extend twelve feet underground. The nest region is divided into special rooms for the king and queen, nursery, and garden.

Living in the termite colony are the queen, king, workers, and soldiers. The queen is the largest of all termites and dominates the colony, with the king next in size and status. Protecting the colony are the female soldiers who have larger heads and jaws than the smaller male workers. Workers repair the mounds and tend to the nursery and royal couple. They gather food, some of which they cultivate in their garden. The cooperative social structure of these termites has allowed them, like ants and bees, to flourish.

The orangutan is one of the three kinds of great apes, the other two being chimpanzee and gorilla. The word orangutan means "wild man," but this is misleading. For although they look fearsome, orangutans would prefer to avoid a fight if possible. However, if cornered, these apes would fight to survive. The appearance of an orangutan is quite strange. Its arm spread can be as wide as eight feet, while the average height, if its body were straightened out, would be four feet or less. The orangutan's reddish, yellow hair is unevenly distributed, being over twelve inches long on the arms, thighs, and shoulders, but nonexistent on the chest and stomach. It is a powerful animal in arms and jaws, for the orangutan can chew through the hard shell of the durian fruit, while humans require an ax to break the shell.

An interesting habit of the orangutan is to build for sleeping a tree-top nest which is constructed from small, leafy branches. It resembles a round, thick, saucer-like platform. The ape uses this nest until it dries and becomes itchy, and then builds a new nest for the daily naps.

The coyote has become a symbol of the American West; its plaintive howl at sunset is a familiar sound for many residents of this area. Hearing the coyote is easier than seeing it, but with binoculars and patience, it is possible. The coyote resembles a small German Shepherd dog with a long, full tail carried low; it wags its tail when it is happy. The coyote's slender legs and easy, flowing movements give an impression of delicacy.

The coyote's delicate appearance is deceiving, because it thrives in great numbers in the West; indeed, the coyote might be called a survivor. When adversity strikes, it modifies its habits to meet the new circumstances. For example, it can adapt to nearly any terrain or climate and exist on almost any type of food, as demonstrated by the successful raising of a coyote family within the limits of one American city. Although preferring to roam day and night, it becomes nocturnal when humans live nearby.

The coyote is, by reputation, a sly and cunning animal that will play tricks to capture prey. In one night, a coyote may raid both a sheep farm and a produce farm, cleverly picking the best of everything for its meal.

Boys like to play the games.
People like to see the games.
They want to see who plays best.
The boys work and work.
Then they are strong.
Some run fast.
Some want to jump.
Some like to throw.

Soon boys will play more games.
But girls will play the games.
They will run, jump, and throw.
They will swim fast.
People will have fun at the games.

A man was working on his land.
He found some parts of an old house.
Some men helped him dig more.
They found a very old city.

There was a wall around the city.
The wall had eight gates.
The streets were made of rocks.
There were many stores and shops.
People were surprised to find swimming pools.
Some houses were big and fine.

Today people go to see the old city.
They like to see how people lived long ago.

Long ago the mail was carried by men upon quick ponies.
The ponies were changed each ten miles.
Each rider rode almost one hundred miles.
Then he stopped to rest.
Then the next man would leave with the mail.
Riders were changed each hundred miles.

Sometimes mail traveled across the country.
Twenty riders would be used to make this trip.
They would use as many as two hundred ponies.
They went as fast as they could.
It still took ten days to finish the trip.
To mail one small letter cost five dollars.
Most people did not write many letters then.

People today use salt to stay healthy. Salt makes their food taste better. Even in the very old days people wanted salt. They knew they needed it to stay alive. Some people followed cattle to salt rocks. Then they carried the rocks to their caves.

Later, some people decided to build their homes on special land. This land was once covered by the sea. The salt water of the sea had slowly disappeared. The salt was left behind. Many early cities were built to be near this salt.

Those who had plenty of salt traded it for other goods. The salt trade became an important business for some people. Some men were even paid with salt for their work.

In the early 1800s, a vehicle almost like the modern bike was designed. The original bike had two wheels, but no pedals. The wheels were joined by a wooden seat. To move forward, riders pushed their feet against the ground.

During the next eighty years, more bike designs were developed. New models had pedals and wheels of different sizes. Inventions like brakes, new tires, and speed gears improved the bike. By 1900 all major bike changes were complete. People liked bikes so much that they wanted more than were made. Bike clubs were formed to tour and race. One American club had over one hundred thousand members.

The invention of cars decreased the need for bikes. Some people still preferred bikes. The cost to own and operate cars has increased today. Bikes are once more recognized as a cheap means of travel.

Silversmiths were an important part of Colonial America. To become a silversmith, young boys became apprentices. They trained with a skilled silversmith for four or more years of intense study and work. At age twenty-one, they could open their own silver shop. There, they shaped the soft metal into bright silver cups, dishes, and jewelry. Coins or other objects were often melted to get the metal with which to work. Most silversmiths took pride in their work. They stamped their names on each piece of value. One of the most famous works made at this time was a large bowl.

Some silver work of our Colonial ancestors is found in museums today. Silver is still used to make jewelry, dishes, and coins. But most modern silver objects are made by machines. Silver is also used to make medicines, mirrors, and photographs.

Quilts are often associated with a bed cover made by stitching soft stuffing between two pieces of cloth. Today some people use quilts made by precision machines.

The making of quilts began in ancient China and Egypt thousands of years ago. This practical art was passed through families and spread throughout the world. For early American settlers quilts met several needs. On cold winter nights, warm covers were needed. The few covers which could be bought were expensive. The women saved scraps of cloth from old clothes, stitching the scraps together by hand to make warm quilts. Designing new quilt patterns helped the women to feel creative. Most of the designs were quite bright and elegant. These added color and decorative charm to the plain homes. Some women met in small groups to make their quilts. These first quilting parties served as a form of entertainment. As friends worked together, the art of quilting flourished.

In the late 1800s rapid growth of American cities generated new problems for builders. This growth of city populations created demand for more businesses. More land was needed on which to build new one-story office buildings. As demand for land increased, so did the prices. The scarcity and high cost of land helped create a new concept in building design. This was the origin of the distinctive American design for tall buildings known as "skyscrapers."

Prior to this time, the design of the elevator had been improved. It was safe to use in buildings of many floors. Some builders tried different ways to build ground floors of buildings strong enough to support upper floors. When, in 1882, a man conceived the idea of using iron rods to support the floors and walls, building skyscrapers became possible. The completion of the first true skyscraper in the 1890s heralded the dawn of a new era in building. Many skyscrapers have been built since 1900, including one of the tallest American buildings with one hundred ten floors.

History first records coffee trees growing wild in remote regions of Africa. According to legend, it was noticed that the goats didn't sleep after they ate from coffee trees. People were intrigued with the stimulating effects of coffee fruit.

No one seems certain when people first drank coffee. Arabs heated coffee beans with water, making the drink at least seven hundred years ago. After cultivation of coffee trees was begun in Arabia, religious leaders and doctors used coffee. Doctors viewed coffee as important medicine, while religious leaders saw the drink as a special part of religious ceremonies. Once travelers tasted the drink, the Arabs were besieged with requests for coffee plants and beans. As the trees were grown in other countries, much of the civilized world acquired a taste for coffee. Turkish law even permitted wives to divorce husbands who failed to provide coffee.

Today South and Central America produce the most coffee grown for the international industry worth billions of dollars. The U.S. buys more coffee per year than other nations, but Finland's people consume the most coffee per person.

Almost two thousand years ago the Chinese printed designs and pictures on cloth. Nearly one hundred years later, the art of printing words was developed by the Chinese. They carved pictures on wood blocks and then pressed the inked blocks onto paper. Both the invention of paper by the Chinese and the need to make copies of their religious texts helped to foster the growth of printing. Other countries adopted this method to print pictures for books, but all the writing was done by hand. This process seriously limited the number of books that could be produced. The sudden awakening of Europe's appreciation for art and literature broadened interest in acquiring books, and greatly increased the demand for printed texts. Then, in 1456, Johann Gutenberg invented the first printing press with movable type fashioned from metal. After this invention, the printing of books was a much faster and less costly process, with positive effects on education.

Over the next five hundred years, as the demand for texts continued to grow, the printing process was greatly improved. Today, most of our magazines, newspapers, and books are printed by using the relief, offset, or engraving process.

The Taj Mahal is one of the most expensive and beautiful buildings to ever be built. The Emperor had it built between 1632 and 1653 by approximately twenty thousand laborers, and specifically named it in memory of his wife. This unique structure stands in northern India neighboring the city of Agra.

The Taj Mahal is an unusual octagonal shaped building, built of white marble which towers one hundred twenty feet above the ground with sides of one hundred thirty feet. At each corner stands a narrow prayer tower, called a minaret, which rises about one hundred thirty-three feet in height.

The main portion of the Taj Mahal, covered by a seventy-foot dome protecting two magnificent monuments, is an area often considered by visitors to be a highlight of the ancient structure. It features rare gems, elaborate mosaic, and inlaid tiles that are considered to be of unequaled beauty. The inside is lit by the daylight which filters through the stone of the dome and the windows.

The building is found in a beautifully landscaped garden region with large pools; it is breathtaking to see the structure reflected in the surrounding pools. The Taj Mahal is considered by some to be one of the world's architectural treasures.

introduction

This story about a man who liked birds happened a long time ago. Let's pretend we were there.

WORD RECOGNITION ERRORS
Insertions ______
Mispronunciations ______
Omissions ______
Refusals ______
Repetitions ______
Reversals ______
Substitutions ______
Phrasing ______
Other: ______

WORD REC/CONTEXT ERRORS		
Ind	Inst	Frus
0–3	4–8	9→

The boy likes birds.

Some days he just looks at birds.

He draws them.

He goes to school to draw.

As a man, he works.

His wife works.

Then he looks at birds.

He draws birds.

He paints pretty pictures of them.

He makes a book of his pictures.

It is one of the best books on birds.

People like it.

It helps them to see the birds.

MI ___ 1. What would be a good name for this story? (The Man and His Birds; Bird Painter or any appropriate response)

D ___ 2. What did the man sometimes do while he looked at the birds? (drew or painted pictures of them)

WM ___ 3. The story says, "The boy LIKES birds." What does LIKES mean? (enjoyed watching them; thought it was fun to draw them)

D ___ 4. Why did the story say the boy went to school? (to draw)

WM ___ 5. The story says the man DRAWS birds; what does "DRAW" mean? (make pictures with a pen or pencil)

	TOTAL COMPREHENSION			FACTUAL (Even #'s)			INTERPRETIVE (Odd #'s)		
Levels:	Ind	Instructional	Frus	Ind	Inst	Frus	Ind	Inst	Frus
Question Errors	0–1	2–3	4→	0	1	2→	0	1	2→
Approx Grade Equiv	Early 1st Grade (1.1–1.3)		Below Primer	Item Analysis: MI__/1; D__/4; I__/1; WM__/2					

D ___ 6. What did the story tell that the man's book helped people to do? (know all about birds)

I ___ 7. According to this story, his book was one of the best books on birds; why do you think it might be better than other books about birds? (pictures; he knew so much about birds)

D ___ 8. What did the man's wife do in the story? (work)

COMMENTS:

introduction

Read this story to find out about the interesting things that Bill could do.

WORD RECOGNITION ERRORS
Insertions ____
Mispronunciations ____
Omissions ____
Refusals ____
Repetitions ____
Reversals ____
Substitutions ____
Phrasing ____
Other: ____

Long ago a boy rode a horse to take the mail.

Sometimes Bill had to ride very fast.

One time Bill helped his country.

He looked for bad people.

His country gave him a prize.

As a man, Bill had a show.

It was a cowboy show.

Many of the cowboys could ride fast.

But Bill could ride faster.

They all could use a rope.

Bill was the star.

People came from far away to see the show.

WORD REC/CONTEXT ERRORS		
Ind	Inst	Frus
0–3	**4–8**	**9→**

MI ___ 1. Tell me a good name for this story. (The Star Cowboy; Bill's Show; or any appropriate title)

D ___ 2. Who is this story about? (Bill)

WM ___ 3. What does the word STAR mean in "Bill was the star?" (famous, important, or well-known)

D ___ 4. What did the story say the boy took when he rode the horse? (mail)

WM ___ 5. In the story the boy took the mail. What is MAIL? (letters; packages)

D ___ 6. What did Bill do to help his country? (looked for bad people)

I ___ 7. What makes us think that people liked Bill's show? (they came from far away to see the show)

D ___ 8. What kind of show did Bill have? (Cowboy; Western)

	TOTAL COMPREHENSION			FACTUAL (Even #'s)			INTERPRETIVE (Odd #'s)		
Levels:	Ind	Instructional	Frus	Ind	Inst	Frus	Ind	Inst	Frus
Question Errors	**0–1**	**2–3**	**4→**	**0**	**1**	**2→**	**0**	**1**	**2→**
Approx Grade Equiv	Late 1 (1.7–1.9)	Mid 1 (1.4–1.6)	Below 1	Item Analysis: MI__/1; D__/4; I__/1; WM__/2					

introduction

This story describes the life of an important writer; read carefully to find out about her.

WORD RECOGNITION ERRORS
Insertions ______
Mispronunciations ______
Omissions ______
Refusals ______
Repetitions ______
Reversals ______
Substitutions ______
Phrasing ______
Other: ______

WORD REC/CONTEXT ERRORS		
Ind	Inst	Frus
0–4	**5–10**	**11→**

Over a hundred years ago a young girl wanted to write plays.

She wanted to act.

She and her sisters gave plays in their barn.

The girl wrote the plays and acted in them.

The family did not have much money.

The girl worked to help her family.

She taught school, made dresses, and was a nurse.

She wrote a story about her family life.

The story became famous.

Then she wrote more about her life.

She was one of the first Americans to write stories just for

boys and girls.

She was able to earn money writing.

She loved her work.

MI ___ 1. Give this story a good name. (A Famous Writer; or any appropriate title)

D ___ 2. When did this story take place? (over a hundred years ago)

WM ___ 3. The story tells of the girl who ACTED; what does the word ACTED mean? (do a show, entertain, talk in front of people)

D ___ 4. Name two types of work the girl performed to help her family. (taught school, made dresses, was a nurse, wrote books/any two)

WM ___ 5. In the story the girl earned money; what does EARN mean? (make money, work for pay)

D ___ 6. For whom were her stories written? (boys and girls or children)

	TOTAL COMPREHENSION				FACTUAL (Even #'s)			INTERPRETIVE (Odd #'s)		
Levels:	Ind	Instructional		Frus	Ind	Inst	Frus	Ind	Inst	Frus
Question Errors	**0–1**	**2**	**3**	**4→**	**0**	**1**	**2→**	**0**	**1**	**2→**
Approx Grade Equiv	Late 2 (2.7–2.9)	Mid 2 (2.4–2.6)	Early 2 (2.1–2.3)	Below 2	Item Analysis: MI__/1; D__/4; I__/1; WM__/2					

I ___ 7. After reading this story, why do you think that this girl was a happy person? (she could earn money doing work she loved; she had always enjoyed writing and acting, and she was finally able to write and earn money)

D ___ 8. Where did the girls in the story give their plays? (in the barn)

COMMENTS:

introduction

Read this story to find out about a boy who did not like school.

WORD RECOGNITION ERRORS
Insertions ______
Mispronunciations ______
Omissions ______
Refusals ______
Repetitions ______
Reversals ______
Substitutions ______
Phrasing ______
Other: ______

WORD REC/CONTEXT ERRORS		
Ind	Inst	Frus
0–5	**6–12**	**13→**

From the first day, the boy did not like school. He bothered the teachers. They said he couldn't learn because he didn't behave. The boy said that the teachers couldn't teach. In the fourth grade, the boy quit school. No one knew then that one day the boy would be quite famous.

His mother began to teach the boy at home. She helped him meet some people. They taught him the mystery of science and machines.

As a man, he invented wax paper and a kind of printing press. He built improved phone parts. His most famous inventions are the record player and the improved light bulb. He created more than one thousand inventions. He said that a little thought and much hard work helped create the inventions.

MI ___ 1. What is a good title for this story? (A Famous Inventor; Drop-Out Who Became Famous; or any appropriate title)

D ___ 2. Who taught the boy at home? (mother)

WM ___ 3. What is meant by he BOTHERED the teachers? (caused trouble; upset them; misbehaved)

D ___ 4. Name his *two* most famous inventions. (record player AND light bulb)

WM ___ 5. What does it mean to be FAMOUS? (well known, distinguished; renowned)

D ___ 6. How did the boy feel about school? (did not like it)

	TOTAL COMPREHENSION				FACTUAL (Even #'s)			INTERPRETIVE (Odd #'s)		
Levels:	Ind	Instructional		Frus	Ind	Inst	Frus	Ind	Inst	Frus
Question Errors	0–1	2–3	4	5→	0	1–2	3→	0	1–2	3→
Approx Grade Equiv	Late 3 (3.7–3.9)	Mid 3 (3.4–3.6)	Early 3 (3.1–3.3)	Below 3	Item Analysis: MI__/1; D__/5; I__/2; WM__/2					

I ___ 7. Why do you think the boy quit school? (disliked it; wasn't learning; disliked teachers)

D ___ 8. How many inventions did the story say that he created? (over one thousand)

I ___ 9. After reading this story, why do you think that people who knew him as a boy were surprised when he became famous? (he couldn't learn in school AND didn't behave; he quit school)

D ___ 10. What two things did the man say helped to create his inventions? (a little thought and much hard work)

COMMENTS:

introduction

Read to find out about a famous inventor.

WORD RECOGNITION ERRORS
Insertions ______
Mispronunciations ______
Omissions ______
Refusals ______
Repetitions ______
Reversals ______
Substitutions ______
Phrasing ______
Other: ______

WORD REC/CONTEXT ERRORS		
Ind	Inst	Frus
0–5	**6–14**	**15→**

Long ago a father taught his son about sounds. The boy wanted to understand how people made sounds. He studied hard for many years.

As a young man, he became a teacher. He taught at a special school for deaf children. It was hard for these children to speak because they had never heard the language. But this man taught them to speak and communicate. He helped the teachers too. One student was so special to the teacher that he married her several years later.

Each day he taught classes, but at night he studied sound. While working on the telegraph, he happened to make a noise. It sounded like a voice. He began to develop a system of producing voice sounds. His teaching was interrupted by his work with sound. He designed and built the first phone.

MI ___ 1. What is a good title for this story? (The Life of an Inventor; A Teacher of the Deaf; The Invention of the Phone)

D ___ 2. Who taught the boy in the story about sound? (his father)

WM ___ 3. The story says that "his teaching was INTERRUPTED by his work with sound." What does INTERRUPTED mean? (stopped; bothered)

D ___ 4. The teacher in the story built a new invention; what was it? (phone)

WM ___ 5. What does it mean when we say that people COMMUNICATE? (talk; share ideas)

D ___ 6. In what kind of school did the young man teach? (school for deaf)

I ___ 7. What makes you think that the teacher in the story was a good one? (he was able to teach the deaf

	TOTAL COMPREHENSION				FACTUAL (Even #'s)			INTERPRETIVE (Odd #'s)		
Levels:	Ind	Instructional		Frus	Ind	Inst	Frus	Ind	Inst	Frus
Question Errors	**0–1**	**2–3**	**4**	**5→**	**0**	**1–2**	**3→**	**0**	**1–2**	**3→**
Approx Grade Equiv	Late 4 (4.7–4.9)	Mid 4 (4.4–4.6)	Early 4 (4.1–4.3)	Below 4	Item Analysis: MI__/1; D__/5; I__/2; WM__/2					

children; he helped the teachers too)

D ___ 8. What does the story tell us the young man did at night? (studied sound)

I ___ 9. Why do you think the teacher stopped teaching to study more about sound? (not enough time for both; thought sound more important; couldn't do both well)

D ___ 10. What was the teacher in the story working on when he began to think about building a phone? (telegraph)

COMMENTS:

introduction

Read this story to find out about the special dances of Dora Duncan.

WORD RECOGNITION ERRORS
Insertions ______
Mispronunciations ______
Omissions ______
Refusals ______
Repetitions ______
Reversals ______
Substitutions ______
Phrasing ______
Other: ______

WORD REC/CONTEXT ERRORS		
Ind	Inst	Frus
0–6	**7–15**	**16→**

Among the greatest dancers in this century was Dora Duncan. She changed the world of ballet. Her early life held little promise of later fame.

Even as a small child she enjoyed dance. When dancing she forgot the holes in her shoes and her empty stomach. She could ignore the school where few understood her. Dora's mother allowed her to quit school at age eleven when the teacher said Dora could not learn.

Dora and her sister began a dancing school at home. They taught the children nature's fascinating movements. Theirs was not like most dance then seen on stage. Dora said that dance should be an expression of mind and heart. Among her dance movements borrowed from nature were those of whirling leaves and flowers opening.

Many people were impressed with Dora's dancing and teaching. Over the next thirty years the world would recognize the value of expressive dancing.

MI ___ 1. What is a good title for this story? (New Dance; A Special Kind of Dancing; The Dancer; or appropriate title)

D ___ 2. What type of dancer was Dora? (ballet; expressionist)

WM ___ 3. In the story you read about FASCINATING movements. What does FASCINATING mean? (unusual; very interesting; intriguing)

D ___ 4. Where did Dora begin her own dancing school? (at home)

	TOTAL COMPREHENSION				FACTUAL (Even #'s)			INTERPRETIVE (Odd #'s)		
Levels:	Ind	Instructional		Frus	Ind	Inst	Frus	Ind	Inst	Frus
Question Errors	**0–1**	**2–3**	**4**	**5→**	**0**	**1–2**	**3→**	**0**	**1–2**	**3→**
Approx Grade Equiv	Late 5 (5.7–5.9)	Mid 5 (5.4–5.6)	Early 5 (5.1–5.3)	Below 5	Item Analysis: MI__/1; D__/5; I__/2; WM__/2					

WM ___ 5. What does it mean when we talk about the VALUE of dancing? (its worth)

D ___ 6. For how many years was Dora a teacher and dancer? (thirty)

I ___ 7. What makes us think that Dora had little money as a child? (there were holes in her shoes and she had an empty stomach)

D ___ 8. Why was Dora allowed to quit school? (her teacher said that she could not learn)

I ___ 9. Why do you think people liked the expressive dancing? (it was different; based on nature)

D ___ 10. What did Dora say that dance should be? (an expression of mind and heart)

COMMENTS:

introduction

Read this story and find out how Winston Churchill became a famous Englishman.

WORD RECOGNITION ERRORS
Insertions ______
Mispronunciations ______
Omissions ______
Refusals ______
Repetitions ______
Reversals ______
Substitutions ______
Phrasing ______
Other: ______

WORD REC/CONTEXT ERRORS		
Ind	Inst	Frus
0–6	**7–16**	**17→**

Churchill found great pleasure in reading. Yet, throughout his school years, Math and Latin were very difficult for him. He was a very active and restless student whose aggressive acts often caused trouble. A teacher once chased him around the school yard to reduce his restlessness in the classroom. Churchill twice failed the test to enter military school. When his father hired a tutor, Churchill passed the test and was admitted.

It was in military school at age nineteen that Churchill began to achieve his first real success. Here, his activity and restlessness were even encouraged. This school marked the beginning of Churchill's vast achievements. He became known as a popular speaker and writer throughout much of the world. His talents and career continued to flourish. For his writing, he was awarded the Nobel Prize. Churchill rose to the highest office in England's government as its leader. He was awarded the greatest honor in his native land when he became a knight.

MI ___ 1. What is a good title for this story? (A Famous Englishman; A Famous Writer; A Famous Speaker and Government Leader; A Poor Student Becomes Great; or appropriate title)

D ___ 2. Why was Churchill chased around the school yard? (to decrease his restlessness in the classroom)

WM ___ 3. What is meant by AGGRESSIVE behavior? (fighting, troublesome, active)

	TOTAL COMPREHENSION				FACTUAL (Even #'s)			INTERPRETIVE (Odd #'s)		
Levels:	Ind	Instructional		Frus	Ind	Inst	Frus	Ind	Inst	Frus
Question Errors	**0–1**	**2–3**	**4**	**5→**	**0**	**1–2**	**3→**	**0**	**1–2**	**3→**
Approx Grade Equiv	Late 6 (6.7–6.9)	Mid 6 (6.4–6.6)	Early 6 (6.1–6.3)	Below 6	Item Analysis: MI__/1; D__/5; I__/2; WM__/2					

D ____ 4. In what kind of school did Churchill achieve his first real success? (military)

WM ____ 5. In this story, what is meant by VAST achievements? (many, great)

D ____ 6. Name two school subjects that were difficult for Churchill. (Math and Latin)

I ____ 7. Why do you think that people who knew Churchill as a young boy might have been surprised when he became such a great man? (he did so poorly in school; he was so restless and active in school)

D ____ 8. What was Churchill's nation's highest honor? (knighthood)

I ____ 9. Why do you think that Churchill did so poorly in school at one time? (couldn't settle down; misbehaved; didn't like subjects except reading)

D ____ 10. Why was Churchill finally able to pass the test to be admitted to military school? (father hired a tutor to teach him)

COMMENTS:

introduction

Read to find out how Clerow became a well-known comedian.

WORD RECOGNITION ERRORS
Insertions ______
Mispronunciations ______
Omissions ______
Refusals ______
Repetitions ______
Reversals ______
Substitutions ______
Phrasing ______
Other: ______

WORD REC/CONTEXT ERRORS		
Ind	Inst	Frus
0–7	**8–17**	**18→**

When the star of the school play became ill, a small boy volunteered to play the girl's part. The class roared with laughter when Clerow Wilson stood up and began to recite the lines perfectly. The boy entertained the school by playing the girl's part in the school program. This performance heralded the beginning of the career of one of today's most famous entertainers, Flip Wilson.

Flip spent his early childhood in a very poor neighborhood. Despite primitive living conditions, Flip always found something to laugh about. He entertained his friends by telling them outlandish stories.

When Flip joined the U. S. Air Force at age sixteen, he continued to entertain the people around him with his wild stories. Here, he acquired the name Flip when someone said that he had "flipped." Flip decided he wanted to become a professional entertainer. Today Flip Wilson has become one of the most successful comedians on stage and TV. Among his distinctive comical acts is one in which he plays the part of a girl.

	TOTAL COMPREHENSION				FACTUAL (Even #'s)			INTERPRETIVE (Odd #'s)		
Levels:	Ind	Instructional		Frus	Ind	Inst	Frus	Ind	Inst	Frus
Question Errors	**0–1**	**2–3**	**4**	**5→**	**0**	**1–2**	**3→**	**0**	**1–2**	**3→**
Approx Grade Equiv	Late 7 (7.7–7.9)	Mid 7 (7.4–7.6)	Early 7 (7.1–7.3)	Below 7	Item Analysis: MI__/1; D__/5; I__/2; WM__/2					

MI ___ 1. What would be a good title for this story? (A Funny Man; A Famous Comedian; How a Comedian Became Famous; any appropriate title)

D ___ 2. Who is this story about? (Flip Wilson)

WM ___ 3. What does HERALDED mean in the phrase, "this performance HERALDED the beginning"? (signaled; proclaimed; gave tidings of)

D ___ 4. In what kind of show did Flip begin his acting career? (school play)

WM ___ 5. What do we mean when we say an act is DISTINCTIVE? (unusual; different)

D ___ 6. According to the story, what is one of Flip's funniest and best liked acts? (the act in which he plays the part of a girl; Geraldine)

I ___ 7. What was so funny about Flip's part in the school play? (he played the part of a girl; a boy playing a girl's part)

D ___ 8. Why was Flip chosen to play a girl's part in the school play? (he volunteered; it was a girl he was replacing; he knew the lines)

I ___ 9. Why do you think Flip is so well liked? (he's so funny; tells wild stories; different)

D ___ 10. How did Clerow Wilson get the name, "Flip"? (some of his Air Force friends thought he had "flipped.")

COMMENTS:

introduction

Read to find out about
Sarah Walker, a famous hair stylist.

WORD RECOGNITION ERRORS
Insertions ______
Mispronunciations ______
Omissions ______
Refusals ______
Repetitions ______
Reversals ______
Substitutions ______
Phrasing ______
Other: ______

WORD REC/CONTEXT ERRORS		
Ind	Inst	Frus
0–7	**8–18**	**19→**

Although Sarah was extremely poor in her early life, she took great pride in her appearance. Sarah wanted to soften the texture and loosen the curl of her hair. Hers was the problem experienced by many women who were African descendants. She discovered that, with the application of various mixtures, she could soften her hair texture, but not loosen the curl. Reluctant to abandon the project, Sarah continued to experiment. In 1905, she developed an ingenious device to remove or loosen the tight hair curls. By styling her hair with a heated metal comb and oil mixtures, she could achieve this goal.

Later Sarah opened a school to train hair stylists to use the ''Walker System'' of straightening hair. Through the sales of her beauty products and system, Sarah Walker became very wealthy. Part of this wealth was shared through her gifts of money to organizations and black institutions.

For many women the heated comb was the solution to their greatest cosmetic problem. Although some women use the ''Walker System'' today, the modern version is an electric hot comb.

MI ___ 1. What is a good title for this story? (Sarah Walker's Invention; The Hot Comb; or any appropriate title)

D ___ 2. How did Sarah feel about the way she looked? (she took pride in her appearance; she didn't like the texture and curl of her hair)

	TOTAL COMPREHENSION				FACTUAL (Even #'s)			INTERPRETIVE (Odd #'s)		
Levels:	Ind	Instructional		Frus	Ind	Inst	Frus	Ind	Inst	Frus
Question Errors	**0–1**	**2–3**	**4**	**5→**	**0**	**1–2**	**3→**	**0**	**1–2**	**3→**
Approx Grade Equiv	Late 8 (8.7–8.9)	Mid 8 (8.4–8.6)	Early 8 (8.1–8.3)	Below 8	Item Analysis: MI__/1; D__/5; I__/2; WM__/2					

WM ___ 3. What does it mean to be RELUCTANT? (hesitant; doubtful; unwilling)

D ___ 4. What is the "Walker System"? (a system for straightening and/or styling hair)

WM ___ 5. The story tells about an INGENIOUS device; what does INGENIOUS mean? (clever; original)

D ___ 6. What was Sarah's major goal in this story? (soften hair texture and curl)

I ___ 7. How did Sarah's financial state change as an adult? (became wealthy)

D ___ 8. What is the modern version of the "Walker System"? (electric hot comb)

I ___ 9. After reading this story, who do you think was the first person to try Sarah's products? (Sarah herself)

D ___ 10. In the story, how did Sarah share part of her wealth? (gave it to organizations and Black institutions/both)

COMMENTS:

introduction

This story is about Susan B. Anthony.
Read the selection to find out about her.

WORD RECOGNITION ERRORS
Insertions ______
Mispronunciations ______
Omissions ______
Refusals ______
Repetitions ______
Reversals ______
Substitutions ______
Phrasing ______
Other: ______

WORD REC/CONTEXT ERRORS		
Ind	Inst	Frus
0–8	**9–19**	**20→**

There have been many important women who, over a period of nearly two hundred years, have been active leaders in the women's suffrage movement. They have led the struggle for women's rights which include the right to vote, equal work, dress reform, and temperance. Beginning by forming the Women's State Temperance Society of New York, Susan B. Anthony became one of the most prominent leaders for women's rights. Susan, who spoke out for issues such as dress reform and even wore bloomers herself, was mainly interested in all women having the right to vote.

In 1851, Ms. Anthony met Elizabeth Stanton and, together, they organized a team for women's suffrage. Susan was famous for her speeches and particularly for her work as editor for a controversial magazine, *The Revolution.*

Susan Anthony was a person who lived what she believed. In 1872, she was determined to vote even though, by law, women were not allowed to vote. Fully aware of possible consequences, she voted and was then arrested. Her trial helped to unite many women across her country. Ms. Anthony served as an example of what one person can accomplish for an entire nation.

	TOTAL COMPREHENSION				FACTUAL (Even #'s)			INTERPRETIVE (Odd #'s)		
Levels:	Ind	Instructional		Frus	Ind	Inst	Frus	Ind	Inst	Frus
Question Errors	**0–1**	**2–3**	**4**	**5→**	**0**	**1–2**	**3→**	**0**	**1–2**	**3→**
Approx Grade Equiv	Late 9 (9.7–9.9)	Mid 9 (9.4–9.6)	Early 9 (9.1–9.3)	Below 9	Item Analysis: MI__/1; D__/5; I__/2; WM__/2					

MI ___ 1. What is an appropriate title for this story? (The Life of Susan B. Anthony; A Famous Leader; or appropriate title)

D ___ 2. What was the name of the organization Ms. Anthony began? (Women's Temperance Society of New York; or Women's Temperance)

WM ___ 3. What does the word PROMINENT mean? (important, well-known, recognized)

D ___ 4. Who was Elizabeth Stanton? (Susan's friend; suffrage leader)

WM ___ 5. The story mentions a CONTROVERSIAL magazine; what does CONTROVERSIAL mean? (debatable; open to dispute)

D ___ 6. Why was Susan Anthony arrested in 1872? (she voted when women were not allowed to vote)

I ___ 7. After reading this story, what do you think is meant by women's suffrage? (women's right to vote)

D ___ 8. Name an issue in addition to voting that concerned Ms. Anthony. (temperance; dress; equal work)

I ___ 9. Why do you think women in the 1800's were not allowed to vote? (men dominated society; women were expccted to be domestic; appropriate response)

D ___ 10. Ms. Anthony was an editor for a magazine; what was the name of the magazine? (*The Revolution*)

COMMENTS:

introduction

This story is about a well-known American anthropologist. Read to learn about her life.

WORD RECOGNITION ERRORS
Insertions ______
Mispronunciations ______
Omissions ______
Refusals ______
Repetitions ______
Reversals ______
Substitutions ______
Phrasing ______
Other: ______

WORD REC/CONTEXT ERRORS		
Ind	Inst	Frus
0–8	**9–20**	**21→**

Margaret Mead was born in 1901, and became one of the most celebrated anthropologists in the world. She was known for her studies of the children and cultures of the Pacific Islands, Russia, and the United States.

Ms. Mead would actually live with the people she studied and, in many instances, ate and acted exactly as they did. For nine months, while studying Samoan adolescents, she lived and interacted with the adolescent girls almost as a sister. This was made possible, in part, due to her small stature; she stood just over five feet tall. Her efforts were the first of any anthropologist, male or female, on such a personal basis.

Margaret Mead, well known for her writing and also for her lectures, was a major influence in scientifically disproving some ideas concerning human behavior. In addition to her studies, Margaret Mead served in important advisory positions for the United States government following World War II. *Coming of Age in Samoa, Growing Up in New Guinea,* and *Sex and Temperament in Three Primitive Societies* are three of the highly acclaimed books which she authored. Margaret Mead's careful studies of children in primitive societies provided fresh insights toward understanding human personality.

	TOTAL COMPREHENSION				FACTUAL (Even #'s)			INTERPRETIVE (Odd #'s)		
Levels:	Ind	Instructional		Frus	Ind	Inst	Frus	Ind	Inst	Frus
Question Errors	**0–1**	**2–3**	**4**	**5→**	**0**	**1–2**	**3→**	**0**	**1–2**	**3→**
Approx Grade Equiv	Late 10 (10.7–.9)	Mid 10 (10.4–10.6)	Early 10 (10.1–10.3)	Below 10	Item Analysis: MI__/1; D__/5; I__/2; WM__/2					

MI ___ 1. What would be a good title for this story? (A Famous American Anthropologist; or appropriate answer)

D ___ 2. In what year was Margaret Mead born? (1901; or about 1900)

WM ___ 3. This story calls Ms. Mead a CELEBRATED anthropologist; what does CELEBRATED mean? (famous; distinguished; honored)

D ___ 4. According to the story, for what did Margaret Mead become known? (her studies of children and cultures; writings; lectures [any two])

WM ___ 5. What does ADVISORY mean in "ADVISORY position"? (guiding; suggesting; or giving of advice)

D ___ 6. Name two places in which Margaret Mead studied. (United States; Russia; Pacific Islands; Samoa; New Guinea/any two)

I ___ 7. Based upon this story, what do you think is the job of an anthropologist? (to study people and cultures)

D ___ 8. About what age people did the story say Ms. Mead studied in Samoa? (teenagers; adolescents)

I ___ 9. What was so special about the way Ms. Mead studied the adolescent Samoan girls? (she lived as a sister with the girls)

D ___ 10. How tall was Margaret Mead? (just over five feet tall)

COMMENTS:

introduction

Read this story to find out about Ladybugs.

WORD RECOGNITION ERRORS	
Insertions	
Mispronunciations	
Omissions	
Refusals	
Repetitions	
Reversals	
Substitutions	
Phrasing	
Other:	

Some children like Ladybugs.

They like to play with them.

They think they are pretty.

Ladybugs are good bugs.

They help people.

Some men did not want bad bugs.

So they set fires.

But they liked Ladybugs.

They wanted to help them.

They said, "Ladybug, Ladybug, fly away home."

Now we need good bugs.

We use new ways to keep Ladybugs.

WORD REC/CONTEXT ERRORS		
Ind	Inst	Frus
0–3	4–8	9→

MI ___ 1. Give this story a name. (All About Ladybugs; Why People Like Ladybugs; Good Bugs)

D ___ 2. The story says we need Ladybugs. How do we keep them now? (use new ways)

WM ___ 3. What does it mean when we say something is PRETTY? (lovely; nice to look at; beautiful)

D ___ 4. Why does the story say that Ladybugs are good bugs? (they help people)

WM ___ 5. The story says we use NEW ways to keep Ladybugs. What does NEW mean? (better, different)

D ___ 6. Why did some men in this story set fires? (some men did not want bad bugs)

I ___ 7. In the story why do you think the men said, "Ladybug, fly away home"? (they didn't want the Ladybugs to be hurt)

D ___ 8. In this story, who likes to play with Ladybugs? (Children)

	TOTAL COMPREHENSION			FACTUAL (Even #'s)			INTERPRETIVE (Odd #'s)		
Levels:	Ind	Instructional	Frus	Ind	Inst	Frus	Ind	Inst	Frus
Question Errors	0–1	2–3	4→	0	1	2→	0	1	2→
Approx Grade Equiv	Early 1st Grade (1.1–1.3)		Below Primer	Item Analysis: MI__/1; D__/4; I__/1; WM__/2					

introduction

Read this story to find out more about skunks.

WORD RECOGNITION ERRORS
Insertions ______
Mispronunciations ______
Omissions ______
Refusals ______
Repetitions ______
Reversals ______
Substitutions ______
Phrasing ______
Other: ______

Skunks are small and pretty.

They are friendly animals.

They like to be near people.

Skunks live near farms and eat bad bugs.

They help farmers.

Many people do not like to be near skunks.

They give off a bad smell.

Skunks are not strong and they cannot run fast.

People run from skunks because they can make people smell bad.

They keep animals away too.

They can make animals smell the same as the skunk.

This is the way skunks stay safe.

WORD REC/CONTEXT ERRORS		
Ind	Inst	Frus
0–3	4–8	9→

MI ___ 1. What is a good title or name for this story? (All About Skunks; Why Skunks Have a Funny Smell; or any appropriate title)

D ___ 2. Based on this story, how do skunks look? (small and pretty)

WM ___ 3. This story tells about MANY people; what is another word for MANY? (several; lots; more than three or four)

D ___ 4. What does the story say that skunks eat? (bad bugs)

WM ___ 5. What does it mean when something is the SAME as something else? (like)

D ___ 6. How does the story say skunks stay safe? (they give off a bad smell)

I ___ 7. After reading this story, why do you think skunks need their bad smell to stay safe? (can't run from enemies AND are not strong)

D ___ 8. Where did the story say that skunks live? (near farms)

	TOTAL COMPREHENSION			FACTUAL (Even #'s)			INTERPRETIVE (Odd #'s)		
Levels:	Ind	Instructional	Frus	Ind	Inst	Frus	Ind	Inst	Frus
Question Errors	0–1	2–3	4→	0	1	2→	0	1	2→
Approx Grade Equiv	Late 1 (1.7–1.9)	Mid 1 (1.4–1.6)	Below 1	Item Analysis: MI__/1; D__/4; I__/1; WM__/2					

introduction

Read to find out how giraffes live.

WORD RECOGNITION ERRORS
Insertions ______
Mispronunciations ______
Omissions ______
Refusals ______
Repetitions ______
Reversals ______
Substitutions ______
Phrasing ______
Other: ______

Giraffes are the tallest animals in the world.

These tall giants are tame and quiet.

Giraffes eat leaves from tree tops.

Much of their water comes from leaves.

Their long necks help them reach high.

Using their long lips and tongues they are able to pick the leaves.

Their color and spots hide them near the trees.

They travel in herds.

Their long necks help them watch for danger.

These quick animals can run from most enemies.

But, when needed, they kick their long legs.

They hit with their strong necks to keep them safe.

Men have kept some giraffes safe in parks.

WORD REC/CONTEXT ERRORS		
Ind	Inst	Frus
0–5	**5–10**	**11→**

MI ___ 1. Give this story a title. (The Story of Giraffes; How Giraffes Live; or any appropriate title)

D ___ 2. What do giraffes eat? (leaves)

WM ___ 3. What does it mean to be ABLE to do something? (capable; can; have the ability)

D ___ 4. Where are some giraffes in this story kept to stay safe? (in parks)

WM ___ 5. What is meant by NEAR the trees? (close by; next to; not far from)

D ___ 6. Name two ways the giraffes in the story protect themselves. (any two: run fast; kick; hit with neck; hide near trees)

I ___ 7. Why do you think giraffes eat leaves from tree tops instead of the lower parts of trees? (more convenient for their long necks; easier; can watch for enemies while eating)

D ___ 8. In the story, how do giraffes pick the leaves from trees? (using their long lips AND tongue)

	TOTAL COMPREHENSION				FACTUAL (Even #'s)			INTERPRETIVE (Odd #'s)		
Levels:	Ind	Instructional		Frus	Ind	Inst	Frus	Ind	Inst	Frus
Question Errors	**0–1**	**2**	**3**	**4→**	**0**	**1**	**2→**	**0**	**1**	**2→**
Approx Grade Equiv	Late 2 (2.7–2.9)	Mid 2 (2.4–2.6)	Early 2 (2.1–2.3)	Below 2	Item Analysis: MI__/1; D__/4; I__/1; WM__/2					

introduction

Read this story to find out what is so special about butterflies.

WORD RECOGNITION ERRORS	
Insertions	
Mispronunciations	
Omissions	
Refusals	
Repetitions	
Reversals	
Substitutions	
Phrasing	
Other:	

WORD REC/CONTEXT ERRORS		
Ind	Inst	Frus
0–5	6–12	13→

Butterflies are quite beautiful insects. Most butterflies have two pairs of wings. Their bodies are covered with small scales or hairs. These give the silent insects their color. The special mouths of butterflies are made like drinking straws. These straws enable the insects to draw juice from flowers. The straws roll up when not in use.

When the weather turns cool, one kind of butterfly flies south. They may fly as many as eighty miles a day. They travel hundreds of miles. There, on a special mountain, they spend the winter. Their body heat becomes the same as the cool outsidc air. The quiet, still insects look like thousands of fall leaves. In spring the butterflies return north to enjoy the flowers.

MI ___ 1. Give this story a title. (All About Butterflies; The Life of Butterflies; Special Features of Butterflies; or any appropriate title)

D ___ 2. How many pairs of wings do butterflics have? (two)

WM ___ 3. What does it mean when we say they TRAVEL? (go somewhere; take a trip)

D ___ 4. Where do some butterflies in the story go in the spring? (north)

WM ___ 5. According to the story, butterflies have SPECIAL mouths; what is another word for SPECIAL? (unusual; different)

D ___ 6. Where do butterflies get their juice? (from flowers)

I ___ 7. In the story, the butterflies' body heat "becomes the same as the cool outside air." How does this help the butterflies? (Keeps them from being uncomfortable; re-

	TOTAL COMPREHENSION				FACTUAL (Even #'s)			INTERPRETIVE (Odd #'s)		
Levels:	Ind	Instructional		Frus	Ind	Inst	Frus	Ind	Inst	Frus
Question Errors	0–1	2–3	4	5→	0	1–2	3→	0	1–2	3→
Approx Grade Equiv	Late 3 (3.7–3.9)	Mid 3 (3.4–3.6)	Early 3 (3.1–3.3)	Below 3	Item Analysis: MI_/1; D_/5; I_/2; WM_/2					

duces the shock of the cool air; allows them to remain motionless, using little stored energy)

D ___ 8. What is special or different about a butterfly's mouth? (made like a drinking straw)

I ___ 9. Why do you think the straw-like mouths of butterflies need to roll up? (to stay out of the way when not in use)

D ___ 10. How many miles a day can some butterflies in the story travel? (as many as eighty)

COMMENTS:

introduction

This story tells about an interesting insect.
Read this story to find out what this insect can do.

WORD RECOGNITION ERRORS
Insertions ____
Mispronunciations ____
Omissions ____
Refusals ____
Repetitions ____
Reversals ____
Substitutions ____
Phrasing ____
Other: ____

WORD REC/CONTEXT ERRORS		
Ind	Inst	Frus
0–5	**6–14**	**15→**

Fleas are not well liked. The small fleas prefer to ride on animals, especially dogs and cats. Fleas have been known to ride on people and even chickens. They make the animals miserable because they tickle. It is hard to get rid of the insects because they multiply quickly.

But some kinds of fleas are intelligent. They can be trained to perform acrobatics. They can jump almost twelve inches. The fleas land on their back legs, facing backward. The patient trainers must first teach the insects to walk instead of jump. Then the fleas can be taught to perform many tricks. They can learn to race, jump sticks and hoops, or even pull wagons. Sometimes the trainers exhibit the performing fleas at a fair. These insects can be a bother. They can also be fun to watch.

MI ___ 1. What is a good title for this story? (Performing Fleas; Tricks of Fleas; or any appropriate title)

D ___ 2. The story tells that fleas prefer to ride on dogs; name two *other* places fleas ride. (cats; people; chickens/two of thrcc)

WM ___ 3. What did ACROBATICS mean in ''they learn to perform ACROBATICS''? (tumbling tricks; jumping tricks)

D ___ 4. According to this story, how far can a flea jump? (twelve inches)

WM ___ 5. The story tells that fleas make the animals MISERABLE; what does MISERABLE mean? (uncomfortable; unhappy; or sad)

D ___ 6. Name two tricks that some fleas can learn. (walk; race; jump sticks and hoops; pull wagons)

I ___ 7. Before teaching the fleas tricks, the trainers must train the fleas to

	TOTAL COMPREHENSION				FACTUAL (Even #'s)			INTERPRETIVE (Odd #'s)		
Levels:	Ind	Instructional		Frus	Ind	Inst	Frus	Ind	Inst	Frus
Question Errors	**0–1**	**2–3**	**4**	**5→**	**0**	**1–2**	**3→**	**0**	**1–2**	**3→**
Approx Grade Equiv	Late 4 (4.7–4.9)	Mid 4 (4.4–4.6)	Early 4 (4.1–4.3)	Below 4	Item Analysis: MI__/1; D__/5; I__/2; WM__/2					

walk instead of jump; based on this story, why do you think that this is so? (when they jump, they land backward—couldn't race that way; also couldn't pull wagons or aim for the sticks or hoops)

D ___ 8. How do the fleas make animals miserable? (tickle them)

I ___ 9. After reading this story, why do you think that flea trainers need to be very patient? (fleas are so small; hard to train)

D ___ 10. Where do fleas sometimes perform in this story? (at a fair)

COMMENTS:

introduction

Read this story to find out about the habits of sponges.

WORD RECOGNITION ERRORS
Insertions ______
Mispronunciations ______
Omissions ______
Refusals ______
Repetitions ______
Reversals ______
Substitutions ______
Phrasing ______
Other: ______

WORD REC/CONTEXT ERRORS		
Ind	Inst	Frus
0–6	**7–15**	**16→**

Sponges are among the most fascinating of the water creatures. All sponges are made of many single cells. But unlike most animals, their systems have no hearts, brains, or lungs. Sponges have no way of moving around in the water.

There are over five thousand known species of sponges. Some live in salt water, while others live in fresh water. Colors may range from the typical tan to bright reds and blues. They range in size from small to large. They may be as small as peas or larger than a man.

Many small animals live among the pores of sponges, and may even share their meals. Sponges protect small sea creatures by hiding them. A broken sponge can attach itself to a new spot and continue to grow. Sponges have extraordinary powers to resist bacteria. By investigating these powers, scientists have developed new ways to help humans resist diseases.

MI ___ 1. What would be a good title for this story? (How Sponges Live; All About Sponges; Why Sponges Are Interesting; or any appropriate title)

D ___ 2. Name two unusual things about the life systems of sponges. (they have no heart; no brain; no lungs/any two of three)

WM ___ 3. According to the story, sponges are FASCINATING; what does FASCINATING mean? (interesting; enchanting; bewitching; charming)

D ___ 4. How do sponges protect small sea creatures? (by hiding them; hiding them in their pores)

	TOTAL COMPREHENSION				FACTUAL (Even #'s)			INTERPRETIVE (Odd #'s)		
Levels:	Ind	Instructional		Frus	Ind	Inst	Frus	Ind	Inst	Frus
Question Errors	**0–1**	**2–3**	**4**	**5→**	**0**	**1–2**	**3→**	**0**	**1–2**	**3→**
Approx Grade Equiv	Late 5 (5.7–5.9)	Mid 5 (5.4–5.6)	Early 5 (5.1–5.3)	Below 5	Item Analysis: MI__/1; D__/5; I__/2; WM__/2					

WM ___ 5. What does the word INVESTIGATING mean in the phrase "investigating these powers"? (studying; examining; researching; looking at closely)

D ___ 6. According to this story, how many known species of sponges are there? (more than five thousand)

I ___ 7. How, according to this story, have sponges been helpful to people? (scientists have developed ways to help people resist diseases by studying sponges)

D ___ 8. The most common sponges are tan; name two other colors of sponges that the story tells about. (red and blue)

I ___ 9. After reading this story, how do you think sponges are able to survive accidents and disease so well? (can grow after being broken AND resist bacteria)

D ___ 10. How large is the largest sponge told about in the story? (larger than a man)

COMMENTS:

introduction

Read this story to find out what is so interesting about the lives of owls.

WORD RECOGNITION ERRORS
Insertions ______
Mispronunciations ______
Omissions ______
Refusals ______
Repetitions ______
Reversals ______
Substitutions ______
Phrasing ______
Other: ______

WORD REC/CONTEXT ERRORS		
Ind	Inst	Frus
0–6	**7–16**	**17→**

Many species of owls flourish in both hemispheres. Most owls are night creatures, who sleep during the day. Some owls make the familiar ''hoo-hoo'' sound; others have an eerie cry. The unique design of the owls' eyes and ears gives them phenomenal vision and hearing. The feathers on their wings are shorter and rounder than those of other birds, making their flight almost silent. Owls usually live alone or in pairs.

Among the least social of these birds are Great Horned Owls. These enormous and aggressive owls sometimes have a wing spread of five feet. They do not like people. The eerie cry of these birds scares many people.

Among the more social owls are those named for their sad, wailing call. The colors of the feathers of Screech Owls resemble the bark of the trees in which they perch. These owls do not mind having humans for neighbors. Because Screech Owls help keep crops safe, farmers appreciate these birds.

MI ___ 1. Give this story a good title. (Night Creatures; All About Owls; The Interesting Lives of Owls; or any appropriate title)

D ___ 2. The story tells that many species of owls flourish where? (in both hemispheres)

WM ___ 3. The story talks about AGGRESSIVE owls; what does AGGRESSIVE mean? (assaulting; attacking; pushy)

D ___ 4. What type of owl in the story likes people? (Screech Owl)

	TOTAL COMPREHENSION				FACTUAL (Even #'s)			INTERPRETIVE (Odd #'s)		
Levels:	Ind	Instructional		Frus	Ind	Inst	Frus	Ind	Inst	Frus
Question Errors	**0–1**	**2–3**	**4**	**5→**	**0**	**1–2**	**3→**	**0**	**1–2**	**3→**
Approx Grade Equiv	Late 6 (6.7–6.9)	Mid 6 (6.4–6.6)	Early 6 (6.1–6.3)	Below 6	Item Analysis: MI__/1; D__/5; I__/2; WM__/2					

WM ___ 5. Owls are said to have PHENOMENAL hearing and vision; what is another word for PHENOMENAL? (very good; extraordinary; great; excellent)

D ___ 6. According to the story how wide may the wing spread of a Great Horned Owl be? (five feet)

I ___ 7. Why do you think someone might be afraid of an owl? (its sound; appearance; associated with night; some are aggressive)

D ___ 8. How do the feathers of owls' wings differ from those of other birds? (shorter AND rounder)

I ___ 9. Based on this story, why do you think some owls might be hard to see? (feathers look like tree bark; blend into surroundings)

D ___ 10. Why do the farmers in this story like Screech Owls? (they help keep crops safe; help protect crops)

COMMENTS:

introduction

Read this story to find out some interesting facts about oysters.

WORD RECOGNITION ERRORS
Insertions ______
Mispronunciations ______
Omissions ______
Refusals ______
Repetitions ______
Reversals ______
Substitutions ______
Phrasing ______
Other: ______

WORD REC/CONTEXT ERRORS		
Ind	Inst	Frus
0–7	**8–17**	**18→**

Oysters are small animals who live mostly in warm ocean waters. Shells provide refuge for their soft fleshy bodies. Each shell has two valves attached by a hinge. A strong muscle attaches the oyster's body to the inside of the shell, allowing the oyster to open and close its shell at will. Once an oyster has attached its left valve to a rock or other object on the sea bottom, it stays there for life.

Oyster shells are lined with a fold of tissue which secretes a lime substance. If an alien object or substance enters the shell, it irritates the oyster's body. In order to protect itself, the oyster secretes a white liquid and surrounds the object. This lime liquid hardens, forming thin sheets over the object. Slowly, more circular layers are added until a pearl is formed.

Some species of oysters create pearls which are highly valued by people. The oyster's method of protection not only provides a more comfortable life for the animal, but also produces something of beauty for people.

MI ___ 1. Give this story a good title. (All About Oysters; How Pearls Are Made; or any appropriate title)

D ___ 2. Where do oysters live, according to this story? (warm ocean water; sea bottom)

	TOTAL COMPREHENSION				FACTUAL (Even #'s)			INTERPRETIVE (Odd #'s)		
Levels:	Ind	Instructional		Frus	Ind	Inst	Frus	Ind	Inst	Frus
Question Errors	**0–1**	**2–3**	**4**	**5→**	**0**	**1–2**	**3→**	**0**	**1–2**	**3→**
Approx Grade Equiv	Late 7 (7.7–7.9)	Mid 7 (7.4–7.6)	Early 7 (7.1–7.3)	Below 7	Item Analysis: MI__/1; D__/5; I__/2; WM__/2					

WM ___ 3. The story says that the shell provides a REFUGE for the oyster; what is a REFUGE? (safe place, retreat; haven)

D ___ 4. What attaches the oyster's body to the inside of the shell? (strong muscle)

WM ___ 5. The story talks about an ALIEN object or substance; what is another word for ALIEN? (foreign; adverse; different)

D ___ 6. What does the oyster do to protect itself from alien objects? (secretes white liquid; secretes limey substance; makes pearls)

I ___ 7. Based on information in this story, what do you think causes some pearls to be larger than others? (larger alien object irritates; or alien object in oyster for longer time)

D ___ 8. What holds the oyster to a rock in this story? (its left valve)

I ___ 9. The story says that some pearls are highly valued by people; why do you think that they are valued? (beautiful; not many of them; used in making jewelry)

D ___ 10. Name two results of the oyster's method of protection. (more comfortable life for oyster AND pearls)

COMMENTS:

introduction

Read this story to learn some interesting facts about termites.

WORD RECOGNITION ERRORS
Insertions ______
Mispronunciations ______
Omissions ______
Refusals ______
Repetitions ______
Reversals ______
Substitutions ______
Phrasing ______
Other: ______

WORD REC/CONTEXT ERRORS		
Ind	Inst	Frus
0–7	**8–18**	**19→**

Termites are considered to be destructive insects; their damage to wooden structures has earned them quite a bad reputation. But certain species of termites are helpful to the ecology of the tropics. There, they loosen and enrich the soil, foster plant growth, and recycle wood matter.

Termites of the tropics have quite an ingenious social structure. The huge columns of the insect mounds may tower six feet above the ground and extend twelve feet underground. The nest region is divided into special rooms for the king and queen, nursery, and garden.

Living in the termite colony are the queen, king, workers, and soldiers. The queen is the largest of all termites and dominates the colony, with the king next in size and status. Protecting the colony are the female soldiers who have larger heads and jaws than the smaller male workers. Workers repair the mounds and tend to the nursery and royal couple. They gather food, some of which they cultivate in their garden. The cooperative social structure of these termites has allowed them, like ants and bees, to flourish.

MI ___ 1. Give this story a good title. (How Termites Live; All About Termites)

D ___ 2. According to the story, what has allowed termites to flourish? (their cooperative or ingenious social structure)

WM ___ 3. The story tells that termites have INGENIOUS social structures.

	TOTAL COMPREHENSION				FACTUAL (Even #'s)			INTERPRETIVE (Odd #'s)		
Levels:	Ind	Instructional		Frus	Ind	Inst	Frus	Ind	Inst	Frus
Question Errors	**0–1**	**2–3**	**4**	**5→**	**0**	**1–2**	**3→**	**0**	**1–2**	**3→**
Approx Grade Equiv	Late 8 (8.7–8.9)	Mid 8 (8.4–8.6)	Early 8 (8.1–8.3)	Below 8	Item Analysis: MI__/1; D__/5; I__/2; WM__/2					

What does INGENIOUS mean? (special aptitude, clever)

D ___ 4. How does this story describe the female soldiers? (larger heads and jaws/both)

WM ___ 5. The story describes the columns of the insect mounds. What are COLUMNS? (tall pillars)

D ___ 6. Name two ways in which some species of termites are helpful to the ecology according to the story. (loosen soil; enrich soil; foster plant growth; recycle wood matter)

I ___ 7. How do you think the cooperative social structure has allowed termites to flourish? (they work together; take care of each other; grow own food)

D ___ 8. Name two things the workers do in this story. (repair mounds; tend nursery and royal couple; gather food; cultivate garden/any two)

I ___ 9. Why do you think the heads and jaws of the soldier termites are larger than those of the workers? (they protect the colony)

D ___ 10. What has earned termites their bad reputation according to this story? (their damage to wooden structures)

COMMENTS:

introduction

Read this selection to find out about orangutans and their habits.

WORD RECOGNITION ERRORS
Insertions ______
Mispronunciations ______
Omissions ______
Refusals ______
Repetitions ______
Reversals ______
Substitutions ______
Phrasing ______
Other: ______

WORD REC/CONTEXT ERRORS		
Ind	Inst	Frus
0–8	**9–19**	**20→**

The orangutan is one of the three kinds of great apes, the other two being chimpanzee and gorilla. The word orangutan means "wild man," but this is misleading. For although they look fearsome, orangutans would prefer to avoid a fight if possible. However, if cornered, these apes would fight to survive. The appearance of an orangutan is quite stange. Its arm spread can be as wide as eight feet, while the average height, if its body were straightened out, would be four feet or less. The orangutan's reddish, yellow hair is unevenly distributed, being over twelve inches long on the arms, thighs, and shoulders, but nonexistent on the chest and stomach. It is a powerful animal in arms and jaws, for the orangutan can chew through the hard shell of the durian fruit, while humans require an ax to break the shell.

An interesting habit of the orangutan is to build for sleeping a tree-top nest which is constructed from small, leafy branches. It resembles a round, thick, saucer-like platform. The ape uses this nest until it dries and becomes itchy, and then builds a new nest for the daily naps.

MI ___ 1. Give this story a title. (Wild Man of the Jungle or appropriate title)

D ___ 2. What are the three kinds of great apes? (orangutan; chimpanzee; gorilla)

WM ___ 3. What does ORANGUTAN mean? (wild man)

D ___ 4. According to the story, what *two* parts of orangutans are powerful? (arms AND jaws)

	TOTAL COMPREHENSION				FACTUAL (Even #'s)			INTERPRETIVE (Odd #'s)		
Levels:	Ind	Instructional		Frus	Ind	Inst	Frus	Ind	Inst	Frus
Question Errors	**0–1**	**2–3**	**4**	**5→**	**0**	**1–2**	**3→**	**0**	**1–2**	**3→**
Approx Grade Equiv	Late 9 (9.7–9.9)	Mid 9 (9.4–9.6)	Early 9 (9.1–9.3)	Below 9	Item Analysis: MI__/1; D__/5; I__/2; WM__/2					

WM ___ 5. What is a DURIAN according to the story? (hard shell jungle fruit)

D ___ 6. What gives the orangutan its strange appearance? (short body with very long arms AND uneven hair distribution)

I ___ 7. After reading this story, why do you think that the orangutan is considered a non-violent animal? (prefers to avoid fights)

D ___ 8. How did the story describe the orangutan's hair? (any two: reddish yellow; unevenly distributed; twelve inches long)

I ___ 9. When might an orangutan be dangerous and why? (when cornered AND because it will fight to survive)

D ___ 10. According to the story, what does the orangutan's bed resemble? (round, thick, saucer-like platform)

COMMENTS:

introduction

Read this selection to find out some interesting facts about coyotes

WORD RECOGNITION ERRORS	
Insertions	______
Mispronunciations	______
Omissions	______
Refusals	______
Repetitions	______
Reversals	______
Substitutions	______
Phrasing	______
Other:	______

WORD REC/CONTEXT ERRORS		
Ind	Inst	Frus
0–8	**9–20**	**21→**

The coyote has become a symbol of the American West; its plaintive howl at sunset is a familiar sound for many residents of this area. Hearing the coyote is easier than seeing it, but with binoculars and patience, it is possible. The coyote resembles a small German Shepherd dog with a long, full tail carried low; it wags its tail when it is happy. The coyote's slender legs and easy, flowing movements give an impression of delicacy.

The coyote's delicate appearance is deceiving, because it thrives in great numbers in the West; indeed, the coyote might be called a survivor. When adversity strikes, it modifies its habits to meet the new circumstances. For example, it can adapt to nearly any terrain or climate and exist on almost any type of food, as demonstrated by the successful raising of a coyote family within the limits of one American city. Although preferring to roam day and night, it becomes nocturnal when humans live nearby.

The coyote is, by reputation, a sly and cunning animal that will play tricks to capture prey. In one night, a coyote may raid both a sheep farm and a produce farm, cleverly picking the best of everything for its meal.

	TOTAL COMPREHENSION				FACTUAL (Even #'s)			INTERPRETIVE (Odd #'s)		
Levels:	Ind	Instructional		Frus	Ind	Inst	Frus	Ind	Inst	Frus
Question Errors	**0–1**	**2–3**	**4**	**5→**	**0**	**1–2**	**3→**	**0**	**1–2**	**3→**
Approx Grade Equiv	Late 10 (10.7–.9)	Mid 10 (10.4–10.6)	Early 10 (10.1–10.3)	Below 10	Item Analysis: MI__/1; D__/5; I__/2; WM__/2					

MI ___ 1. Suggest a title for this story. (The Symbol of the American West; The Sly Coyote; or appropriate title)

D ___ 2. How does the story tell that it is possible to see coyotes? (with binoculars AND patience)

WM ___ 3. What does PLAINTIVE mean? (sad; sorrowful)

D ___ 4. What breed of dog does the coyote resemble? (German Shepherd)

WM ___ 5. What does NOCTURNAL mean? (moving at night; active by night)

D ___ 6. Why is the coyote's appearance deceiving? (appears delicate, but survives)

I ___ 7. Why might the coyote be called a "survivor"? (changes to fit the situation, climate, terrain; it is crafty and can outwit others)

D ___ 8. When does the coyote become nocturnal? (when it lives near humans)

I ___ 9. Why do you think the coyote is considered to be a symbol of the American West? (thrives there; lots of them there; its howl is so common and familiar there)

D ___ 10. What does the story say gives the coyote its delicate appearance? (slender legs and easy flowing movements)

COMMENTS:

introduction

This story about special games happened long ago. *Let's pretend that we were there.*

WORD RECOGNITION ERRORS
Insertions ______
Mispronunciations ______
Omissions ______
Refusals ______
Repetitions ______
Reversals ______
Substitutions ______
Phrasing ______
Other: ______

WORD REC/CONTEXT ERRORS		
Ind	Inst	Frus
0–3	4–8	9→

Boys like to play the games.

People like to see the games.

They want to see who plays best.

The boys work and work.

Then they are strong.

Some run fast.

Some want to jump.

Some like to throw.

Soon boys will play more games.

But girls will play the games.

They will run, jump, and throw.

They will swim fast.

People will have fun at the games.

MI ___ 1. Give this story a good name. (Special Games: Girls and Boys Play; The Olympic Games; Games People Like; any appropriate title)

D ___ 2. Name two games that the boys played. (running; jumping; throwing)

WM ___ 3. The story tells that the boys work and work to be strong; what does WORK AND WORK mean? (tried very hard; practiced; trained; worked-out)

D ___ 4. Why did the story say that the boys played the games? (because boys like to play the games; people liked to see the games)

WM ___ 5. The story says that people will HAVE FUN; what does it mean to HAVE FUN? (be happy; to enjoy; have a good time)

	TOTAL COMPREHENSION			FACTUAL (Even #'s)			INTERPRETIVE (Odd #'s)		
Levels:	Ind	Instructional	Frus	Ind	Inst	Frus	Ind	Inst	Frus
Question Errors	0–1	2–3	4→	0	1	2→	0	1	2→
Approx Grade Equiv	Early 1st Grade (1.1–1.3)		Below Primer	Item Analysis: MI__/1; D__/4; I__/1; WM__/2					

D ___ 6. In the story, why did the people like to see the games? (they wanted to see who played best)

I ___ 7. The story tells about games that will soon be played; why do you think these games may be more fun to watch than the first ones in the story? (boys AND girls will play; more games)

D ___ 8. In the games soon to be played, who will play? (boys AND girls)

COMMENTS:

introduction

Read this story to find out about an exciting discovery.

WORD RECOGNITION ERRORS
Insertions ______
Mispronunciations ______
Omissions ______
Refusals ______
Repetitions ______
Reversals ______
Substitutions ______
Phrasing ______
Other: ______

A man was working on his land.

He found some parts of an old house.

Some men helped him dig more.

They found a very old city.

There was a wall around the city.

The wall had eight gates.

The streets were made of rocks.

There were many stores and shops.

People were surprised to find swimming pools.

Some houses were big and fine.

Today people go to see the old city.

They like to see how people lived long ago.

WORD REC/CONTEXT ERRORS		
Ind	Inst	Frus
0–3	**4–8**	**9→**

MI ___ 1. What is a good name for this story? (Lost City; Old Town; How People Lived Long Ago)

D ___ 2. How many gates were mentioned in the story? (eight)

WM ___ 3. There were MANY stores and shops in the story; what does MANY mean? (several; a lot; lots; more than one)

D ___ 4. What were the people in the story surprised to find in the old city? (swimming pools)

WM ___ 5. What is another name for PEOPLE? (humans; boys and girls; men and women)

D ___ 6. Why do people go to see the old city? (like to see how people lived long ago)

I ___ 7. Why do you think that there was a wall around the city? (for safety; for protection; to stay safe)

D ___ 8. What were the streets made of in the old city? (rocks)

	TOTAL COMPREHENSION			FACTUAL (Even #'s)			INTERPRETIVE (Odd #'s)		
Levels:	Ind	Instructional	Frus	Ind	Inst	Frus	Ind	Inst	Frus
Question Errors	**0–1**	**2–3**	**4→**	**0**	**1**	**2→**	**0**	**1**	**2→**
Approx Grade Equiv	Late 1 (1.7–1.9)	Mid 1 (1.4–1.6)	Below 1	Item Analysis: MI__/1; D__/4; I__/1; WM__/2					

introduction

Read this story to find out about early mail service.

WORD RECOGNITION ERRORS
Insertions ______
Mispronunciations ______
Omissions ______
Refusals ______
Repetitions ______
Reversals ______
Substitutions ______
Phrasing ______
Other: ______

WORD REC/CONTEXT ERRORS		
Ind	Inst	Frus
0–4	**5–10**	**11→**

Long ago the mail was carried by men upon quick ponies.

The ponies were changed each ten miles.

Each rider rode almost one hundred miles.

Then he stopped to rest.

Then the next man would leave with thc mail.

Riders were changed each hundred miles.

Sometimes mail traveled across the country.

Twenty riders would be used to make this trip.

They would use as many as two hundred ponies.

They went as fast as they could.

It still took ten days to finish the trip.

To mail one small letter cost five dollars.

Most people did not write many letters then.

MI ___ 1. What is a good title for this story? (The Mail Run; Pony Express; or any appropriate title)

D ___ 2. How many riders were needed to carry the mail across the country? (twenty)

WM ___ 3. What does FINISH mean in "to FINISH the trip"? (complete; get through; be done)

D ___ 4. How often were the riders changed? (every one hundred miles)

WM ___ 5. The story tells that the mail was CARRIED by men; what does CARRIED mean? (taken; transported; driven; conveyed; delivered)

D ___ 6. How long did it take to deliver a letter across the country? (ten days)

	TOTAL COMPREHENSION				FACTUAL (Even #'s)			INTERPRETIVE (Odd #'s)		
Levels:	Ind	Instructional		Frus	Ind	Inst	Frus	Ind	Inst	Frus
Question Errors	0–1	2	3	4→	0	1	2→	0	1	2→
Approx Grade Equiv	Late 2 (2.7–2.9)	Mid 2 (2.4–2.6)	Early 2 (2.1–2.3)	Below 2	Item Analysis: MI__/1; D__/4; I__/1; WM__/2					

I ___ 7. Based on this story give two reasons why you think that only a few people wrote letters long ago? (any two: cost too much; delivery too slow; many people didn't know how to write letters)

D ___ 8. How much did it cost to mail a small letter then? ($5.00)

COMMENTS:

introduction

Read this story to find out about people of ancient times and their use of salt.

WORD RECOGNITION ERRORS
Insertions ______
Mispronunciations ______
Omissions ______
Refusals ______
Repetitions ______
Reversals ______
Substitutions ______
Phrasing ______
Other: ______

WORD REC/CONTEXT ERRORS		
Ind	Inst	Frus
0–5	**6–12**	**13→**

People today use salt to stay healthy. Salt makes their food taste better. Even in the very old days people wanted salt. They knew they needed it to stay alive. Some people followed cattle to salt rocks. Then they carried the rocks to their caves.

Later, some people decided to build their homes on special land. This land was once covered by the sea. The salt water of the sea had slowly disappeared. The salt was left behind. Many early cities were built to be near this salt.

Those who had plenty of salt traded it for other goods. The salt trade became an important business for some people. Some men were even paid with salt for their work.

MI ___ 1. Give this story a good title. (The Story of Salt; Salt and Ancient People; or an appropriate title)

D ___ 2. What *two* reasons for people using salt are given in the story? (to make food taste better AND to stay healthy)

WM ___ 3. The story tells about "homes built on SPECIAL land." What does SPECIAL mean? (unusual; exceptional; different)

D ___ 4. Why did people follow cattle in ancient times? (to find salt)

WM ___ 5. What does it mean when something is BUILT? (constructed; put together; made)

D ___ 6. The men who worked in the salt business were probably paid with money; what else was used as payment for their work? (salt)

I ___ 7. Why do you think the cattle wanted salt? (they needed it to stay alive)

D ___ 8. How did the people in the story use salt to get other goods? (trade)

	TOTAL COMPREHENSION				FACTUAL (Even #'s)			INTERPRETIVE (Odd #'s)		
Levels:	Ind	Instructional		Frus	Ind	Inst	Frus	Ind	Inst	Frus
Question Errors	**0–1**	**2–3**	**4**	**5→**	**0**	**1–2**	**3→**	**0**	**1–2**	**3→**
Approx Grade Equiv	Late 3 (3.7–3.9)	Mid 3 (3.4–3.6)	Early 3 (3.1–3.3)	Below 3	Item Analysis: MI__/1; D__/5; I__/2; WM__/2					

I ___ 9. Name two jobs that might have been performed by people in the salt business. (mining of salt; loading; hauling; delivery; selling; trading)

D ___ 10. According to this story, what caused salt to be on the special land? (sea covered the land, and left behind its salt)

COMMENTS:

introduction

Read this story and find out more about bikes.

WORD RECOGNITION ERRORS
Insertions ____
Mispronunciations ____
Omissions ____
Refusals ____
Repetitions ____
Reversals ____
Substitutions ____
Phrasing ____
Other: ____

WORD REC/CONTEXT ERRORS		
Ind	Inst	Frus
0–5	**6–14**	**15→**

In the early 1800s, a vehicle almost like the modern bike was designed. The original bike had two wheels, but no pedals. The wheels were joined by a wooden seat. To move forward, riders pushed their feet against the ground.

During the next eighty years, more bike designs were developed. New models had pedals and wheels of different sizes. Inventions like brakes, new tires, and speed gears improved the bike. By 1900 all major bike changes were complete. People liked bikes so much that they wanted more than were made. Bike clubs were formed to tour and race. One American club had over one hundred thousand members.

The invention of cars decreased the need for bikes. Some people still preferred bikes. The cost to own and operate cars has increased today. Bikes are once more recognized as a cheap means of travel.

MI ___ 1. Give this story a good title. (How Bikes Began; More About Bikes; or appropriate title)

D ___ 2. Name two inventions that the story told about which helped to improve bikes. (brakes, new tires, and speed gears/two of three)

WM ___ 3. What is another word for PREFERRED? (liked; picked)

D ___ 4. How did the rider move forward on the original bike? (pushed with feet)

WM ___ 5. The story tells about the ORIGINAL bike; what does ORIGINAL mean? (first; beginning)

D ___ 6. What invention decreased the need for bikes? (car)

	TOTAL COMPREHENSION				FACTUAL (Even #'s)			INTERPRETIVE (Odd #'s)		
Levels:	Ind	Instructional		Frus	Ind	Inst	Frus	Ind	Inst	Frus
Question Errors	**0–1**	**2–3**	**4**	**5→**	**0**	**1–2**	**3→**	**0**	**1–2**	**3→**
Approx Grade Equiv	Late 4 (4.7–4.9)	Mid 4 (4.4–4.6)	Early 4 (4.1–4.3)	Below 4	Item Analysis: MI__/1; D__/5; I__/2; WM__/2					

I ___ 7. Give at least two reasons why the early bikes were harder to ride than bikes of today. (had to push with feet; wooden instead of soft seat; no brakes; no gears)

D ___ 8. Around what year were most major changes in bike design completed? (1900)

I ___ 9. After the invention of cars, some people still preferred bikes; give two reasons why you think this was so. (cheaper; no parking problems; more versatile; can ride many different places; too young for car/any two)

D ___ 10. Name one activity of the bike clubs. (touring, racing)

COMMENTS:

introduction

A smith is someone who works with metals.
Read this story to find out about silversmiths.

WORD RECOGNITION ERRORS
Insertions ____
Mispronunciations ____
Omissions ____
Refusals ____
Repetitions ____
Reversals ____
Substitutions ____
Phrasing ____
Other: ____

WORD REC/CONTEXT ERRORS		
Ind	Inst	Frus
0–6	**7–15**	**16→**

Silversmiths were an important part of Colonial America. To become a silversmith, young boys became apprentices. They trained with a skilled silversmith for four or more years of intense study and work. At age twenty-one, they could open their own silver shop. There, they shaped the soft metal into bright silver cups, dishes, and jewelry. Coins or other objects were often melted to get the metal with which to work. Most silversmiths took pride in their work. They stamped their names on each piece of value. One of the most famous works made at this time was a large bowl.

Some silver work of our Colonial ancestors is found in museums today. Silver is still used to make jewelry, dishes, and coins. But most modern silver objects are made by machines. Silver is also used to make medicines, mirrors, and photographs.

MI ___ 1. What would be a good title for this story? (The Work of Silversmiths; Uses of Silver; or appropriate title)

D ___ 2. Name two silver products the silversmiths in the story made. (jewelry; cups; dishes/any two)

WM ___ 3. What is meant by INTENSE study? (concentrated; hard work; serious)

D ___ 4. How old did a person have to be before opening a silver shop in this story? (twenty-one)

WM ___ 5. The story told about our Colonial ANCESTORS. What are ANCESTORS? (people who lived before us and were related to us)

	TOTAL COMPREHENSION				FACTUAL (Even #'s)			INTERPRETIVE (Odd #'s)		
Levels:	Ind	Instructional		Frus	Ind	Inst	Frus	Ind	Inst	Frus
Question Errors	**0–1**	**2–3**	**4**	**5→**	**0**	**1–2**	**3→**	**0**	**1–2**	**3→**
Approx Grade Equiv	Late 5 (5.7–5.9)	Mid 5 (5.4–5.6)	Early 5 (5.1–5.3)	Below 5	Item Analysis: MI__/1; D__/5; I__/2; WM__/2					

D ___ 6. What were the people called while they were training to become silversmiths? (apprentices)

I ___ 7. Why do you think silversmiths stamped their name on their works? (they were proud of them)

D ___ 8. Silver is used in making other kinds of products today; name *two* mentioned in the story. (medicine, mirrors, and photographs)

I ___ 9. Why do you think modern silver objects are not usually made by hand today? (machines can do it faster and cheaper)

D ___ 10. Where can we find some of the early silver work that was made in Colonial times? (museums)

COMMENTS:

introduction

Read this story to learn about quilts.

WORD RECOGNITION ERRORS
Insertions ______
Mispronunciations ______
Omissions ______
Refusals ______
Repetitions ______
Reversals ______
Substitutions ______
Phrasing ______
Other: ______

WORD REC/CONTEXT ERRORS		
Ind	Inst	Frus
0–6	**7–16**	**17→**

Quilts are often associated with a bed cover made by stitching soft stuffing between two pieces of cloth. Today some people use quilts made by precision machines.

The making of quilts began in ancient China and Egypt thousands of years ago. This practical art was passed through families and spread throughout the world. For early American settlers quilts met several needs. On cold winter nights, warm covers were needed. The few covers which could be bought were expensive. The women saved scraps of cloth from old clothes, stitching the scraps together by hand to make warm quilts. Designing new quilt patterns helped the women to feel creative. Most of the designs were quite bright and elegant. These added color and decorative charm to the plain homes. Some women met in small groups to make their quilts. These first quilting parties served as a form of entertainment. As friends worked together, the art of quilting flourished.

MI ___ 1. Give this story a good title. (Quilting; Quilt Making; Early Quilting; or any appropriate title)

D ___ 2. Name one country where quilt making began thousands of years ago. (China or Egypt)

WM ___ 3. What is another word for ELEGANT? (fine; refined; beautiful)

D ___ 4. How did the story say that the early American settlers made their quilts? (stitching scraps together by hand)

WM ___ 5. The story tells about PRECISION machines. What is meant by PRECISION? (exacting; careful; very accurate)

	TOTAL COMPREHENSION				FACTUAL (Even #'s)			INTERPRETIVE (Odd #'s)		
Levels:	Ind	Instructional		Frus	Ind	Inst	Frus	Ind	Inst	Frus
Question Errors	**0–1**	**2–3**	**4**	**5→**	**0**	**1–2**	**3→**	**0**	**1–2**	**3→**
Approx Grade Equiv	Late 6 (6.7–6.9)	Mid 6 (6.4–6.6)	Early 6 (6.1–6.3)	Below 6	Item Analysis: MI__/1; D__/5; I__/2; WM__/2					

D ___ 6. Give two reasons early American settlers needed quilts. (to keep warm; for decoration)

I ___ 7. How did quilting provide entertainment for early American settlers? (gave them a reason for having a party, for meeting with friends; it was a fun time with friends)

D ___ 8. Where did early settlers get the material for quilts? (clothing scraps)

I ___ 9. Why do you think more quilts are made today by machine than are made by hand? (machines are faster and cheaper; people don't know how to make by hand; don't have time to make by hand)

D ___ 10. Why did the settlers have to use scraps to make quilts? (cloth was expensive and scarce)

COMMENTS:

introduction

Read this story to find out about a special kind of building.

WORD RECOGNITION ERRORS
Insertions ______
Mispronunciations ______
Omissions ______
Refusals ______
Repetitions ______
Reversals ______
Substitutions ______
Phrasing ______
Other: ______

WORD REC/CONTEXT ERRORS		
Ind	Inst	Frus
0–7	**8–17**	**18→**

In the late 1800s rapid growth of American cities generated new problems for builders. This growth of city populations created demand for more businesses. More land was needed on which to build new one-story office buildings. As demand for land increased, so did the prices. The scarcity and high cost of land helped create a new concept in building design. This was the origin of the distinctive American design for tall buildings known as "skyscrapers."

Prior to this time, the design of the elevator had been improved. It was safe to use in buildings of many floors. Some builders tried different ways to build ground floors of buildings strong enough to support upper floors. When, in 1882, a man conceived the idea of using iron rods to support the floors and walls, building skyscrapers became possible. The completion of the first true skyscraper in the 1890s heralded the dawn of a new era in building. Many skyscrapers have been built since 1900, including one of the tallest American buildings with one hundred ten floors.

MI ___ 1. Give this story a title. (Tall Buildings; How Skyscrapers Began; or any appropriate title)

D ___ 2. The use of what metal made building skyscrapers possible? (iron)

	TOTAL COMPREHENSION				FACTUAL (Even #'s)			INTERPRETIVE (Odd #'s)		
Levels:	Ind	Instructional		Frus	Ind	Inst	Frus	Ind	Inst	Frus
Question Errors	**0–1**	**2–3**	**4**	**5→**	**0**	**1–2**	**3→**	**0**	**1–2**	**3→**
Approx Grade Equiv	Late 7 (7.7–7.9)	Mid 7 (7.4–7.6)	Early 7 (7.1–7.3)	Below 7	Item Analysis: MI__/1; D__/5; I__/2; WM__/2					

WM ___ 3. What does the word GENERATED mean in the phrase, "the growth of cities GENERATED new problems"? (created; made)

D ___ 4. Why did people see a need for skyscrapers? (land was expensive; allowed for better use of land)

WM ___ 5. What does the word DISTINCTIVE mean in the phrase "the DISTINCTIVE American design"? (unusual; different; unique)

D ___ 6. The story tells of one of the tallest buildings; how many floors does the building have? (one hundred ten)

I ___ 7. How did the development of safe elevators help to make the building of skyscrapers possible? (people could get up and down the many stories safely and easily)

D ___ 8. In what country was the first skyscraper built? (America)

I ___ 9. Why do you think skyscrapers were not built until the late 1890s? (little need; not as many people; more land; people didn't know how to build them/at least two)

D ___ 10. In what type of places were skyscrapers built? (cities; crowded)

COMMENTS:

introduction

Read this story to find out where coffee originated and how it became popular.

WORD RECOGNITION ERRORS
Insertions ______
Mispronunciations ______
Omissions ______
Refusals ______
Repetitions ______
Reversals ______
Substitutions ______
Phrasing ______
Other: ______

History first records coffee trees growing wild in remote regions of Africa. According to legend, it was noticed that the goats didn't sleep after they ate from coffee trees. People were intrigued with the stimulating effects of coffee fruit.

No one seems certain when people first drank coffee. Arabs heated coffee beans with water, making the drink at least seven hundred years ago. After cultivation of coffee trees was begun in Arabia, religious leaders and doctors used coffee. Doctors viewed coffee as important medicine, while religious leaders saw the drink as a special part of religious ceremonies. Once travelers tasted the drink, the Arabs were besieged with requests for coffee plants and beans. As the trees were grown in other countries, much of the civilized world acquired a taste for coffee. Turkish law even permitted wives to divorce husbands who failed to provide coffee.

Today South and Central America produce the most coffee grown for the international industry worth billions of dollars. The U.S. buys more coffee per year than other nations, but Finland's people consume the most coffee per person.

WORD REC/CONTEXT ERRORS		
Ind	Inst	Frus
0–7	**8–18**	**19→**

	TOTAL COMPREHENSION				FACTUAL (Even #'s)			INTERPRETIVE (Odd #'s)		
Levels:	Ind	Instructional		Frus	Ind	Inst	Frus	Ind	Inst	Frus
Question Errors	**0–1**	**2–3**	**4**	**5→**	**0**	**1–2**	**3→**	**0**	**1–2**	**3→**
Approx Grade Equiv	Late 8 (8.7–8.9)	Mid 8 (8.4–8.6)	Early 8 (8.1–8.3)	Below 8	Item Analysis: MI__/1; D__/5; I__/2; WM__/2					

MI ____ 1. Give the story a title. (Growing Coffee; The History of Coffee; How Coffee Became Popular; or appropriate title)

D ____ 2. In what country do people drink the most coffee per person? (Finland)

WM ____ 3. The story tells of people being INTRIGUED with the effects of coffee; what is another word for INTRIGUED? (fascinated; interested; puzzled)

D ____ 4. What effect did coffee have on animals in the story? (kept them from sleeping; after they ate it, they didn't sleep)

WM ____ 5. What does it mean "to be BESIEGED with requests"? (flooded; inundated; overwhelmed; harassed by requests)

D ____ 6. In what part of the world is most of the coffee grown? (South and Central America)

I ____ 7. Based on this story, how do we know the Turkish people thought that coffee was very important? (husbands could even be divorced for not providing coffee to their wives)

D ____ 8. For what purposes did doctors and religious leaders use coffee? (doctors for medicine, religious leaders as part of ceremonies/both)

I ____ 9. Based on this story, how do we know people in the U.S. like coffee? (so much sold in U.S.; U.S. buys more coffee than other nations)

D ____ 10. Where does history first record coffee trees being grown? (Africa)

COMMENTS:

introduction

Read this selection to find out about the history of printing.

WORD RECOGNITION ERRORS	
Insertions	
Mispronunciations	
Omissions	
Refusals	
Repetitions	
Reversals	
Substitutions	
Phrasing	
Other:	

WORD REC/CONTEXT ERRORS		
Ind	Inst	Frus
0–8	**9–19**	**20→**

Almost two thousand years ago the Chinese printed designs and pictures on cloth. Nearly one hundred years later, the art of printing words was developed by the Chinese. They carved pictures on wood blocks and then pressed the inked blocks onto paper. Both the invention of paper by the Chinese and the need to make copies of their religious texts helped to foster the growth of printing. Other countries adopted this method to print pictures for books, but all the writing was done by hand. This process seriously limited the number of books that could be produced. The sudden awakening of Europe's appreciation for art and literature broadened interest in acquiring books, and greatly increased the demand for printed texts. Then, in 1456, Johann Gutenberg invented the first printing press with movable type fashioned from metal. After this invention, the printing of books was a much faster and less costly process, with positive effects on education.

Over the next five hundred years, as the demand for texts continued to grow, the printing process was greatly improved. Today, most of our magazines, newspapers, and books are printed by using the relief, offset, or engraving process.

	TOTAL COMPREHENSION				FACTUAL (Even #'s)			INTERPRETIVE (Odd #'s)		
Levels:	Ind	Instructional		Frus	Ind	Inst	Frus	Ind	Inst	Frus
Question Errors	**0–1**	**2–3**	**4**	**5→**	**0**	**1–2**	**3→**	**0**	**1–2**	**3→**
Approx Grade Equiv	Late 9 (9.7–9.9)	Mid 9 (9.4–9.6)	Early 9 (9.1–9.3)	Below 9	Item Analysis: MI__/1; D__/5; I__/2; WM__/2					

MI ___ 1. Suggest a title for this story. (Printing Past and Present; or appropriate title)

D ___ 2. What people did the first printing? (Chinese)

WM ___ 3. What does POSITIVE EFFECTS mean? (good results; helpful results)

D ___ 4. How did the story describe the printing press invented by Johann Gutenberg? (with movable type fashioned from metal)

WM ___ 5. What does FASHIONED from metal mean? (made; created)

D ___ 6. What *two* things helped the growth of the printing process in China? (their invention of paper AND the need to make copies of religious texts)

I ___ 7. Why was the printing of books severely limited before the 15th century? (all books had to be hand copied, a very slow process)

D ___ 8. Name *two* printing processes used to print most of our magazines, books, and newspapers today. (any two: relief; offset; or engraving process)

I ___ 9. What do you think were the positive effects on education due to the printing of books? (more books sooner; greater access and spread of knowledge)

D ___ 10. What event in Europe greatly increased the demand for printed texts? (Europe's sudden interest in art and literature)

COMMENTS:

introduction

This story is about the Taj Mahal (tahj-muh-hahl); read to learn about this famous building.

The Taj Mahal is one of the most expensive and beautiful buildings to ever be built. The Emperor had it built between 1632 and 1653 by approximately twenty thousand laborers, and specifically named it in memory of his wife. This unique structure stands in northern India neighboring the city of Agra.

The Taj Mahal is an unusual octagonal shaped building, built of white marble which towers one hundred twenty feet above the ground with sides of one hundred thirty feet. At each corner stands a narrow prayer tower, called a minaret, which rises about one hundred thirty-three feet in height.

The main portion of the Taj Mahal, covered by a seventy-foot dome protecting two magnificent monuments, is an area often considered by visitors to be a highlight of the ancient structure. It features rare gems, elaborate mosaic, and inlaid tiles that are considered to be of unequaled beauty. The inside is lit by the daylight which filters through the stone of the dome and the windows.

The building is found in a beautifully landscaped garden region with large pools; it is breathtaking to see the structure reflected in the surrounding pools. The Taj Mahal is considered by some to be one of the world's architectural treasures.

WORD RECOGNITION ERRORS
Insertions ______
Mispronunciations ______
Omissions ______
Refusals ______
Repetitions ______
Reversals ______
Substitutions ______
Phrasing ______
Other: ______

WORD REC/CONTEXT ERRORS		
Ind	Inst	Frus
0–8	**9–20**	**21→**

	TOTAL COMPREHENSION				FACTUAL (Even #'s)			INTERPRETIVE (Odd #'s)		
Levels:	Ind	Instructional		Frus	Ind	Inst	Frus	Ind	Inst	Frus
Question Errors	**0–1**	**2–3**	**4**	**5→**	**0**	**1–2**	**3→**	**0**	**1–2**	**3→**
Approx Grade Equiv	Late 10 (10.7–.9)	Mid 10 (10.4–10.6)	Early 10 (10.1–10.3)	Below 10	Item Analysis: MI__/1; D__/5; I__/2; WM__/2					

MI ___ 1. Give this story a good title. (A Famous Building; or appropriate title)

D ___ 2. Describe what the Taj Mahal looks like. (any two: octagonal; long sides; towers; surrounded by gardens and pools; beautiful tiles and mosaics)

WM ___ 3. The story tells of an OCTAGONAL building; what does OCTAGONAL mean? (eight sides)

D ___ 4. For whom was the Taj Mahal named? (Emperor's wife)

WM ___ 5. What is a MINARET? (narrow prayer tower)

D ___ 6. About how many people did it take to build the Taj Mahal? (about twenty thousand)

I ___ 7. Why do you think it took so long to build this building? (building was big; made of marble; no modern tools were used)

D ___ 8. Where is the Taj Mahal located? (India; near Agra)

I ___ 9. The story tells that the dome area is lit by daylight; why do you think the Emperor chose this means of lighting? (no electricity; unusual; prettier)

D ___ 10. How tall is the Taj Mahal? (one hundred twenty feet)

COMMENTS:

IEP/r
GRADED PASSAGE RECORD FORM

Student Name	Age	Grade	Number Yrs/School	Date	Diagnostician
______	___	___	______	___	______

DIRECTIONS: Enter Form and Level of each passage and circle how each story is read (O = Orally; S = Silently; L = Listening). For each passage on which student is tested, indicate correct responses by placing a check (✓) beside appropriate question numbers and write incorrect responses. The number of oral word recognition errors should be noted with appropriate comments offered. As each set of story questions is answered, indicate which comprehension level and word recognition in context level that story represents for that student according to scoring criteria on Teacher's copy by circling Independent, Instructional, or Frustration.

STORY						
LEVEL:	______	______	______	______	______	
FORM:	___	___	___	___	___	
	Read: O S L	Read: O S L	Read: O S L	Read: O S L	Read: O S L	
MI	1. ______	1. ______	1. ______	1. ______	1. ______	MI
D	2. ______	2. ______	2. ______	2. ______	2. ______	D
WM	3. ______	3. ______	3. ______	3. ______	3. ______	WM
D	4. ______	4. ______	4. ______	4. ______	4. ______	D
WM	5. ______	5. ______	5. ______	5. ______	5. ______	WM
D	6. ______	6. ______	6. ______	6. ______	6. ______	D
I	7. ______	7. ______	7. ______	7. ______	7. ______	I
D	8. ______	8. ______	8. ______	8. ______	8. ______	D
I	9. ______	9. ______	9. ______	9. ______	9. ______	I
D	10. ______	10. ______	10. ______	10. ______	10. ______	D
COMP LEVEL:	Ind Ins Frs	Ind Ins Frs	Ind Ins Frs	Ind Ins Frs	Ind Ins Frs	
WR/CON:	# of errors___	# of errors___	# of errors___	# of errors___	# of errors___	
LEVEL:	Ind Ins Frs	Ind Ins Frs	Ind Ins Frs	Ind Ins Frs	Ind Ins Frs	

STORY						
LEVEL:	______	______	______	______	______	
FORM:	___	___	___	___	___	
	Read: O S L	Read: O S L	Read: O S L	Read: O S L	Read: O S L	
MI	1. ______	1. ______	1. ______	1. ______	1. ______	MI
D	2. ______	2. ______	2. ______	2. ______	2. ______	D
WM	3. ______	3. ______	3. ______	3. ______	3. ______	WM
D	4. ______	4. ______	4. ______	4. ______	4. ______	D
WM	5. ______	5. ______	5. ______	5. ______	5. ______	WM
D	6. ______	6. ______	6. ______	6. ______	6. ______	D
I	7. ______	7. ______	7. ______	7. ______	7. ______	I
D	8. ______	8. ______	8. ______	8. ______	8. ______	D
I	9. ______	9. ______	9. ______	9. ______	9. ______	I
D	10. ______	10. ______	10. ______	10. ______	10. ______	D
COMP LEVEL:	Ind Ins Frs	Ind Ins Frs	Ind Ins Frs	Ind Ins Frs	Ind Ins Frs	
WR/CON:	# of errors___	# of errors___	# of errors___	# of errors___	# of errors___	
LEVEL:	Ind Ins Frs	Ind Ins Frs	Ind Ins Frs	Ind Ins Frs	Ind Ins Frs	

COMMENTS: ______________________________

IEP/r
STUDENT SUMMARY SHEET

NAME:______________ DATE:_____ TEACHER:______________________ GRADE:____
AGE:____ # YRS IN SCHOOL____ CLASSIFICATION:____ DIAGNOSTICIAN:__________

SKILL AREA

1. Visual Skills
A. Visual Discrimination__________
B. Visual Memory__________
C. Sound Visualization__________

2. Auditory Skills
A. Auditory Discrimination__________
B. Auditory Memory__________

3. WORD RECOGNITION PATTERNS
(Isolation & Context)

A. Sight Vocabulary __________

C. Word Recognition in Context____
____

D. Specialized Vocabulary__________
____

B. Word Analysis:__________
1. Beginning Consonants______
2. Ending Consonants______
3. Short Vowels __________
4. Long Vowels __________
5. Silent e__________
6. Blends __________
7. Digraphs __________
8. Special Vowels______
9. Prefixes __________
10. Suffixes __________
11. Compounds________
12. Contractions________
13. Other:__________

4. ORAL READING

A. Insertions __________
B. Mispronunciations ________
C. Omissions __________
D. Refusals__________
E. Repetitions__________
F. Reversals __________
G. Substitutions__________
H. Phrasing__________
I. Other:__________

5. COMPREHENSION PATTERNS

Total Comprehension Analysis

Questions Correct 3 Instructional Levels				Question Type	Questions Attempted 3 Instructional Levels				Total %
Oral	Silent	Lstng	Total		Oral	Silent	Lstng	Total	Correct
				Main Idea (#1)					% *
				Detail (#2, 4, 6, 8, 10)					% *
				Word Meaning (#3, 5)					% *
				Inference (#7, 9)					% *

Percentages under 70% indicate areas of instructional need

FACTUAL COMPREHENSION (Even # Questions)			INTERPRETIVE COMPREHENSION (Odd # Questions)		
Ques Correct	Ques Attempted	% Correct	Ques Correct	Ques Attempted	% Correct
		% *			% *

COMPREHENSION STYLE:	LEVEL:

IEP/r
STUDENT PLANNING SHEET FOR READING PRESCRIPTION

Name: ____________
Grade: ______ Age: ______
Years in School ______
Examiner: ____________
Date: ____________

READING LEVELS:	Comprehension			Word Recognition	
	ORAL	SILENT	LSTNG	SIGHT	CONTEXT
INSTRUCTIONAL					
INDEPENDENT					
***COMPREHENSION STYLE (circle) ORAL SILENT**					

Stories Administered (Circle)
Oral—L/A, S/A, H/A Silent—L/B, S/B, H/B Listening—L/B, S/B, H/B

Analysis of Reading Skills			
Acquired Skills	IEP # Skill Area	Prioritized Needs	Comments
	1. VISUAL SKILLS A. Visual Discrimination . . . . B. Visual Memory . . . . C. Visualization of Sounds . . . . 2. AUDITORY SKILLS A. Auditory Discrimination . . . . B. Auditory Memory . . . . 3. WORD RECOGNITION PATTERNS A. Sight Vocabulary . . . . B. Word Analysis . . . . 1. Beginning Consonants . . . . 2. Ending Consonants . . . . 3. Short Vowels . . . . 4. Long Vowels . . . . 5. Silent e . . . . 6. Blends . . . . 7. Digraphs . . . . 8. Special Vowel Sounds . . . . 9. Prefixes . . . . 10. Suffixes . . . . 11. Compound Words . . . . 12. Contractions . . . . 13. Other: ____________ C. Word Recognition in Context . . . . . . D. Specialized Vocabulary . . . . 4. ORAL READING A. Insertions . . . . B. Mispronunciations . . . . C. Omissions . . . . D. Refusals . . . . E. Repetitions . . . . F. Reversals . . . . G. Substitutions . . . . H. Phrasing . . . . I. Other: ____________ 5. COMPREHENSION PATTERNS A. Main Idea . . . . B. Detail . . . . C. Word Meaning . . . . D. Inference . . . . E. Other: ____________		

INDIVIDUAL EVALUATION PROCEDURES FOR READING

Summary of Reading Diagnosis

NAME ______________________ BIRTH DATE ______________________
SCHOOL __________ GRADE __________ # YEARS IN SCHOOL __________
HOMEROOM TEACHER __________ CLASSIFICATION __________
EXAMINER ______________________ DATE ______________________

INTEREST INVENTORY

High Interest Strand: ______________________
Neutral Interest Strand: ______________________

WORD RECOGNITION LISTS

Instructional Level: ______________________
Independent Level: ______________________

GRADED PASSAGES

READING LEVELS:	COMPREHENSION			WORD REC
	Oral	Silent	Listening	Context
Instructional—				
Independent—				
	*COMPREHENSION STYLE: Oral Silent			

VISUAL TESTS

☐ Vis (1) Dis Shapes
Results: __________

☐ Vis (2) Dis L Shapes
Results: __________

☐ Vis (3) Dis Letters I
Results: __________

☐ Vis (4) Dis Letters II
Results: __________

☐ Vis (5) Dis Words
Results: __________

☐ Vis (6) Dis Words II
Results: __________

☐ Vis (7) Mem Symbols
Results: __________

☐ Vis (8) Mem Letters I
Results: __________

☐ Vis (9) Mem Letters II
Results: __________

☐ Vis (10) Sounds/Words
Results: __________

AUDITORY TESTS

☐ Aud (1) Discrim
Results: ______

☐ Aud (2) Mem Words
Results: __________

☐ Aud (3) Mem Letters II
Results: __________

WORD ANALYSIS SURVEY

☐ Phonic Analysis Survey
Results: __________

☐ Structural Analysis Survey
Results: __________

SPECIALIZED VOCABULARY

☐ Survival Voc I
Results: ________

☐ Survival Voc II
Results: ______

☐ 16 Essential Sight Wds
Results: __________

☐ ECOLOGICAL SURVEY

Results: ____

IEP/r Supplementary Evaluation Procedures

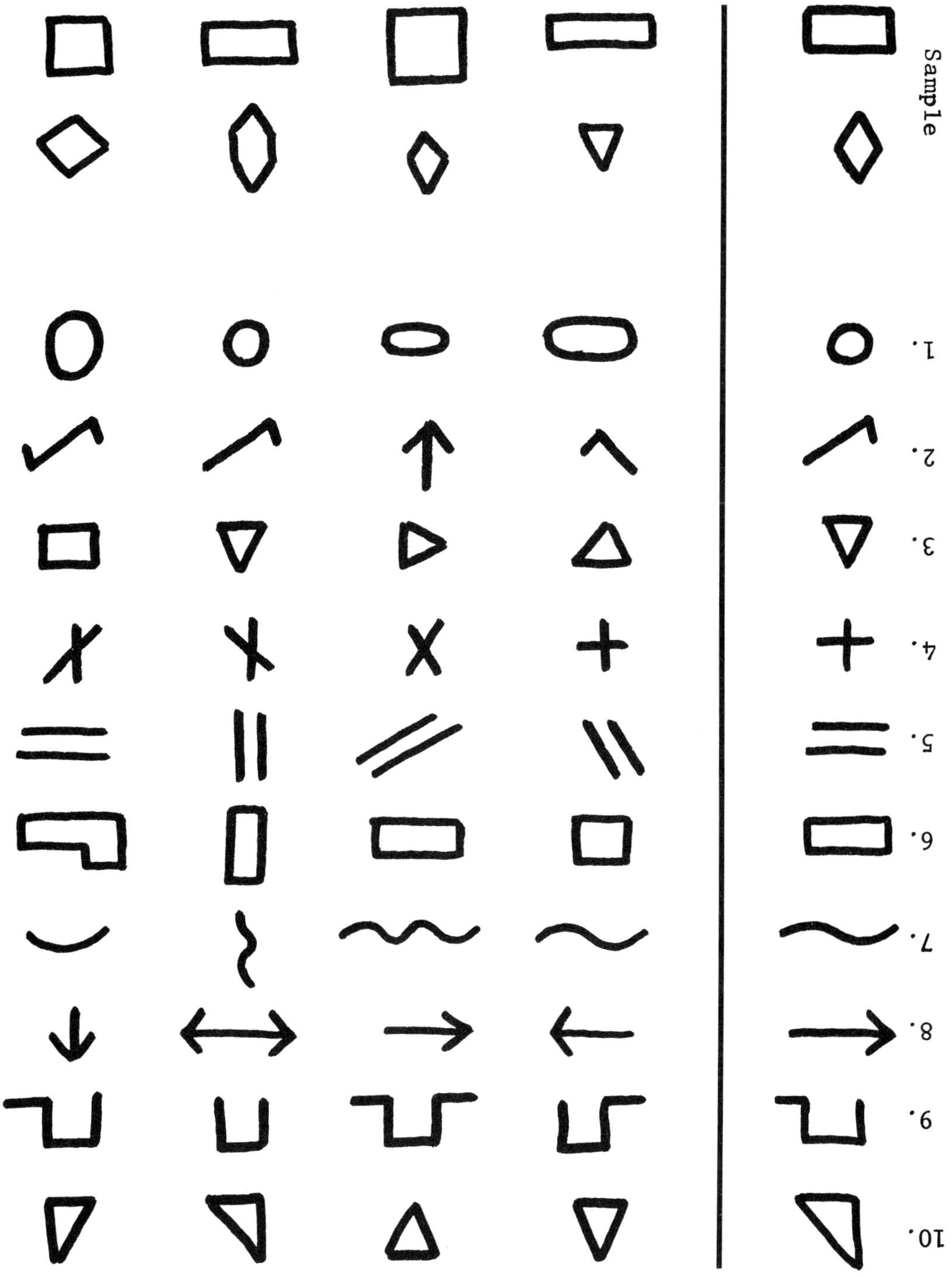

VISUAL TEST ONE

Visual Discrimination of Shapes and Symbols

Directions: Point to the symbol that looks like the first one.

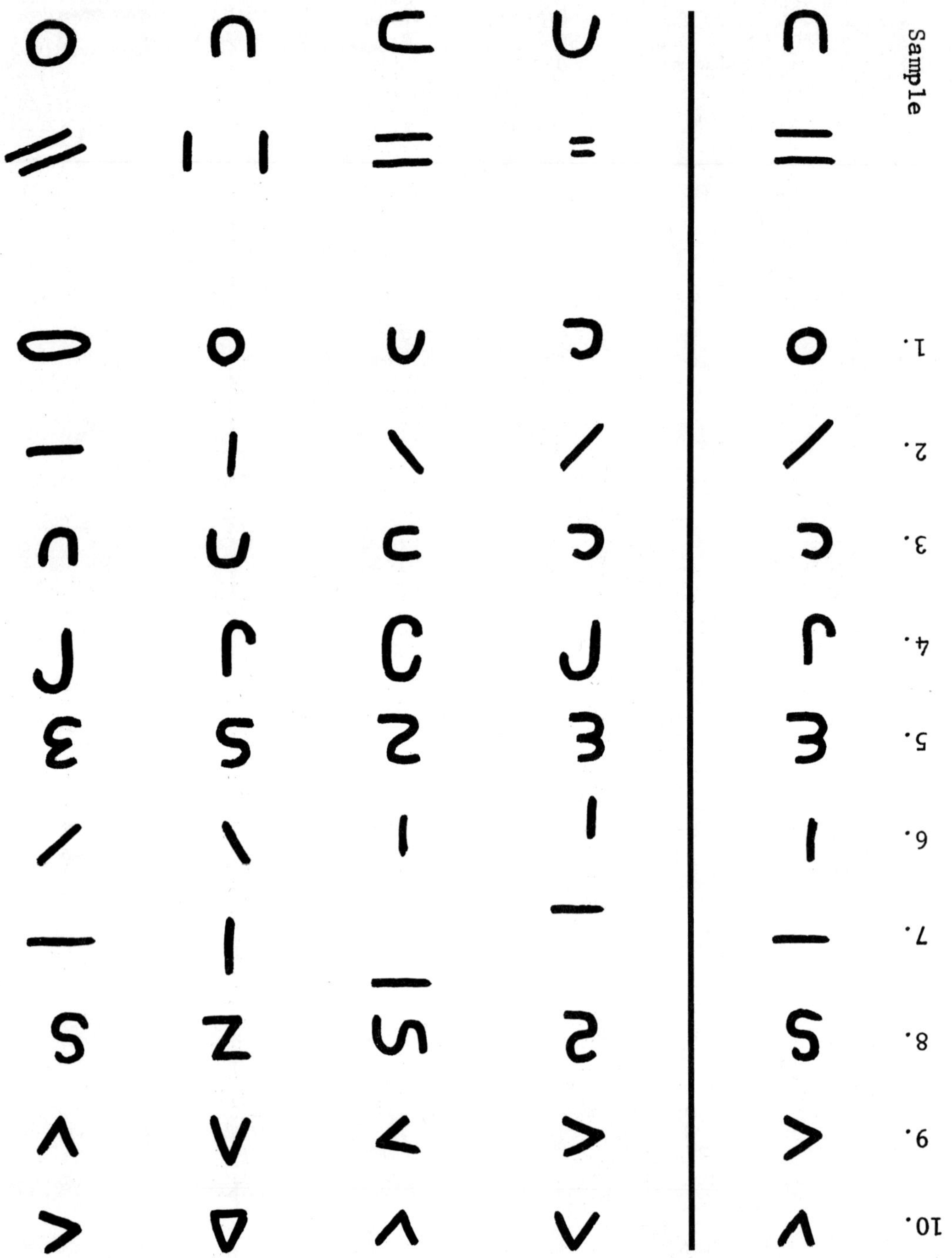

VISUAL TEST TWO

Discrimination of Letter Shapes

Directions: Point to the shape that looks like the first one.

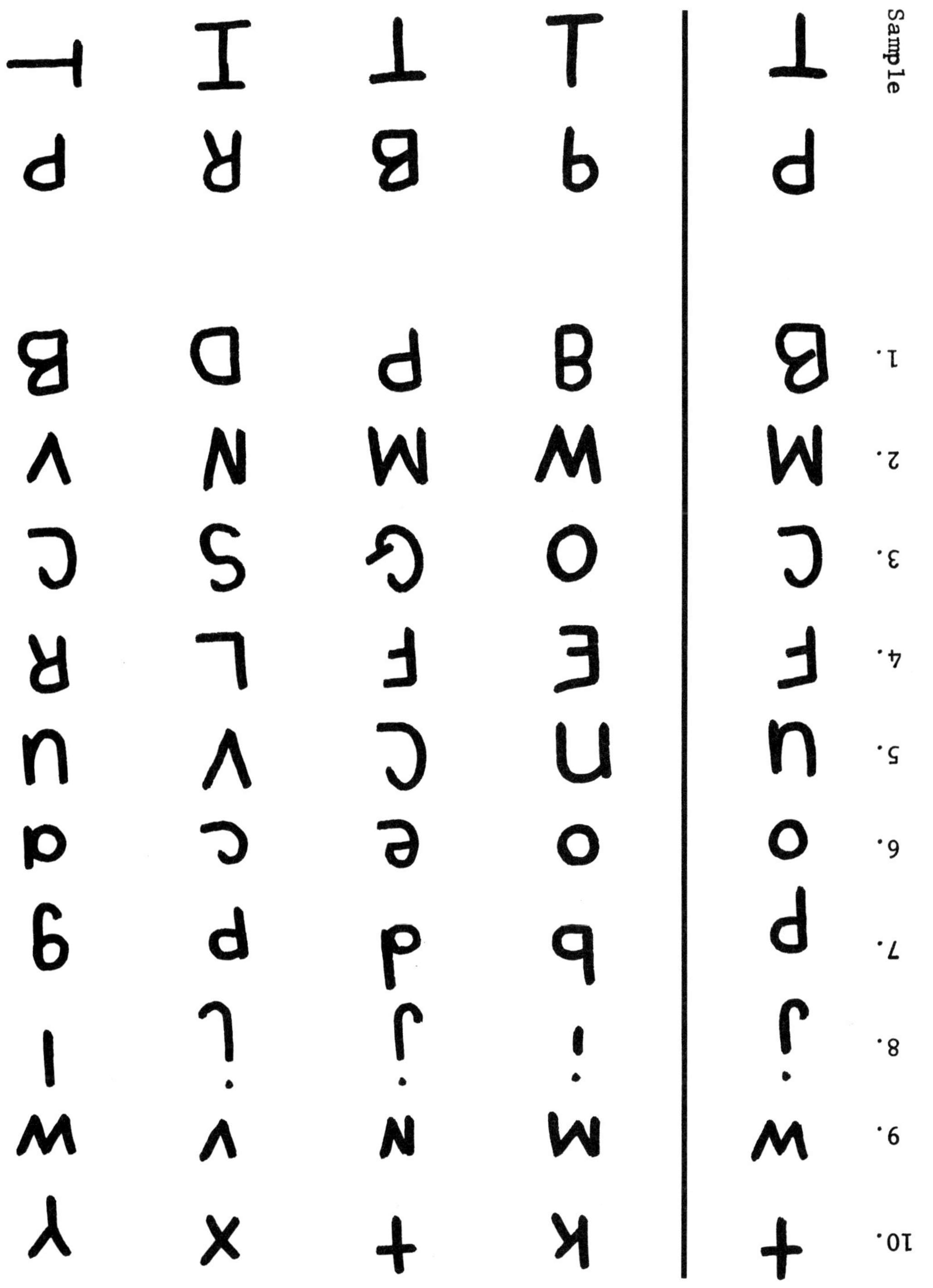

VISUAL TEST THREE

Visual Discrimination of Letters I

Directions: Point to the letter that looks like the first one.

Sample	TX	TT	XX	XT	TX
	VW	WA	WV	VW	WW
1.	AV	VA	AL	AW	AV
2.	PB	PB	BP	PR	DB
3.	NE	NL	NI	NE	EN
4.	OG	OC	OG	OO	OQ
5.	TZ	TZ	TL	TK	ZT
6.	sc	se	sc	so	sr
7.	uv	uu	vu	nv	uv
8.	yh	yn	yl	yh	yt
9.	fm	fm	fn	fw	fh
10.	pb	bp	pb	pd	gb

VISUAL TEST FOUR

Discrimination of Letters II

Directions: Point to the group of letters that look like the first group.

Sample				
car	can	cat	con	car
bag	bet	beg	bag	bug
1. red	fed	red	led	wed
2. map	map	mad	mat	may
3. tan	tin	ton	tan	ten
4. got	jot	pot	got	dot
5. cab	cat	can	car	cab
6. pin	pen	pan	pun	pin
7. joy	toy	boy	joy	soy
8. bed	beg	bed	ben	bet
9. set	sit	set	sot	sat
10. pet	bet	pet	let	jet
11. tin	bin	fin	tin	win
12. pot	pat	pit	pot	pet

VISUAL TEST FIVE

Discrimination of Words I

Directions: Point to the word that looks the same as the first word.

VISUAL TEST SIX

Discrimination of Words II

Directions: Point to the word that is the same as the first word.

Sample	jump	lump	bump	dump	jump
	bear	tear	fear	bear	dear
1.	fable	table	fable	cable	gable
2.	warn	warm	wart	warp	warn
3.	cook	coop	cool	coon	cook
4.	sock	sock	sack	suck	sick
5.	park	dark	park	bark	lark
6.	band	bond	bind	bend	band
7.	toll	tell	till	toll	tall
8.	cart	part	chart	cart	dart
9.	mole	male	mole	mule	mile
10.	dart	dart	dark	dare	darn
11.	wide	side	hide	wide	ride
12.	harp	hard	harp	hare	harm

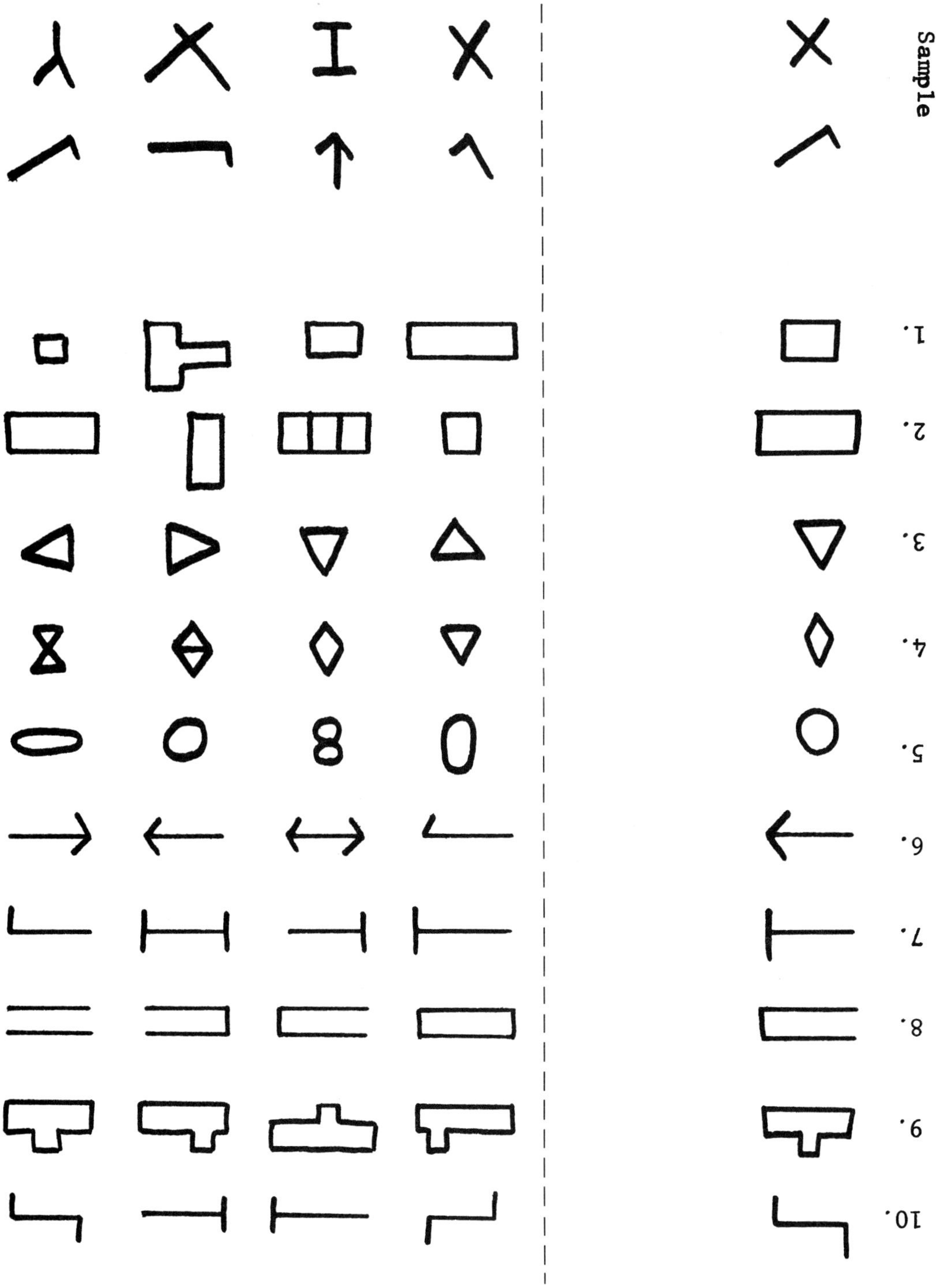

VISUAL TEST SEVEN

Visual Memory of Symbols

Directions: Look at each symbol and try to remember what you see. The symbol will be covered up after you see it. Then I will ask you to point to the symbol that looks like the one you saw.

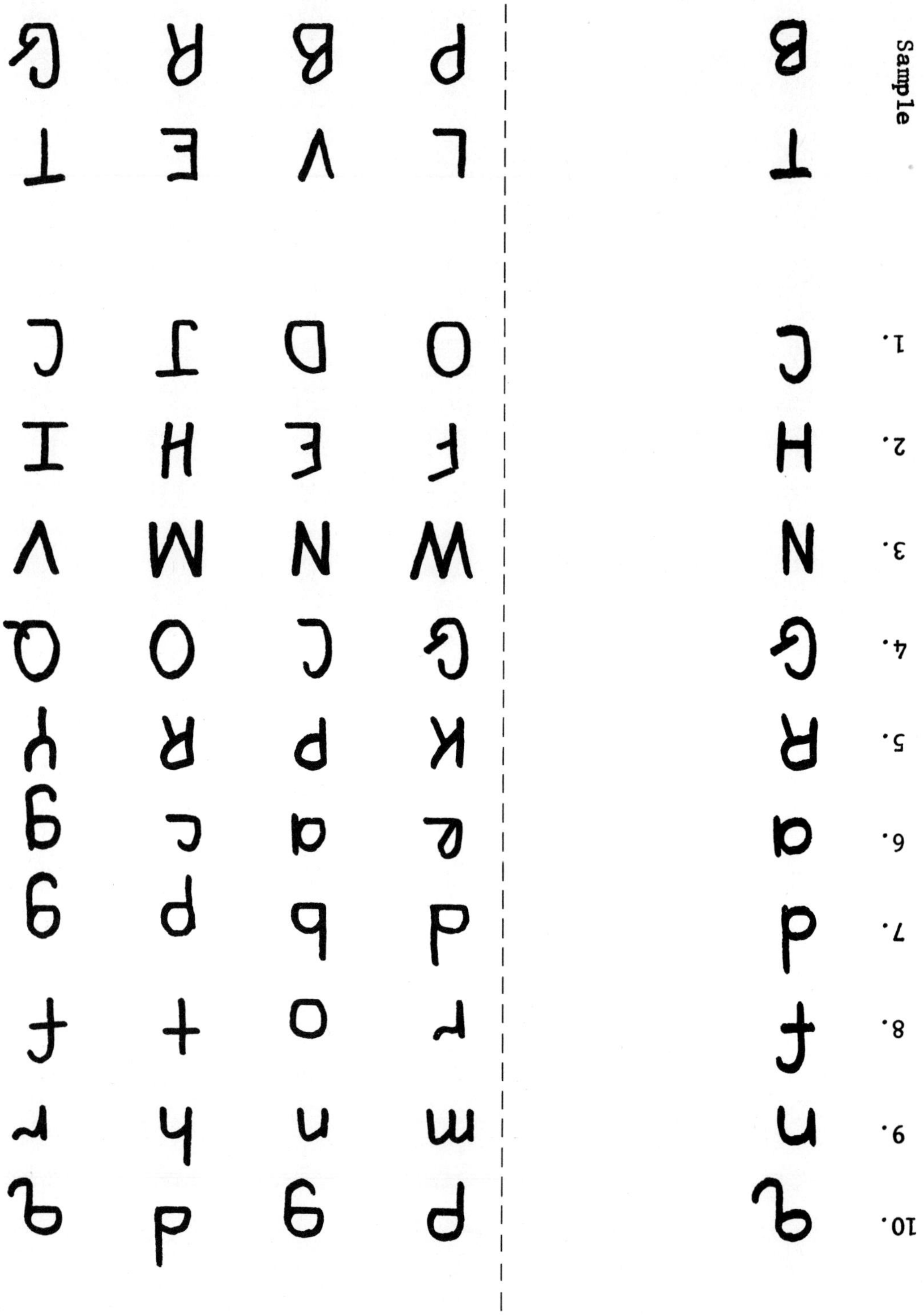

VISUAL TEST EIGHT

Visual Memory of Letters I

Directions: Look at each letter and try to remember what you see. The letter will be covered up after you have seen it. Then you will be asked to point to the same letter you just saw.

Sample	mw	cn	mw	ns	nm
	tl	zl	xt	tl	wn
1.	sk	cl	at	st	sk
2.	ae	ac	co	ae	ea
3.	zht	slt	znh	zht	wbl
4.	gvn	jnv	gvn	dnm	qwn
5.	frsv	trcw	frsv	vsfr	fvsr
6.	cfkp	cfkp	otkp	ctkq	sftd
7.	bxcfl	dxctl	bxcfl	dtcfd	pwctl
8.	jbhmr	gbhnr	jbhmr	ghbmt	jdnrh
9.	lkmynp	lknpny	klmymp	lhnymp	lkmynp
10.	xftvwn	xtfvvn	zftwmv	xftvwn	xklwvm
11.	bdpsqnc	dbgspnc	bdpsqnc	dbpzgnc	bdpcgns
12.	clkmpry	clkmpry	rlkcpmy	ctknpry	clknrvp

VISUAL TEST NINE

Visual Memory of Letters II

Directions: Look carefully at each group of letters as it is flashed. Then point to the same group of letters when you see it in the row on the right.

Beginning	cat	cut	cell	man
Sample:	boy	beg	tag	bit
1.	moon	take	late	come
2.	dish	runt	beach	lead
3.	plum	motor	pop	boat
4.	shine	clown	wish	down
5.	learn	enter	chair	spain
Ending	shop	skip	have	were
Sample:	skip	class	cube	clad
6.	meat	look	cream	mail
7.	frog	fern	lettuce	sent
8.	jumpy	candle	cage	manage
9.	hanger	spend	happen	hurt
10.	that	team	budget	chair
Medial	cure	tack	cope	cake
Sample:	mask	leave	poor	cup
11.	table	note	teeth	tub
12.	push	bush	pint	wave
13.	tube	master	watch	movie
14.	grown	sweet	year	grasp
15.	great	them	floor	grand

VISUAL TEST TEN

Visualizing Sounds in Words

Read: "I am going to say some words. For each word you will have to point to another word that has the same (beginning or ending or medial) sound. The first practice word is '——.' Point to the word that has the same (beginning or ending or medial) as '——.' The next practice word is '——.'"

Directions: Read the key word and then wait for the child to point to a word in each row that has the same beginning, ending, or medial sound.

AUDITORY TEST ONE

Auditory Discrimination of Words

Directions: Have the child sit facing away from you. This will eliminate the opportunity for lip reading during this test.

Read: "I am going to say two words. I want you to listen carefully and then tell me if I repeat the same word. If I say the same word both times, say "YES." If the words are *not* alike say "NO."

Sample:	mat	mat	run	fun
	tip	flip	mop	mop

Read: "Do you understand what to do?"

1. go	no	________	(B)	14. took	look	________	(B)
2. cob	cab	________	(M)	15. still	still	________	
3. run	run	________		16. pat	bat	________	(B)
4. met	mat	________	(M)	17. sun	sum	________	(E)
5. car	car	________		18. chair	chair	________	
6. mow	mow	________		19. will	well	________	(M)
7. find	mind	________	(B)	20. hide	hide	________	
8. bad	bag	________	(E)	21. mop	mob	________	(E)
9. fix	fix	________		22. park	part	________	(E)
10. sit	set	________	(M)	23. room	room	________	
11. was	was	________		24. rub	rob	________	(M)
12. bug	buzz	________	(E)	25. first	thirst	________	(B)
13. fast	fast	________					

AUDITORY TEST TWO

Auditory Memory of Words

Directions: Say each word or words clearly and at a normal rate of speech. Do not repeat any word or group of words. Mark the responses as they are given.

Read: "I am going to pronounce some words. You are to listen to the words I say and repeat them back to me. Try to say them back just the way I said them to you."

Sample:	day	am	out	ring	
	sky	tin	boy	ice	rug

(2)	1. cake	bus				
	2. pen	sock				
(3)	3. nose	map	sea			
	4. wind	tape	horn			
(4)	5. yard	book	fog	lady		
	6. milk	log	ant	box		
(5)	7. house	nickle	sail	ranch	adult	
	8. plane	apple	team	bird	ribbon	
(6)	9. board	pipe	trip	cushion	skate	artist
	10. vegetable	rodeo	lamp	acorn	marble	truck
(7)	11. airplane flashlight	horses	window	swing	paper	sent
	12. jam soap	towel	floor	picture	moon	telephone

AUDITORY TEST THREE

Auditory Memory of Sentences

Directions: Read each sentence to the child. Do not repeat the sentence. Then ask the child to repeat the sentence back to you.

Read: "I am going to read some sentences to you. Listen carefully and then say the sentence back to me."

Sample: I like my school.
The day has been nice.

(5) 1. Look at the birds fly.
2. We almost lost the race.
(7) 3. Be sure to tell her I called.
4. People seem to like what she says.
(8) 5. When we get the chance we can leave.
6. Pretend we will be able to go today.
(9) 7. My home is almost three miles away from here.
8. The television was broken so we cleaned our room.
(10) 9. Try not to spill your food on the new rug.
10. I have a surprise waiting for you in the car.
(11) 11. We just stopped and watched as the leaves began to fall.
12. The park was empty by the time we made our trip.
(12) 13. Running is a great activity for some people when they need exercise.
14. Famous singers have eaten here many times both before and after work.
(13) 15. You could help us begin the program if you have the time now.
16. We could hardly believe the contest was over before we really got started.
(14) 17. Reading is a habit that can bring joy, knowledge, and relaxation to us all.
18. The pool was closed so we were not able to begin our lessons today.
(15) 19. My brother was sunburned so badly that he almost had to stay home from work.
20. From time to time we spend an hour or two just talking on the phone.
(16) 21. Help arrived just before the problem became so bad that we would lose the game.
22. The people realized that everyone was not going to join in the group's special events.
(17) 23. Our town was not very big but we had our share of nice farms and good people.
24. First of all we need the type of support the students are capable of giving to us.
(18) 25. One day we will begin to notice the people who are really responsible for our new meeting hall.
26. The newspaper story was what started the whole investigation about the way the group had run its business.
(19) 27. Our team was recognized for being fast, smart, and, for the most part, really staying cool under pressure.
28. The day of the picnic we were not able to get enough ice for making the homemade ice cream.
(20) 29. The service was one that everyone was pleased to have seen, but the leaders were not able to stop early.
30. We managed to gather up enough bread, meat, drinks, and dessert to make a real party out of the trip.

VISUAL TESTS 1-6

1. Visual Discrimination: SHAPES AND SYMBOLS	2. Visual Discrimination: LETTER SHAPES	3. Visual Discrimination: LETTERS 1
1. 2. 3. 4. 5. 6. 7. 8. 9. 10.	1. 2. 3. 4. 5. 6. 7. 8. 9. 10.	1. 2. 3. 4. 5. 6. 7. 8. 9. 10.
Grade: Correct: K-2 70% 3-5 90%	Grade: Correct: K 70% 1 90%	Grade: Correct: K-1 80% 2-up 100%

4. Vis Discrim: LETTERS II	5. Visual Discrimination: WORDS I	6. Visual Discrimination WORDS II
1. VA AL AW AV 2. PB BP PR DB 3. NL NI NE EN 4. OC OG OO OQ 5. TZ TL TK ZT 6. se sc so sr 7. uu vu nv uv 8. yn yl yh yt 9. fm fn fw fh 10. bp pb pd gb	1. fed red led wed (B) 2. map mad mat may (E) 3. tin ton tan ten (M) 4. jot pot got dot (B) 5. cat can car cab (E) 6. pen pan pun pin (M) 7. toy boy joy soy (B) 8. beg bed ben bet (E) 9. sit set sot sat (M) 10. bet pet let jet (B) 11. bin fin tin win (E) 12. pat pit pot pet (M)	1. table fable cable gable (B) 2. warm wart warp warn (E) 3. coop cool coon cook (E) 4. sock sack suck sick (M) 5. dark park bark lark (B) 6. bond bind bend band (M) 7. tell till toll tall (M) 8. part chart cart dart (B) 9. male mole mule mile (M) 10. dart dark dare darn (E) 11. side hide wide ride (B) 12. hard harp hare harm (E)
GR: Correct: K-2 80% 3-up 100%	__/4 (B: 1,4,7,10) __/4 (M: 3,6,9,12) __/4 (E: 2,5,8,11) Grade: Correct: K-2 75% 3-up 100%	__/4 (B: 1,5,8,11) __/4 (M: 4,6,7,9) __/4 (E: 2,3,10,12) Grade: Correct: K-3 75% 4-up 100%

VISUAL TESTS 7-10

7. Visual Memory: SYMBOLS	8. Visual Memory: LETTERS I	9. Visual Memory: LETTERS II
1.	1. O D J C	1. cl at st sk (2)
2.	2. F E H I	2. ac co ae ea
3.	3. W N M V	3. slt znh zht wbl (3)
4.	4. G C O Q	4. jnv gvn dnm qwn
5.	5. K P R Y	5. trcw frsv vsfr fvsr (4)
6.	6. e a c g	6. cfkp otkp ctkq sftd
7.	7. d b p g	7. dxctl bxcfl dtcfd pwctl (5)
8.	8. r o t f	8. gbhnr jbhmr ghbmt jdnrh
9.	9. m n h r	9. lknpny klmymp lhnymp lkmynp (6)
10.	10. p g d q	10. xtfvvn zftwmv xftvwn xklwvm
		11. dbgspnc bdpsqnc dbpzgnc bdpcgns (7)
		12. clkmpry rlkcpmy ctknpry clknrvp

Grade	Correct
2	80%
3-up	100%

Grade	Correct
K	70%
1	80%
2-up	100%

Grade	K-2	3	4	5	6	7
# Letters	2	3	4	5	6	7

10. Visualizing Sounds in Words

Stimulus Words: (Examiner must read aloud the stimulus words)

a. make	cat, cut, cell, man	(B)
b. tell	boy, beg, tag, bit	(B)
1. tame	1. moon, take, late, come	(B)
2. blue	2. dish, runt, beach, lead	”
3. plan	3. plum, motor, pop, boat	”
4. want	4. shine, clown, wish, down	”
5. chain	5. learn, enter, chair, spain	”
a. war	shop, skip, have, were	(E)
b. miss	skip, class, cube, clad	(E)
6. milk	6. meat, look, cream, mail	(E)
7. fence	7. frog, fern, lettuce, sent	”
8. candy	8. jumpy, candle, cage, manage	”
9. hard	9. hanger, spend, happen, hurt	”
10. temper	10. that, team, budget, chair	”
a. hole	cure, tack, cope, cake	(M)
b. seen	make, leave, poor, cup	(M)
11. toad	11. table, note, teeth, tub	(M)
12. paint	12. push, bush, pint, wave	”
13. music	13. tube, master, watch, movie	”
14. green	14. grown, sweet, year, grasp	”
15. storm	15. great, them, floor, grand	”

Gr:	# Correct (B)	# Correct (E)	# Correct (M)
1	3	3	—
2	4	4	3
3	5	5	4
4	—	—	5

AUDITORY TESTS

1. Auditory Discrimination: WORDS

Total Scoring: ____/25

(B)__/5; (M)__/5; (E)__/5

GR: 1 2 2

(B)100% (M)100% (E)100%

2. Auditory Memory: WORDS

Highest number of words recalled exactly ________

Highest number of words recalled ________

3. Auditory Memory: SENTENCES

Longest sentence recalled exactly ________

Longest sentence correctly rephrased ________

COMMENTS: ________

WORD ANALYSIS SURVEY

Directions to student: I am going to show you lists of words which you probably have not seen before. Look at each word, then pronounce the word. If you are not sure how to say the word, please try anyway. If you can't say all of a word, say the sounds you know.

I-X PHONIC ANALYSIS SURVEY		XI-XIV STRUCTURAL ANALYSIS SURVEY	
1. bef	glite	1. un/cake/s	1. can't
2. fod	twate	2. a/talk/ed	2. I'm
3. von	smote	3. in/help/ing	3. didn't
4. zim	plyte	4. mis/run/ful	4. I'll
5. juh	snute	5. en/pet/ly	5. isn't
6. cas	prete	6. im/tree/less	6. don't
7. hec	skeal	7. dis/ask/er	7. I've
8. nuv	frayl	8. ex/bed/est	8. it's
9. mik	driel	9. de/from/tion	9. we've
10. suz	greel	10. pro/hand/en	10. won't
11. yeg	clail	11. re/much/ies	11. he's
12. raf	croel	12. pre/long/ward	12. you're
13. lub	sloal	13. inter/work/ment	13. we're
14. dit	tror	14. con/let/ous	14. they're
15. pir	flur	15. per/girl/ish	15. we'll
16. gax	brar	16. non/tell/ious	16. hasn't
17. waq	swir	17. tri/new/et	17. I'd
18. tel	bler	18. trans/all/able	18. you'll
19. kip	chure	19. sub/slow/ure	19. hadn't
	20. thore	20. intro/that/in	20. wasn't
	21. shere	21. super/call/ity	21. haven't
	22. phare	22. inway	22. doesn't
	23. whire	23. dogpage	23. aren't
	24. shroil	24. takeman	24. she's
	25. splew	25. letsome	25. wouldn't
	26. thraul	26. talkway	26. weren't
	27. sproyl	27. allrun	27. here's
	28. strool	28. wordcall	28. who's
	29. scroul	29. handboy	
	30. chreil	30. roomwork	
		31. homeplay	

WORD ANALYSIS SURVEY RECORD FORM

Directions to Examiner: Place WORD ANALYSIS SURVEY so that stimulus words face student. Read DIRECTIONS TO STUDENT aloud. Mark each sound correctly pronounced with a check (✓), and encircle incorrect sounds. Summarize needed skills for Test Columns I-XIV at bottom of this record form.

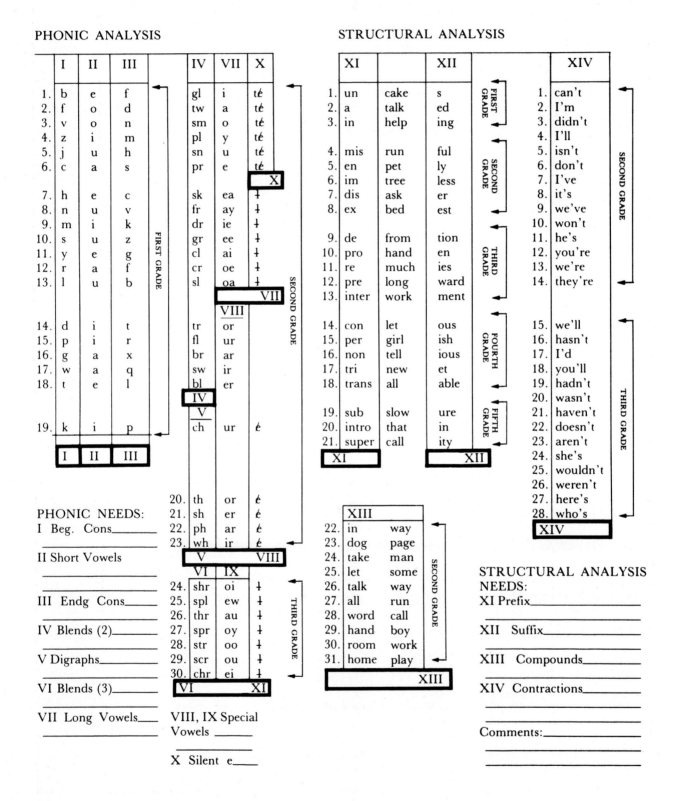

PHONIC ANALYSIS

	I	II	III	
1.	b	e	f	FIRST GRADE
2.	f	o	d	
3.	v	o	n	
4.	z	i	m	
5.	j	u	h	
6.	c	a	s	
7.	h	e	c	
8.	n	u	v	
9.	m	i	k	
10.	s	u	z	
11.	y	e	g	
12.	r	a	f	
13.	l	u	b	
14.	d	i	t	
15.	p	i	r	
16.	g	a	x	
17.	w	a	q	
18.	t	e	l	
19.	k	i	p	
	I	II	III	

	IV	VII	X	
1.	gl	i	té	SECOND GRADE
2.	tw	a	té	
3.	sm	o	té	
4.	pl	y	té	
5.	sn	u	té	
6.	pr	e	té	
			X	
7.	sk	ea	ŧ	
8.	fr	ay	ŧ	
9.	dr	ie	ŧ	
10.	gr	ee	ŧ	
11.	cl	ai	ŧ	
12.	cr	oe	ŧ	
13.	sl	oa	ŧ	
		VII		
		VIII		
14.	tr	or		
15.	fl	ur		
16.	br	ar		
17.	sw	ir		
18.	bl	er		
	IV			
	V			
19.	ch	ur	é	
20.	th	or	é	
21.	sh	er	é	
22.	ph	ar	é	
23.	wh	ir	é	
	V	VIII		
	VI	IX		
24.	shr	oi	ŧ	THIRD GRADE
25.	spl	ew	ŧ	
26.	thr	au	ŧ	
27.	spr	oy	ŧ	
28.	str	oo	ŧ	
29.	scr	ou	ŧ	
30.	chr	ei	ŧ	
	VI		XI	

PHONIC NEEDS:

I Beg. Cons______

II Short Vowels______

III Endg Cons______

IV Blends (2)______

V Digraphs______

VI Blends (3)______

VII Long Vowels______

VIII, IX Special Vowels ______

X Silent e____

STRUCTURAL ANALYSIS

	XI		XII	
1.	un	cake	s	FIRST GRADE
2.	a	talk	ed	
3.	in	help	ing	
4.	mis	run	ful	SECOND GRADE
5.	en	pet	ly	
6.	im	tree	less	
7.	dis	ask	er	
8.	ex	bed	est	
9.	de	from	tion	THIRD GRADE
10.	pro	hand	en	
11.	re	much	ies	
12.	pre	long	ward	
13.	inter	work	ment	
14.	con	let	ous	FOURTH GRADE
15.	per	girl	ish	
16.	non	tell	ious	
17.	tri	new	et	
18.	trans	all	able	
19.	sub	slow	ure	FIFTH GRADE
20.	intro	that	in	
21.	super	call	ity	
	XI		XII	

	XIV	
1.	can't	SECOND GRADE
2.	I'm	
3.	didn't	
4.	I'll	
5.	isn't	
6.	don't	
7.	I've	
8.	it's	
9.	we've	
10.	won't	
11.	he's	
12.	you're	
13.	we're	
14.	they're	
15.	we'll	THIRD GRADE
16.	hasn't	
17.	I'd	
18.	you'll	
19.	hadn't	
20.	wasn't	
21.	haven't	
22.	doesn't	
23.	aren't	
24.	she's	
25.	wouldn't	
26.	weren't	
27.	here's	
28.	who's	
	XIV	

	XIII		
22.	in	way	SECOND GRADE
23.	dog	page	
24.	take	man	
25.	let	some	
26.	talk	way	
27.	all	run	
28.	word	call	
29.	hand	boy	
30.	room	work	
31.	home	play	
		XIII	

STRUCTURAL ANALYSIS NEEDS:

XI Prefix______

XII Suffix______

XIII Compounds______

XIV Contractions______

Comments:______

SPECIALIZED VOCABULARY LISTS ONE AND TWO

Survival Vocabulary I

A	B
1. go	closed
2. in	doctor
3. up	toilet
4. men	private
5. out	caution
6. pull	hospital
7. walk	emergency
8. down	directions
9. help	no fires
10. push	no minors
11. boys	no swimming
12. stop	don't walk
13. girls	keep off
14. exit	fire escape
15. wait	deep water
16. open	keep out
17. phone	post office
18. women	hands off
19. quiet	do not enter
20. enter	out of order
21. poison	do not handle
22. danger	beware of dog
23. ladies	do not use near heat
24. police	shelter

Survival Vocabulary II

1. left	no smoking
2. taxi	go slow
3. right	no admittance
4. detour	bus stop
5. warning	no turns
6. fragile	wet paint
7. external	no trespassing
8. teaspoon	help wanted
9. internal	no parking
10. entrance	fire extinguisher
11. stairway	school zone
12. elevator	public telephone
13. ambulance	deposit coin
14. flammable	hospital zone
15. restrooms	dangerous curve
16. tablespoon	restricted area
17. prohibited	temporarily closed
18. explosives	lost and found
19. combustible	stop for pedestrians
20. escalator	emergency exit

SPECIALIZED VOCABULARY LISTS

Sixteen Essential Sight Words III

1. a
2. in
3. to
4. is
5. it
6. for
7. not
8. see
9. the
10. and
11. but
12. can
13. look
14. said
15. with
16. little

SPECIALIZED VOCABULARY LISTS RECORD FORM

Survival Vocabulary I (Ages 7–11)

A	B
1.__go ______	__closed ______
2.__in ______	__doctor ______
3.__up ______	__toilet______
4.__men ______	__private______
5.__out ______	__caution______
6.__pull______	__hospital ______
7.__walk ______	__emergency ______
8.__down ______	__directions______
9.__help ______	__no fires______
10.__push ______	__no minors______
11.__boys ______	__no swimming ______
12.__stop______	__don't walk ______
13.__girls ______	__keep off ______
14.__exit______	__fire escape ______
15.__wait ______	__deep water ______
16.__open ______	__keep out ______
17.__phone______	__post office______
18.__women ______	__hands off______
19.__quiet ______	__do not enter ______
20.__enter ______	__out of order______
21.__poison______	__do not handle______
22.__danger ______	__beware of dog______
23.__ladies ______	__do not use near heat______
24.__police______	__shelter ______

Survival Vocabulary II (Ages 12–up)

A	B	Sixteen Essential Sight Words III
1.__left ______	__no smoking______	__a ______
2.__taxi ______	__go slow ______	__in ______
3.__right______	__no admittance______	__to ______
4.__detour______	__bus stop ______	__is ______
5.__warning ______	__no turns ______	__it ______
6.__fragile ______	__wet paint______	__for______
7.__external ______	__no trespassing______	__not ______
8.__teaspoon ______	__help wanted ______	__see______
9.__internal ______	__no parking______	__the______
10.__entrance ______	__fire extinguisher ______	__and ______
11.__stairway ______	__school zone ______	__but ______
12.__elevator ______	__public telephone______	__can ______
13.__ambulance ______	__deposit coin______	__look ______
14.__flammable ______	__hospital zone ______	__said ______
15.__restrooms ______	__dangerous curve______	__with ______
16.__tablespoon ______	__restricted area______	__little ______
17.__prohibited ______	__temporarily closed ______	
18.__explosives ______	__lost and found______	
19.__combustible______	__stop for pedestrians______	
20.__escalator ______	__emergency exit ______	

ECOLOGICAL SURVEY: CHECKLIST OF STUDENT LEARNING PREFERENCE

Indicate below the optimal learning conditions for this student.

I. LEARNER Characteristics which should be considered in planning for individualized reading instruction:

A. When presented with a new reading task, student learns best by
__hearing __seeing __reading __doing __writing
__seeing and hearing __saying and writing

B. When asked for answers, responds best by
__telling __writing __selecting correct answers

C. Practice and long term memory are best reinforced by
__games __workbooks __discussions __drill activities

D. Self-concept is
__low __moderate __high __unrealistic

E. Frustration tolerance is
__poor __low __moderate __high

II. CLASSROOM Characteristics which help student to study and perform best include

A. Time. . . __early morning __mid-day __afternoon __evening
B. Temperature. . . __warm __cold __comfortable for most people
C. Noise. . . __quiet __slight __moderate __radio __TV
D. Need for Movement. . . __none __little __average __high
E. Period of Study. . . __5 minutes __15 minutes __30 minutes

III. TEACHER Characteristics which contribute to student success include

A. Supervision. . . __none __little __moderate __high
B. Extra help from. . . __teacher __peer __older student
__parent __other adult
C. Need for Encouragement. . . __frequent __average __seldom
D. Proximity. . . __very close __near __moderate distance __far

IV. METHODS which appear to best enhance the student's learning include

A. Type. . . __discovery method __direct instruction __combination
B. Grouping. . . __large group __small group __one peer __alone
C. Need for structure. . . __high __average __low
D. Tests. . . __essay __fill blanks __multiple choice __oral
__true/false

V. MATERIALS suited to this student's needs should be those that are

A. Format. . . __traditional __very colorful __little distraction
B. Organization. . . __small units __long units __varying activities
C. Level. . . __above grade __on grade __below grade

SUMMARY of Student Learning Preferences:

I. Learner Characteristics: ______________________________
II. Classroom: ______________________________
III. Teacher: ______________________________
IV. Methods: ______________________________
V. Materials: ______________________________

Projected Achievement Level Formula:

$$\left(\frac{\text{AAL}}{\text{Yrs/Sch}} \times \text{Time} + \text{AAL} = \text{PAL}\right)$$

For those who feel the need to quantify both past and future reading achievement, the Projected Achievement Level Formula is presented as a means to roughly estimate such data. The user is cautioned against considering the numbers thus obtained as fixed or statistically pure. Because so many factors impinge upon student learning, quantification of ALL pertinent factors is impossible. Nonetheless teachers and diagnosticians are frequently asked to predict student reading progress over a given period of time or to set reading goals for the student. This becomes particularly important in the formulation of IEP long term goals.

In the past, reading specialists have relied upon reading expectancy formulae, based upon IQ scores, to predict a theoretical reading or learning capacity level. It is herein suggested that past learning rate, rather than IQ score, is a less biased, readily obtained, and more realistic means of projecting achievement levels. While the past learning rate partially reflects intellectual powers, it includes only the quantity, not quality, of past academic experiences. The diagnostician may need to critically analyze a student's academic history and consider these findings when interpreting PAL.

THREE FACTORS

In order to more realistically estimate the *minimal* reading progress to be expected of a student, three (3) factors should be considered: (1) Actual Achievement Level; (2) Years in School; and (3) Time.

1. Actual Achievement Level. The Actual Achievement Level, or AAL, of the student, is the present test score expressed in approximate grade equivalent form. Thus, Student A whose highest comprehension instructional level is found to be at mid-fourth (4th) grade level, would have an AAL of 4.4–4.6, or roughly 4.5.

2. Years in School. The number of years in school is the total time the student has been officially enrolled in school, beginning with first grade, expressed in grade equivalent form. Each school month is counted as 1/10 or .1 year, with the student's present school year and portion thereof included in the count. In order to convert actual time in school to grade equivalent form, it is necessary to add one year to the total count. A student who repeated first grade, and is now in the sixth month of the seventh grade, would be considered to have been in school 8.6 years (two years in 1st grade; one year for each grade 2–6; .6 years in 7th; plus one year for grade equivalent conversion).

3. Time. The time factor is the length of the specialized instruction interval for which predictions are to be made. If one is concerned with projecting progress for one school year, then TIME = 1, or one year. If the period of instruction before retest is to be eight (8) months, then TIME = .8.

COMPUTING PROJECTED ACHIEVEMENT LEVELS

1. Learning Rate. Setting the two factors, AAL and Years in School, in ratio form, a student's average learning rate can be estimated. If Student A has an AAL, or reading test score, of 4.5, and has been in school 8.6 years, then the learning rate is .52, or 52%. The student has progressed 5.2 months for every year in school, or has mastered 52% of the curriculum in that area for each year in school, as indicated in the equation.

$$\frac{\text{AAL}}{\text{Yrs/Sch}} = \frac{4.5}{8.6} = .52 \text{ or } 52\% \text{ Learning Rate}$$

2. Projected Achievement Gain. Multiplying the Learning Rate by the Time of instruction yields an estimate of the *minimum* Projected Achievement Gain. This computation represents the *least* amount of achievement gain to be expected of this student over the given time of specialized instruction, based upon the student's past learning rate. Student A, whose AAL is 4.5, who has been in school for 8.6 years, and who will be given specialized instruction for eight (8) months, will thus be expected to evidence achievement gains equal to at least 4.2 months.

$$\frac{\text{AAL}}{\text{Yrs/Sch}} \times \text{TIME} = \frac{4.5}{8.6} \times .8 = .416 = .42 = 4.2 \text{ months}$$

It is anticipated that, because of specialized instruction, achievement gains will be even greater than the minimum.

3. Projected Achievement Level (PAL). In order to predict the *minimum* level at which the student is expected to perform at the end of the time period of instruction, the original test score, or AAL, is added to the Projected Achievement Gain. Student A is expected to attain, on retest, an approximate grade equivalent of at least 4.9 as indicated by using the equation.

$$\left(\frac{\text{AAL}}{\text{Yrs/Sch}} \times \text{Time}\right) + \text{AAL} = \left(\frac{4.5}{8.6} \times .8\right) + 4.5 = 4.92 \text{ PAL}$$

USE AND INTERPRETATION

The Projected Achievement Level may be used to predict estimated achievement levels for formulating IEP's and in setting more realistic instructional goals. Following the specialized instructional period, retest scores may be compared to Projected Achievement Level scores to estimate appropriateness of instruction. The PAL has proven to be particularly valuable in explaining to parents the significance of a student's achievement gain. While a reading gain of six (6) months, following a year of specialized instruction (L.R. = 60%) may not at first appear impressive, when interpreted using PAL, the accomplishments of the student who previously progressed only three (3) months per year (L.R. = 30%) become apparent. Acceptance by parents of realistic IEP goals is also fostered by explaining the use of the PAL in setting these goals.

The use of the PAL is not restricted to interpretation of IEP/r scores, or even to the area of reading; it is appropriate for use in many areas of educational assessment. However, caution must be exercised in the use and interpretation of PAL data. The diagnostician MUST remember that this procedure is but a means of ESTIMATING MINIMUM progress and predicting gains. While it is recognized that the PAL procedure is subject to many of the same criticisms as most quantification methods, the need for such procedures is acknowledged. Further, it must be assumed that the professional who is industrious enough to accomplish these PAL computations is similarly cautious enough to judiciously interpret and use the data.

Individual Educational Prescriptions for Reading

Directions: The IEP goals and objectives which follow can be used to plan educational programs and/or as a teaching resource. Upon completion of the reading diagnosis, determine the skill area numbers of the student's prioritized needs from the Student Planning Sheet. Find those skill area numbers in the pages which follow for sample goal statements and instructional objectives. From the presented goals and objectives, select, modify, or formulate those which will be most specific to student diagnosed needs. For a more detailed discussion of appropriate use of this section, refer to page 17.

VISUAL SKILLS

1. GOAL: The student will evidence increased skills in the visual areas associated with reading by visually recalling and reproducing 20 (*appropriate # of letters*) — letter words at the ______ (*student's instructional level*) level with 95% accuracy.

A. Visual Discrimination

The student will orally match by visual features each of 10 stimulus symbols with its like symbol selected from 4 similar choices with 90% accuracy.

Given each of 10 stimulus letter shapes, the student will choose and underline from 4 similar shapes the like symbol with 90% accuracy.

When presented with each of 10 random letters, the student will circle the matching letter from a choice of 4, with 90% accuracy.

From a selection of 4 similar letter pairs, the student will point to the matching letter pairs for each of 10 2-letter stimuli, 9 of 10 attempts correct.

Given each of 10 3-letter words and 10 sets of 4 similar words, the student will underline the matching pairs with 90% accuracy.

When presented with each of 10 5-letter words and 10 sets of 5 similar words, the student will encircle the matching words with 100% accuracy.

B. Visual Memory

Given a 5-second exposure to each of 10 symbols, the student will select and point to from memory each matching symbol from a set of 5 with 90% accuracy.

When presented with each of 10 letters exposed to student view for 5 seconds, the student will, from memory, underline the matching letter from sets of 4 with 90% accuracy.

The student will encircle from memory each of 10 matching 7-letter words exposed to student view for 5 seconds, selected from a choice of 4 similar words with 90% accuracy.

C. Visualizing Sounds in Words

When presented with each of 10 oral stimulus words, the student will underline the one word in a set of 4 which has the same beginning sound as the stimulus word with 90% accuracy.

Given each of 10 oral words, the student will underline the one word in a set of 4 which has the matching ending sound with 90% accuracy.

The student will underline the one word in a set of 4 which has the same medial sound as each of 10 oral stimulus words with 90% accuracy.

1 line short

AUDITORY SKILLS

2. GOAL: The student will evidence increased skills in those auditory areas associated with reading by orally repeating each of 10 (*appropriate # of words*)—word sentences, with every word recalled in sequence.

A. Auditory Discrimination

When orally presented each of 10 pairs of similar words, the student will indicate those words which are identical and those which are not by stating "yes," or "no," with 100% accuracy.

When orally presented each of 10 pairs of words 1/2 with different beginning sounds, the student will indicate those words which are identical and those which are not by stating "yes" or "no" with 100% accuracy.

When orally presented each of 10 pairs of words 1/2 with different medial sounds, the student will indicate those words which are identical and those which are not by stating "yes" or "no" with 100% accuracy.

When orally presented each of 10 pairs of words 1/2 of which have different ending sounds, the student will indicate those words which are identical and those which are not by stating "yes" or "no" with 100% accuracy.

B. Auditory Memory

When orally presented each of 5 groups of (*appropriate # of words*) words, the student will repeat all of the words.

Given each of 5 oral lists of (*appropriate # of words*) words, the student will correctly repeat the words in proper sequence, 100% accuracy.

When orally presented each of 5 (*appropriate # words/sentence*)—word sentences, the student will orally repeat each sentence, including all major details, 4/5 attempts.

When orally presented each of 5 (*appropriate # words/sentence*)—word sentences, the student will correctly repeat each sentence in proper sequence, 4/5 attempts.

WORD RECOGNITION PATTERNS

3. GOAL: The student will demonstrate expanded word recognition skills by correctly pronouncing (*appropriate #*) previously unknown words on the (*student's Projected Achievement Level*) level with 95% accuracy.

A. Sight Vocabulary

Given a one second exposure per word to the (*appropriate word list*) list at the (*instructional level*) level, the student will pronounce each word with 90% accuracy.

When presented a vocabulary list at the (*instructional level*), the student will pronounce each word with 90% accuracy.

Given 20 sentences containing the (*instructional level*) level sight word list, the student will pronounce the words in context with 95% accuracy.

B. Word Analysis

1. Beginning Consonants

When given the sound of (*needed sound*) and shown 5 picture cards, the student will point to the 3 pictures that begin with the stimulus sound.

Given 10 words beginning with _____ and _____ (*needed sounds*), the student will pronounce the beginning sound of each word with 100% accuracy.

When presented with 10 unknown words beginning with letters ______,

_____, _____, and _____ (*needed sounds*), the student will pronounce the beginning sound of each word with 100% accuracy.

2. Ending Consonants

   When given a series of 10 picture cards, the student will correctly point to the 5 cards with the (*needed sound*) ending sound.

   Given 10 words ending with _____ and _____ (*needed sounds*) consonant sounds, the student will pronounce the ending sound of each word with 100% accuracy.

   When presented with 10 unknown words ending with letters _____, _____, _____, and _____, (*needed sounds*) the student will pronounce the ending sound of each word with 100% accuracy.

3. Short Vowels

   When given a series of 10 picture cards, the student will point to the 5 cards with the short sound of (*needed sound*) with 100% accuracy.

   The student will correctly match short vowel sound with 5 picture cards with the (*needed sound*) sound and 5 with the (*needed sound*) sound.

   Given a list of 20 words at the (*instructional level*) grade level, the student will circle the short vowel sound pronounced by the teacher with 90% accuracy.

4. Long Vowels

   When given 10 picture cards, the student will point to the 5 cards with the long sound of (*needed sound*) with 100% accuracy.

   The student will point to the 5 picture cards with the long sound of _____ and _____ (*needed sounds*) from a set of 10 with 100% accuracy.

   Given a list of 20 words at the (*instructional level*) level, the student will circle the long vowel sound in the words pronounced by the teacher with 90% accuracy.

   The student will correctly pronounce the long vowel sounds in 20 words at the (*instructional level*) level.

5. Silent e

   Given a list of 10 words, the student will circle the words that contain the silent e pattern with 100% accuracy.

   When presented a list of 20 words at the (*instructional level*) level, 1/2 of which have silent e, the student will pronounce each word with 95% accuracy.

6. Blends

   When presented the beginning blend sounds in 20 words, the student will pronounce the beginning blend sounds for _____ (*needed sound*) with 100% accuracy.

   The student will point to the 5 picture cards representing the blends of _____ and _____ (*needed sounds*) with 90% accuracy.

   Given a list of 20 unknown words with blends, the student will pronounce the blends with 90% accuracy.

7. Digraphs

   When presented the digraph sound (*needed sound*), the student will point to the picture cards that begin with the stimulus sound with 100% accuracy.

   When given the letters and a word card, the student will pronounce the digraph (*needed sound*) with 100% accuracy.

   When presented words orally that include digraphs _____, _____, _____, _____, and _____ (*needed sounds*), the student will pronounce the digraph sounds with 100% accuracy.

   Given the digraphs _____, _____, _____, _____, and _____ (*needed sounds*), the student will point to the picture cards representing the sounds with 100% accuracy.

Given 20 word cards at the (*instructional level*), the student will read the digraph words with 100% accuracy.

8. Special Vowel Sounds

Given a list of 20 words at the (*instructional level*) level, the student will circle the words containing the special vowel sounds _____ (*needed sounds*) with 90% accuracy.

When shown 10 word cards, the student will pronounce each digraph word with 90% accuracy.

Given a list of 20 words having special vowel sounds, the student will pronounce each word with 90% accuracy.

9. Prefixes

When given a list of 10 words, the student will circle the words containing prefixes with 100% accuracy.

Given a list of 10 common prefixes, the student will pronounce each correctly, 9 of 10 attempts.

When given a list of 20 words having prefixes at the (*instructional level*), the student will pronounce prefixes with 90% accuracy.

10. Suffixes

When given a list of 10 words, the student will circle the words containing suffixes with 100% accuracy.

Given a list of 10 common suffixes, the student will pronounce each correctly 9 of 10 attempts.

When given a list of 20 words having suffixes, the student will pronounce the suffixes with 100% accuracy.

11. Compound Words

Given a list of 20 words, the student will draw lines to join the word parts to make compound words with 90% accuracy.

When presented a list of compound words, the student will circle the word parts with 90% accuracy.

When shown two word parts, the student will pronounce the compound word with 100% accuracy.

12. Contractions

When presented a list of 10 words, the student will circle the contractions with 90% accuracy.

When presented word cards, the student will read the contractions _____, _____, _____, _____, and _____ (*needed contractions*) with 100% accuracy.

When given contractions _____, _____, _____ (*needed contractions*) orally the student will state the words from which the contractions are derived, 100% accuracy.

When given word parts of contractions _____, _____, _____, _____, and _____, the student will state the contractions with 90% accuracy.

C. Word Recognition in Context

The student will complete a 10 sentence Cloze exercise at the (*instructional level*) level by circling the correct word from a list of 25 with 80% accuracy.

Given a 10-sentence Cloze exercise at the (*instructional level*) level, the student will orally supply the missing words with 80% accuracy.

The student will complete a 10-sentence Cloze exercise at the (*instructional level*) by writing the missing word with 80% accuracy.

D. Specialized Vocabulary

The student will pronounce the words from (specify *Special Vocabulary List*) list with 100% accuracy.

ORAL READING

4. GOAL: The student will read aloud each of three (3) passages at the (*student's minimum PAL in oral reading*), reading fluently and correctly pronouncing each word with 100% accuracy.

A. Insertions
The student will orally read each of 3 passages at the (*Instructional level*) level with no oral insertions.

B. Mispronunciations
Given each of 3 reading passages at the (*instructional level*) level the student will read orally, correctly pronouncing each word.

C. Omissions
The student will orally read each of 3 passages at the (*instructional level*) level, pronouncing every word.

D. Refusals
When presented each of 3 passages at the (*instructional level*) level the student will attempt to read aloud and pronounce every word.

E. Repetitions
Given each of 3 reading passages at the (*instructional level*) level, the student will fluently read aloud, making no repetitions.

F. Reversals
The student will read aloud each of 3 passages at the (*instructional level*) level, pronouncing each word correctly and in proper sequence.

G. Substitutions
The student will read aloud each of 3 passages at the (*instructional level*) level, correctly pronouncing each word, and making no substitutions.

H. Phrasing
Given each of 3 passages at the (*instructional level*) level, the student will orally read, reading fluently at a moderate rate, and with appropriate phrasing.

COMPREHENSION PATTERNS

5. GOAL: The student will demonstrate increased reading comprehension skills by (*highest comprehension style*) reading of paragraphs at the (*student's minimum projected achievement level*) level and answering comprehension questions with 75% accuracy.

A. Main Idea
After (*comprehension style*)—reading of each of 5 short paragraphs at (*instructional level*) level, the student will select from 3 oral choices the paragraph topic with 100% accuracy.
When presented with each of 5 short paragraphs at the (*instructional level*) level, the student will (*comprehension style*) read and state the paragraph topic with 100% accuracy.
The student will (*comprehension style*) read each of 5 short paragraphs at the (*instructional level*) and then underline the topic sentence of each selection with 100% accuracy.
The student will (*comprehension style*) read each of 5 short paragraphs at the (*instructional level*) level, selecting from 3 choices the main idea of each selection with 80% accuracy.
When presented 5 short paragraphs at the (*instructional level*) level, the student will (*comprehension style*) read and say an appropriate title for each selection, 4 of 5 attempts.

The student will (*comprehension style*) read each of 5 short passages at the (*instructional level*) level, and make up a main idea type question and answer for each, with 5/5 appropriate questions.

B. Detail

When presented each of 5 sentences at the _____ (*student's instructional level*) the student will _____ (*comprehension style*) read and retell each with correct reproduction 9/10 attempts.

The student will _____ (*comprehension style*) _____ read each of 5 short paragraphs at the _____ (*instructional level*) _____ level, orally retelling the paragraph and including 4/5 of the details of each.

The student will _____ (*comprehension style*) _____ read each of 5 short paragraphs at the _____ (*instructional level*) _____ and indicate accurate detail statement by circling "true" or "false" for 10 statements about each with 90% accuracy.

Given each of 5 short paragraphs at the (*instructional level*) level, the student will _____ (*comprehension style*) _____ read and encircle the 10 answers to detail questions about each with 90% accuracy.

The student will _____ (*comprehension style*) _____ read 5 short paragraphs at the _____ (*instructional level*) _____ level and underline facts which appear in the material with 80% accuracy.

After _____ (*comprehension style*) _____ reading each of 5 short paragraphs at the _____ (*instructional level*) level, the student will list the 5 most important details.

The student will _____ (*comprehension style*) _____ read each of 5 short stories at the (*instructional level*) _____ level and formulate 3 factual questions and answers based upon what was read with 100% accuracy.

C. Word Meaning

When presented 5 sentences at the _____ (*instructional level*) _____ level, the student will verbally select a synonym for 10 underlined words from the list given 90% accuracy.

Given 10 sentences at the _____ (*instructional level*) _____ level, the student will encircle an antonym for the underlined words with 90% accuracy.

Given 10 pairs of words of similar meaning, the student will verbalize one way in which the word meanings are alike and one way in which they are different with 90% accuracy.

The student will supply the missing word for 10 incomplete 4-word analogies with 90% accuracy.

The student will formulate five 4-word analogies with 80% accuracy.

D. Inference

The student will _____ (*comprehension style*) _____ read each of 5 incomplete "if, then" sentences at the _____ (*instructional level*) _____ level, orally selecting from three choices the "then" ending for each sentence with 100% accuracy.

The student will _____ (*comprehension style*) _____ read each of 5 incomplete "if, then" sentences at the _____(*instructional level*) _____ level, and then state the "then" ending for each sentence with 100% accuracy.

When given 5 descriptive paragraphs at the (*instructional level*) _____ level, the student will _____ (*comprehension style*) _____read each and verbally select from 3 choices the title of the described object with 80% accuracy.

When given 5 descriptive paragraphs at the (*instructional level*) _____ level, the student will _____ (*comprehension style*) _____ read each and state the title of the described object with 80% accuracy.

Presented 5 partial short paragraphs at the (*instructional level*) _____ level, the student will (*comprehension style*) _____ read each and orally select from 3 choices the appropriate endings with 100% accuracy.

Presented 5 partial short paragraphs at the (*instructional level*) _____ level, the student will (*comprehension style*) _____ read each and state the appropriate endings with 100% accuracy.

The student will _____ (*comprehension style*) _____ read each of 5 short paragraphs at the (*instructional level*) _____ level and state the correct answers to inference questions.

After _____ (*comprehension style*) _____ reading each of 5 passages at the (*instructional level*) _____ level, the student will formulate one appropriate inference question for each.

Prescriptive Resource References

1. **Alexander, J. Estill.** *Teaching Reading.* Boston: Little, Brown and Co., 1979.
2. **Bader, Lois A.** *Reading Diagnosis and Remediation in Classroom and Clinic.* New York: The Macmillan Co., 1980.
3. **Bailey, Evalyn James.** *Academic Activities for Adolescents with Learning Disabilities.* Evergreen: Learning Pathways, 1975.
4. **Bond, Guy L., Miles A. Tinker** and **Barbara B. Watson.** *Reading Difficulties: Their Diagnosis and Correction.* Englewood Cliffs: Prentice-Hall, Inc., 1979.
5. **Burns, Paul C.** and **Betty D. Roe.** *Teaching Reading In Today's Elementary Schools.* Chicago: Rand McNally, 1976.
6. **Bush, Clifford** and **Mildred H. Huebner.** *Strategies for Reading in the Elementary Schools.* 2nd ed. New York: The Macmillan Co., 1979.
7. **Cheek, Martha Collins** and **Earl H. Cheek, Jr.** *Diagnostic-Prescriptive Reading Instruction.* Dubuque: Wm. C. Brown Co., 1980.
8. **Cohen, Sandra B.** and **Stephen P. Plaskon.** *Language Art for the Mildly Handicapped.* Columbus: Charles E. Merrill, 1980.
9. **Cook, Jimmie E.** and **Elsie C. Earlley.** *Remediating Reading Disabilities.* Germantown: Aspen System Corp., 1979.
10. **Cramer, Ronald L.** *Writing, Reading, and Language Growth.* Columbus: Charles E. Merrill, 1978.
11. **Dallmann, Martha, Roger L. Rouch, Lynette Y. C. Char,** and **John J. DeBoer.** *Teaching of Reading.* New York: Holt, Rinehart, Winston, 1978.
12. **Dauzat, Jo Ann** and **Sam V. Dauzat.** *Reading—The Teacher and the Learner.* New York: John Wiley and Sons, 1981.
13. **Dechant, Emerald.** *Diagnosis and Remediation of Reading Difficulties.* Englewood Cliffs: Prentice-Hall, Inc., 1981.
14. **Durkin, Delores.** *Teaching Young Children to Read.* 3rd ed. Boston: Allyn and Bacon, Inc., 1980.
15. **Ekwall, Eldon E.** *Locating and Correcting Reading Difficulties.* 3rd ed. Columbus: Charles E. Merrill, 1981.
16. **Faas, Larry A.** *Children with Learning Problems.* Boston: Houghton Mifflin, 1980.
17. **Fisher, Carol J.** and **C. Ann Terry.** *Children's Language and the Language Arts.* New York: McGraw-Hill, 1982.
18. **Gearheart, Bill R.** *Special Education for the '80s.* St. Louis: C.V. Mosby Co., 1980.
19. **Gearheart, Bill R.** and **Mel W. Weishahn.** *The Handicapped Student in the Classroom.* St. Louis: C.V. Mosby Co., 1980.
20. **Gillespie, Patricia H.** and **Lowell E. Johnson.** *Teaching Reading to the Mildly Retarded Child.* Columbus: Charles E. Merrill, 1974.
21. **Gillet, Jean Wallace** and **Charles Temple.** *Understanding Reading Problems Assessment and Instruction.* Boston: Little, Brown and Co., 1982.
22. **Grzynkowicz, Wineva, Diane Spurgeon Wirtz,** and **Grances Marling.** *Basic Education for Children with Learning Disabilities.* Springfield: Charles C. Thomas, 1979.
23. **Hall, Mary Ann.** *Teaching Reading as a Language Experience.* 3rd ed. Columbus: Charles E. Merrill, 1981.
24. **Hammill, Donald D.** and **Nettie R. Bartel.** *Teaching Children with Learning and Behavior Problems.* Boston: Allyn and Bacon, 1978.
25. **Hardman, Michael L., M. Winston Egan,** and **Elliott D. Landau.** *What Will WE Do in the Morning?* Dubuque: Wm. C. Brown, 1981.
26. **Haring, Norris G.** and **Barbara Bateman.** *Teaching the Learning Disabled Child.* Englewood Cliffs: Prentice-Hall, 1977.
27. **Harris, Albert J.** and **Edward R. Sipay.** *How To Teach Reading.* Longman, Inc., 1979.
28. **Harris, Larry A.** and **Carl B. Smith.** *Reading Instruction—Diagnostic Teaching in the Classroom.* New York: Holt, Rinehart and Winston, 1980.
29. **Harris, Larry A.** and **Carl B. Smith.** *Reading Instruction.* New York: Holt, Rinehart, Winston, 1976.
30. **Heilman, Arthur W., Timothy R. Blair,** and **William H. Rupley.** *Principles and Practices of Teaching Reading.* Columbus: Charles E. Merrill, 1981.
31. **Heward, William L.** and **Michael D. Orlansky.** *Exceptional Children.* Columbus: Charles E. Merrill, 1980.
32. **Hull, Marion A.** *Phonics for the Teacher of Reading.* Columbus: Charles E. Merrill, 1981.
33. **Kaluger, George** and **Clifford J. Kolson.** *Reading and Learning Disabilities,* 2nd ed. Columbus: Charles E. Merrill, 1978.
34. **Karlin, Robert.** *Teaching Elementary Reading: Principles and Strategies,* 3rd ed. New York: Harcourt, Brace, Jovanovich, Inc., 1980.
35. **Kirk, Samuel A., Sister Joanne Marie Kliebhan,** and **Janet W. Lerner.** *Teaching Reading to Slow and Disabled Learners.* Boston: Houghton Mifflin Co., 1978.
36. **McGinnis, Dorothy J.** and **Dorothy E. Smith.**

Analyzing and Treating Reading Problems. New York: The Macmillan Co., 1982.

37. **McNeil, John D., Lisbeth Donant,** and **Marvin C. Alkin.** *How to Teach Reading Successfully.* Boston: Little, Brown and Co., 1980.
38. **Mangrum, Charles T. II** and **Harry W. Forgan.** *Developing Competencies in Teaching Reading.* Columbus: Charles E. Merrill, 1979.
39. **Mann, Lester, Libby Goodman,** and **J. Lee Wiederholt.** *Teaching the Learning Disabled Adolescent.* Boston: Houghton Mifflin, 1978.
40. **Otto, Wayne** and **Richard J. Smith.** *Corrective and Remedial Teaching.* Boston: Houghton Mifflin, 1980.
41. **Payne, James S., Edward A. Polloway, James E. Smith, Jr.,** and **Ruth Ann Payne.** *Strategies for Teaching the Mentally Retarded.* Columbus: Charles E. Merrill, 1981.
42. **Reid, D. Kim** and **Wayne P. Hresko.** *A Cognitive Approach to Learning Disabilities.* New York: McGraw-Hill, 1981.
43. **Ross, Alan O.** *Psychological Aspects of Learning Disabilities and Reading Disorders.* New York: McGraw-Hill, 1976.
44. **Savage, John F.** and **Jean F. Mooney.** *Teaching Reading to Children with Special Needs.* Boston: Allyn and Bacon, 1979.
45. **Silver, Patricia Gillespie.** *Teaching Reading to Children with Special Needs.* Columbus: Charles E. Merrill, 1979.
46. **Smith, Nila B.** and **H. Alan Robinson.** *Reading Instruction for Today's Children.* Englewood Cliffs: Prentice-Hall, Inc., 1980.
47. **Smith, Richard J.** and **Dale D. Johnson.** *Teaching Children to Read.* Addison-Wesley Co., 1980.
48. **Spache, George D.** *Diagnosing and Correcting Reading Disabilities.* Boston: Allyn and Bacon, Inc., 1976.
49. **Stauffer, Russell G., Jules C. Abrams** and **John J. Pikulski.** *Diagnosis, Correction, and Prevention of Reading Disabilities.* New York: Harper and Row, 1978.
50. **Stoodt, Barbara.** *Reading Instruction.* Boston: Houghton Mifflin, 1981.
51. **Stowitschek, Joseph J., Robert A. Gable,** and **Jo Mary Hendrickson.** *Instructional Materials for Exceptional Children.* Germantown: Aspen Publications, 1980.
52. **Swanson, B. Marion** and **Diane J. Willis.** *Understanding Exceptional Children and Youth.* Chicago: Rand McNally, 1979.
53. **Wehman, Paul** and **Phillip J. McLaughlin.** *Program Development in Special Education.* New York: McGraw-Hill, 1981.
54. **Wiig, Elizabeth Hemmersam** and **Eleanor Missing Semel.** *Language Assessment and Intervention.* Columbus: Charles E. Merrill, 1980.
55. **Wilson, Robert M.** *Diagnostic and Remedial Reading.* Columbus: Charles E. Merrill, 1981.
56. **Zintz, Miles V.** *Corrective Reading,* 4th ed. Dubuque: Wm. C. Brown, 1981.
57. **Zintz, Miles V.** *Reading Process: The Teacher and Learner.* Dubuque: Wm. C. Brown, 1980.

Prescriptive Resource Guide

Directions: Each skill area listed in the left margin below corresponds with the major numbered skill areas on the Student Planning Sheet. Once a student's specific skill needs are identified thru diagnosis additional teacher resources may be located by referring to the references listed. The authors' names are numbered and arranged alphabetically across the top of each page, with the complete reference information given in the Prescriptive Resource Guide which follows. Skill areas and referenced pages appear cross-referenced. This list is representative of selected resources available but is not intended to be comprehensive in its listings.

SKILL AREA		REFERENCE	1) Alexander	2) Bader	3) Bailey	4) Bond
1. VISUAL	A.	Vis Discrimination	41-42	74-75		
	B.	Vis Memory			74-76	78
2. AUDITORY	A.	Aud Discrimination	41-42	74-75	48	304-305
	B.	Aud Memory				
3. WORD RECOGNITION	A.	Sight Vocabulary	51-71	39-42	295	225-229
	B.	Word Analysis				254
	(1)	Begin Consonants	75-76,84-85		288	254,257
	(2)	End Consonants	88-90		288	254,257
	(3,4,5)	Short/Long Vowels,ȼ	76-79,91-94		288-289	256
	(6)	Blends	85,98-90		288	254-255,258
	(7)	Digraphs	79,85,90		288	255
	(8)	Spec Vowel Sounds	79,85,94			
	(9,10)	Prefixes/Suffixes	104,120-123, 408		288-289	
	(11,12)	Compd/Contractions				
4. ORAL READING	A.	Insertions			296,312	
	B.	Mispronunciations				
	C. D.	Omissions, Refusals				
	E.	Repetitions				
	F.	Reversals			312	284
	G.	Substitutions			297,312	
	H.	Phrasing		162-165	315-316	401-402
5. COMPREHENSION	A.	Main Idea	141,234	156-162	317	
	B.	Detail	141-142			
	C.	Word Meaning			305,310	232-235
	D.	Inference	139-140,144			
		General Discussions: Teaching Reading to Exceptional Students				

5) Burns	6) Bush	7) Cheek	8) Cohen	9) Cook
		252-253	371	68-69
		245-246,252	371-372	48
	109	254-255	370	88
		254-255		
128-135	70-73	58,151,276 279	384	48,57-61
138-142	78		387	81-85
138-142			387	85-87
143-144	78-84		387	91-94,97,117
137			387	89,91,257
143-145				89,91
143-145				96-98
153-156	88,91-92	44	387	125-129,130
159-160				
453-456			383	
453-456			383	
453-456			383	
453-456			383	
453-456			383	
453-456			383	
495	108		392	
208-209	118-119	38	389-391	171-172
209-211	119		389-391	192-194
164-169	97-98	224	389-391	
	122-123	39	389-391	
		338-359		

SKILL AREA

	REFERENCE	10) Cramer	11) Dallman	12) Dauzat	13) Dechant
1. VIS-UAL	A. Vis Discrimination		115-117	33,45-46	258-261
	B. Vis Memory			46	258
2. AUDI-TORY	A. Aud Discrimination	48-49,154	113-115	46	249-252
	B. Aud Memory				180,252
3. WORD RECOGNITION	A. Sight Vocabulary	242-243	139-141, 170-173	58-65,89-90	219,269-274
	B. Word Analysis				
	(1) Begin Consonants	235-236	149	104-108	277-280
	(2) End Consonants	235-236	149	104-108	284-286
	(3,4,5) Short/Long Vowels,¢		150	103-114	280,292-295
	(6) Blends	235-236	149	428	288-292
	(7) Digraphs		149	107-111	
	(8) Spec Vowel Sounds		149	111	
	(9,10) Prefixes/Suffixes	239-240	154,183-184	69	300-303
	(11,12) Compd/Contractions			70	299-300
4. ORAL READING	A. Insertions				333
	B. Mispronunciations		265		
	C. D. Omissions, Refusals				332-333
	E. Repetitions				335-336
	F. Reversals			433	
	G. Substitutions				333-335
	H. Phrasing		203,265		338
5. COMPREHENSION	A. Main Idea	200-201	198,223	145-146	341-343
	B. Detail	200-201	198-199		
	C. Word Meaning	201-204	142-144	138	316-320
	D. Inference	200-201		143,146	351-352
	General Discussions: Teaching Reading to Exceptional Students				

14) Durkin	15) Ekwall	16) Faas	17) Fisher	18) Gearheart
97-97,155				
170-172,367		101		
312-313	29-38		97-115	
332-337	56-65			
355-362	56-65			
337-342	66-71			
336-339,376	72-73			
338-339	72-73			
339	72-73			
399-412	74-80		104	
401-402				
	24-25			
	15-16			
	18			
	20			
	21-23			
	26-27			
	9-13			
	92-95		332-334	
	95			
	81-83			
439-440				
		125-146		214-246

SKILL AREA	REFERENCE	19)Gearheart	20)Gillespie	21)Gillet	22)Grzynkowicz
1. VISUAL	A. Vis Discrimination				259
	B. Vis Memory				
2. AUDITORY	A. Aud Discrimination	125		313,333	260
	B. Aud Memory				
3. WORD RECOGNITION	A. Sight Vocabulary	152-153,179	209,261	112,115-116	
	B. Word Analysis		36-39	116-117,141	
	(1) Begin Consonants				
	(2) End Consonants				
	(3,4,5) Short/Long Vowels, ɇ				
	(6) Blends				
	(7) Digraphs				
	(8) Spec Vowel Sounds				
	(9,10) Prefixes/Suffixes		39	141-142	
	(11,12) Compd/Contractions			216,218	
4. ORAL READING	A. Insertions			102-107	
	B. Mispronunciations		109	102-107	
	C. D. Omissions, Refusals		109	102-107	
	E. Repetitions		109	102-107	
	F. Reversals			102-107	
	G. Substitutions		109	102-107	
	H. Phrasing			102-107	
5. COMPREHENSION	A. Main Idea		43		
	B. Detail		43		
	C. Word Meaning				
	D. Inference				
	General Discussions: Teaching Reading to Exceptional Students			161-202	

23) Hall	24)Hammill	25)Hardman	26)Haring	27)Harris, A.
102-104	368			41,68-70
102-104	369	134	130-131	42
105-107	364-365	125	132-135	43-44
		125		
	92-93	121	140	241-264
				559-563
115,117	43			
124	43			
	44			
	42	134	140,196	
	44			
	96-98			277-278
	54-59			216-219
	54-59			216-219
	54-59			216-219
	54-59			216-219
	54-59			216-219
	54-59			216-219
	98			322-323
	98			335-337
	49			331-333
	95			300-302
		123		332-333
	22-98			

SKILL AREA		REFERENCE	28)Harris,L.	29)Harris,L.	30)Heilman	31)Heward
	1. VIS-UAL	A. Vis Discrimination	106,120	149-157	104-105	
		B. Vis Memory		158-160		
	2. AUDI-TORY	A. Aud Discrimination		144-147	106-109	
		B. Aud Memory				
	3. WORD RECOGNITION	A. Sight Vocabulary		168,172-173	154-155	
		B. Word Analysis		190-199		
		(1) Begin Consonants	145,147	191	193-194	
		(2) End Consonants	162-163			
		(3,4,5) Short/Long Vowels, ¢	145-146	192-195	163-164	
		(6) Blends		196	200-202	
		(7) Digraphs		197-198	202-204	
		(8) Spec Vowel Sounds	146,163		213-215	
		(9,10) Prefixes/Suffixes	193-196	208-216	449-451	
		(11,12) Compd/Contractions		215-216		
	4. ORAL READING	A. Insertions				
		B. Mispronunciations				
		C. D. Omissions, Refusals				
		E. Repetitions				
		F. Reversals				
		G. Substitutions				
		H. Phrasing		352-354	303-306	
	5. COMPREHENSION	A. Main Idea		275-276		
		B. Detail		271-273		
		C. Word Meaning	183-185	219-221	248-251	
		D. Inference		264		
		General Discussions: Teaching Reading to Exceptional Students				151-177

32) Hull	33) Kaluger	34) Karlin	35) Kirk	36) McGinnis
		181-185	61-62	
			63	
		181-185	63-64	227
	255-259			
		243-249	97-102	206-208
18-51	308	259-261	237-238	228
			237-238	228
69-92	309-310	253-254	238	223,238
61-64	308	254-255,262	112	223
52-60,96-98	308	254-255		223
93-96			238	224,229
	272-273	296-297		216,217,219
				216-219
			164	69
	344			69
			164	69
			165	69
	386-387		165	69
			164	69
				69
				254
				254
	295			
	291-296			

SKILL AREA	REFERENCE	37) McNeil	38) Mangrum	39) Mann	40) Otto
1. VISUAL	A. Vis Discrimination		113		168
	B. Vis Memory		113	177	
2. AUDITORY	A. Aud Discrimination	93-94,206-208	127,151	144-146	
	B. Aud Memory		126		169
3. WORD RECOGNITION	A. Sight Vocabulary	217-218	170-176		170-171
	B. Word Analysis				
	(1) Begin Consonants	100-101	180		176-177
	(2) End Consonants	100-101	180		
	(3,4,5) Short/Long Vowels,	104-105, 110-113	183-185		179-181
	(6) Blends	102-103	181-182,186	54,180-181	177-178
	(7) Digraphs	111	182,184,186		178
	(8) Spec Vowel Sounds	111	184		181
	(9,10) Prefixes/Suffixes	136-137, 225-226	187		182
	(11,12) Compd/Contractions				
4. ORAL READING	A. Insertions		84-85	177	119-120
	B. Mispronunciations		84	177	119-120
	C. D. Omissions, Refusals		84-85	177	119-120
	E. Repetitions			177	119-120
	F. Reversals			177	119-120
	G. Substitutions		83,85	177	119-120
	H. Phrasing		87,89		
5. COMPREHENSION	A. Main Idea	197-198	86,276		262-264
	B. Detail		410-411		
	C. Word Meaning	139-140	176-179		185
	D. Inference		86,288-289		
	General Discussions: Teaching Reading to Exceptional Students			169-200	

41) Payne	42) Reid	43) Ross	44) Savage	45) Silver
194			162	210
194				210-211
171-172			122-123,135	212
208-209			26	
			27	309-311
206				
207				
194				
207				
207				
193			95	312-317
193			95	312-317
193			95	312-317
193			95	312-317
			95	312-317
			95	312-317
	260			
209			29-32	302
187-214	229-263	141-166		

SKILL AREA	REFERENCE	46)Smith,N.	47)Smith,R.	48) Spache	49)Stauffer
1. VIS-UAL	A. Vis Discrimination	70,73-74	35-37	36-40	269
	B. Vis Memory			36	
2. AUDI-TORY	A. Aud Discrimination	70,74	33-35	57-60	330
	B. Aud Memory			58	
3. WORD RECOGNITION	A. Sight Vocabulary	144-150	68-71		289-315
	B. Word Analysis	153-161	100-109	215-221	290-329
	(1) Begin Consonants				
	(2) End Consonants				
	(3,4,5) Short/Long Vowels,		105-107		319
	(6) Blends				
	(7) Digraphs				
	(8) Spec Vowel Sounds	162,164	110-111	222-224	
	(9,10) Prefixes/Suffixes				295
	(11,12) Compd/Contractions				
4. ORAL READING	A. Insertions				
	B. Mispronunciations				
	C. D. Omissions, Refusals				
	E. Repetitions				
	F. Reversals				
	G. Substitutions				
	H. Phrasing		307,400-401	306-308	273-275
5. COMPREHENSION	A. Main Idea		142		
	B. Detail	216-218	140-142		
	C. Word Meaning	142-144	113-117		
	D. Inference				
	General Discussions: Teaching Reading to Exceptional Students				

50) Stoodt	51)Stowitschek	52)Swanson	53)Wehman	54) Wiig
89-90,103		176-177		
127,130-133			331	
			332-333	
145-149				
146-147				
137-139				
	171			
	171			
59				
91-92				
	171			
	173-176			
180-182,194		323	335	
194				
133-136				
197-198				
		253-290		367-397

		REFERENCE	55)Wilson	56) Zintz	57) Zintz	
SKILL AREA	1. VIS-UAL	A. Vis Discrimination	241-245		196	
		B. Vis Memory			82,196	
	2. AUDI-TORY	A. Aud Discrimination	237-240		83	
		B. Aud Memory				
	3. WORD RECOGNITION	A. Sight Vocabulary	262-280	224	198-204	
		B. Word Analysis	282-292		209-214	
		(1) Begin Consonants		240-243		
		(2) End Consonants				
		(3,4,5) Short/Long Vowels,				
		(6) Blends				
		(7) Digraphs		244		
		(8) Spec Vowel Sounds				
		(9,10) Prefixes/Suffixes	292-293	234	217-218	
		(11,12) Compd/Contractions				
	4. ORAL READING	A. Insertions	122-125	102		
		B. Mispronunciations	122-125	102		
		C. D. Omissions, Refusals	122-125	102		
		E. Repetitions	122-125	102-204		
		F. Reversals	122-125	86-88,219	477-478	
		G. Substitutions	122-125	102		
		H. Phrasing		102	311-313	
	5. COMPREHENSION	A. Main Idea		266-268	248-250	
		B. Detail			240-241	
		C. Word Meaning			206,247-248	
		D. Inference				
		General Discussions: Teaching Reading to Exceptional Students	195-208			

Skill Area		REFERENCE				
1. VISUAL		A. Vis Discrimination				
		B. Vis Memory				
2. AUDITORY		A. Aud Discrimination				
		B. Aud Memory				
3. WORD RECOGNITION		A. Sight Vocabulary				
		B. Word Analysis				
		(1) Begin Consonants				
		(2) End Consonants				
		(3,4,5) Short/Long Vowels,				
		(6) Blends				
		(7) Digraphs				
		(8) Spec Vowel Sounds				
		(9,10) Prefixes/Suffixes				
		(11,12) Compd/Contractions				
4. ORAL READING		A. Insertions				
		B. Mispronunciations				
		C. D. Omissions, Refusals				
		E. Repetitions				
		F. Reversals				
		G. Substitutions				
		H. Phrasing				
5. COMPREHENSION		A. Main Idea				
		B. Detail				
		C. Word Meaning				
		D. Inference				
		General Discussions: Teaching Reading to Exceptional Students				

Index

ORDER FROM PRENTICE-HALL, INC., ENGLEWOOD CLIFFS, N.J. 07632

Attention: Mail Order Billing Department

Please send me ( ) copies of INDIVIDUAL EVALUATION PROCEDURES IN READING by Thomas A. Rakes, Joyce S. Choate, and Gayle Lane Waller @ $19.95 clothbound (45722-6) and ( ) copies @ $14.95 paperback (45721-8). Enclosed is my ( ) check or ( ) money order for $________.

On prepaid orders, publisher pays all shipping and handling charges.
Or call our convenient toll-free number to order: 800-526-0485.

Name____

Address______________________________________

____

City________________State________________ZIP________________

Prices subject to change without notice.

ORDER FROM PRENTICE-HALL, INC., ENGLEWOOD CLIFFS, N.J. 07632

Attention: Mail Order Billing Department

Please send me ( ) copies of INDIVIDUAL EVALUATION PROCEDURES IN READING by Thomas A. Rakes, Joyce S. Choate, and Gayle Lane Waller @ $19.95 clothbound (45722-6) and ( ) copies @ $14.95 paperback (45721-8). Enclosed is my ( ) check or ( ) money order for $________.

On prepaid orders, publisher pays all shipping and handling charges.
Or call our convenient toll-free number to order: 800-526-0485.

Name____

Address______________________________________

____

City________________State________________ZIP________________

Prices subject to change without notice.